A BASIC GUIDE TO
THE PRADO

A BASIC GUIDE TO THE PRADO

J. Rogelio Buendia

Photography Eleonor Dominguez

Silex

Declared a «Book of Touristic Interest» by the Director General of Tourism in his Resolution of October 15, 1973.

Translated by
PATRICIA S. PARRENT

© SILEX®: 1984

Original title: El Prado Básico

I.S.B.N.: 84-85041-22-4
Depósito legal: VI. 706 - 1984

Printed in Spain by:
H. Fournier, S.A. - Vitoria

Layout: J. M. Domínguez

(Printed in Spain)

CONTENTS

PREFACE

I

A View of Art, in Perspective, in the Museum.—During many years art history has been taught with a historicist criterion. Today the parallelism between history and art history lacks meaning if it is a departure from the direct study of the works. New methodologies have, in recent years, attempted to provide new systematics for the science of artistic study; but, in general, procedures created for other sciences have been borrowed, and, thus, theories proceeding from the psychological, sociological or philological (structuralism, semiology...) fields have been applied to art, applied with greater or lesser success by the vanguard of criticism. Thus, the sociology of art translates into its particular language the artistic vision and relates it to the whole of the society which surrounds it; there is an attempt to consider the work of art an object with the same characteristics which other natural objects have, while the psychologists of art rightly consider it to possess mysterious and invisible forces for the community of human beings. There is no doubt that many of these theories are reasonable as long as they are directed along logical lines, nevertheless, the psychology or sociology of art should be employed with precautions. Some psychologists limit the work of art to the moment of its creation by the artist, even finding in it the stimuli produced by repression or other problems of a psychological order. And certain sociologists forget that besides the human surroundings favorable for artistic creation, there also exist particular meanings, often supported by tradition, which are only understandable through iconography and other auxiliary sciences of art history. Thus, the aesthetics or philosophy of art, when it investigates the artistic beauty of a specific and concrete form —art works cannot exist without aesthetic values— helps the observer to be able to draw near to these «unattainable heights» which, according to Hauser, are the works of art.

Although the methods for interpreting an art work are diverse, there is no doubt that a familiarization with the works themselves makes it possible to perceive their meaning more clearly. He who speaks of art without directly confronting the creations risks the danger of elaborating fallacious theories, for these latter cannot be explained without taking the former into account. Since Felipe de Guevara —as we shall later see— in the XVIth century, there has been an insistence upon a dialogue between the spectator and the artistic creations, since these are expressed by means of a special language, perceptible for the social environment in which they were created, which will be more or less accesible to the present observer: the more background he has, the better

7

equipped he will be to perceive their meaning, since a change in the historical context or the need for the use of symbolism on occasion makes its deciphering difficult. Now then, like every human language, if at the beginning its study is very tiring, later its knowledge will make it possible to read the aestheic, historical, sociological, and iconographic values with which the full and integral comprehension of the art work is achieved.

The visitor to a museum, in this case the Prado, in his first visits, should have a general itinerary following a chronological-stylistic order, which will give him an overall view of the works exhibited with a «perspectivistic» projection. Then he can go into each work in depth in terms of its aesthetic and social context, beginning with the genesis of its creative process, but without disintegrating it with an excessive analysis which can arrive at the destructive decomposition of the work of art. Therefore in the second part of this study we try to help the spectator to enter into the admirable collections in the Prado following stylistic sequences and covering its rooms step by step. In the third part, we study in more detail one hundred selected works using an analytical process, but attempting to point out their abstract values. Perhaps we have overstressed iconographic problems in the commentaries, but we haven't been able to avoid the influence of the Warburg Institute —by way of our professors and reading— on our university training, for one of its most important members, Panofsky, «has brought forth a new method for the overall and universal comprehension of works of art» (Francastel). Now, neither have we forgotten that the artist does not transport his ideas to the canvas or the sculpture without a perfect mastery of technique, which confers upon the work of art, not only its quality, but its very existence.

A Brief History of the Collections.—In the Medieval period the paintings in the royal collections had a mission similar to that of the tapestries: they served, in general, to decorate the palaces where the sovereigns provisionally resided. The monarchs of the various peninsular states specially commissioned painters to do works to be donated to chapels founded by royalty and very seldom ordered their portraits done. Even in the XVth century royal collectors, such as John II and Isabella the Catholic, were continually moving their artistic treasures around; upon their deaths, following the custom, the works were put up for public auction. Some of the pictures, though, were donated to churches and monasteries; thus, a good part of Isabella's collection was given over to the Royal Chapel in Granada, where it is partially preserved.

Charles V, on the other hand, leaves the majority of the works assembled by him to the heir to the throne. It will be Philip II who for the first time converts a palace —that of El Pardo— into a *picture gallery*, making a reality the desire of Don Felipe de Guevara, an attendant of his father's, that the pictures be exhibited, «because covered up and hidden away they lose their value, which rests in the eyes and opinions of them belonging to men of good judgement and imagination». This is made possible when Philip II fixes the Court in Madrid. In the *Inventory* of El Pardo of 1564 works are cited which are presently in the Prado, such as the «Danaë» by Titian; but the greater part of the paintings brought together in this palace were destroyed by fire in 1604. This gallery could only be visited by people of noble or intellectual distinction. On the other hand, open to a larger public was the collection put together by the King himself in the Monastery of El Escorial; already in the *Inventory of Jewels, Paintings... 1571-98*, published by Zarco, some 1,150 paintings appear. For the first time on the Iberian Peninsula an authentic picture gallery was opened.

Philip IV, grandson of the Prudent King, will achieve the possession of a collection unequalled in his time, for not only does he surround himself with the most important Spanish artists of the moment, but among his royal painters, besides the admirable Velasquez, he includes foreigners such as Rubens himself. But he is not satisfied with the acquisition of contemporary masterpieces, and he orders his ambassadors to buy the most imporant paintings which appear in the liquidation of the great estates. Thus he acquires, through his ambassador Cárdenas, such important works as the one by Mantegna or the «Self-portrait» by Dürer in the auction of the property of Charles I of England (d. 1645), or the Titian and other masterpieces by Van Dyck or Rubens himself in this latter's testamentary execution. And he commissions Velasquez to search for sculptures and paintings in Italy, which he will bring back in 1651. A large part of these works, especially the religious ones, enriched even more the San Lorenzo Monastery at El Escorial. Thus Velasquez, in 1656, personally brings in «forty-one original paintings, which were described and noted by the painter». Among them was the splendid «St. Alphonsus» by El Greco, which along with the «St. Peter» constitutes the revaluation of the artist from Crete. This monastery was the most direct antecedent, as a museum, of the Prado, and to a large extent one of the principal sources for its collection —along with the royal palaces— since in the XIXth century one hundred forty paintings were moved from El Escorial to the Madrilenian museum, and at the end of the last civil war, works of the importance of Van der Weyden's «Deposition» and Bosch's «Garden of Delights» were added.

The idea of a museum of paintings in Madrid already appears in 1774 in a letter from Mengs to the erudite traveler Ponz, in which he says: «I wish that in this Royal Palace (Oriente) there could be found together all the precious paintings which are spread out among all the other Royal Seats and that they could be placed in a Gallery»; the Czech painter suggested, as well, that it be done systematically. But not until the Society of Jesus is suppressed and the works which belonged to it are moved to the San Fernando Academy is a truly public gallery established in the capital of Spain. There were put, although in this instance in closed rooms, the *nudes* collected by Charles V, Philip II and Philip IV, when they were in danger of perishing due to the pressure of Charles III's confessor, the ominous Frair Joaquín de Eleta; but the intervention of the Marquis of Santa Cruz —a counsellor of the Academy— saved these masterpieces, although they remained locked up until 1827. During the Napoleonic occupation of Madrid they were exhibited, but two works of Titian's were also lost: «The Sleeping Venus» and a «Danaë».

Joseph Bonaparte, in 1810, decreed the formation of a Museum of Painting which should be formed with funds coming from the religious orders and Godoy, but the project did not prosper. It is with the restoration of Ferdinand VII in 1814 that the erection of a National Museum of Paintings is decided upon, making use of the Buenavista Palace. But on November 20, it is ordered that the collections be exhibited in the building which Juan de Villanueva had planned in the year 1785 as a Museum of Natural Sciences and which in 1808 was virtually finished. This masterpiece of the Neoclassical style, since it was situated in a central and busy locale —the Prado Boulevard— was, then, the ideal place. Thus, on November 26, the Royal Order for its definitive creation is promulgated. María Isabel de Braganza, to whom Ferdinand was married in 1816, takes charge of speeding up the work of adapting the building. On February 4, 1819, the King officially visits the Museum and inspects the finishing touches. Two weeks later, in a quiet manner —which will become traditional in all the Prado's events— the museum is opened to the public. Only three hundred eleven paintings were exhibited and Luis Eusebi, the Main Curator, composed a brief *Catalog* of them.

When on September 29, 1833, Ferdinand VII dies, tragedy almost overcomes the fledgling museum, for in his will the treasures of the Prado are considered property to be divided between his two daughters. Fortunately, a faultless deciding commission opined «that monuments of our glories and past greatness, which from very remote times... the monarchs have possessed should not have been inventoried». So that the division would not take place it is recommended that the sister of Isabel II be awarded compensation. Finally, three years later, the directing Junta of the Museum is constituted; among the members are the painters Vicente López and José de Madrazo. This is fruitful: the Museum is expanded, new rooms are opened and a meticulous *Catalog* is made up; its publication will take place five years later. Finally, en 1865, the Museum is included among the property of the Crown's Patrimony and seven years later it is enriched with the works from the Trinidad Convent, part of which are deposited in other places, which has, even now, made impossible an overall vision of the Madrilenian school.

Along with the directors, the administrative organism of the Prado will be the Patronato, which is created in 1912. Since influential politicians are members, between 1914 and 1920 it is possible to carry out expansions. Meanwhile, in 1918, the scandalous robbery of the jewels from the «Dauphin's Treasure» takes place. Later, successive important improvements will be made, such as the vaulting of the central gallery with reinforced concrete in 1927 and in 1931 the installation of the Fernández-Durán legacy, in the upper rooms, where it still awaits the placing of each object in its corresponding spot.

With the civil war, the Museum closes its doors on August 30, 1936; in November the evacuation of the works of art begins, first to Valencia and near the end of the war to Switzerland. The only one which is damaged is «The Charge of the Mamelucos» by Goya, when it falls out of the truck in which it was being carried. In 1939, on July 7, the Prado again opens its doors: pictures which are then being exhibited in Geneva with an unprecedented success are missing, but the beginning of World War II causes its hurried closing, and the works are returned to their country along secondary rail lines in unlighted cars, but once more luck was with the Prado. In 1941, in an exchange with France, the «Soult Immaculate Conception» by Murillo and the «Dama de Elche» are reincorporated; (this last one has recently been transferred to the National Museum of Archaeology). And in this same year, Don Mariano de Zayas makes a donation of important ancient sculptures. In 1942 is built the staircase which gives simultaneous access to the main and upper floors, an architectonic organization used by Haan, a follower of Villanueva's, in the old University of Toledo, today an Institute of Secondary Education. The replacement of wooden floors with stone ones is also begun, for reasons of fireproofing;

cause for nostalgia is the loss of the extremely lovely central gallery similar to the one preserved in the Louvre. And in 1956, the new expansion toward the Jerónimos Church is carried out.

With the death of the painter Alvarez de Sotomayor, on March 17, 1960, who since the end of the Civil War had held the position of director, for the first time in the history of the Prado, an art historian, Don Francisco J. Sánchez-Cantón, achieves the position of Director. Since then the administrative heads have been selected from among prestigious scientists; thus, his work has been continued by Don Diego Angulo Iñiguez, among whose achievements stands out the acquisition of the portrait of the «Duke of Lerma» by Rubens, and most recently Don Francisco Xavier de Salas, a specialist in museology, who with the collaboration of an efficient team (today there are three subdirectors) carries out the systematization and reformations which improve the collections. Thus, the present administration and Patronato hope very soon to air-condition the rooms to protect their treasures from air pollution. Recently a monumental project has been presented for the future expansion of the Prado, making use of the cloister and other outlying buildings of the old Jerónimos Monastery.

In 1971, the collections of XIXth-century Spanish painting, preserved in the old Museum of Modern Art, were incorporated and installed in the Casón del Buen Retiro; but since it has a separate subdirector and administration which gives it a certain interdependence, it departs from the theme discussed here.

But this expansion by bringing the Prado's collection closer to the art of our times, revitalizes it, changing it, not only due to the importance of its pictorial collection, into one of the most important pinacothecas in the world —only weak in its collections of Dutch and Primitive Italian paintings due to historical reasons— but into the *living museum* which we all desire.

I express here my gratitude to Don Diego Angulo, Don José Manuel Pita Andrade and Doña María Elena Gómez Moreno who initiated me in a direct acquaintance with the paintings in the Prado. Also very useful have been my conversations throughout the years with Don José Camón Aznar and the Marquis of Lozoya, to whom in great part I owe my aesthetic interests. I cannot help but remember the previous Director of the Museum, Don Francisco Javier Sánchez Cantón, who since my first year at the university patiently answered my questions and listened to my suggestions, some of which are mentioned in his Catalog. *I also thank the present Director Don Francisco Xavier de Salas, and my colleague Subdirector Don Alfonso Pérez Sánchez for aid given, and also Don Manuel Cruz Valdovinos, collaborator in the thankless task of the correction of proofs. Nor do I forget to mention the Foundation for Aid to Research of the Ministry of National Education, without which results obtained in certain investigations given here would have been impossible.*

MEDIEVAL PAINTING

II

THE ROMANESQUE STYLE

Along with Western civilization, art after the fall of Rome is submerged in shadows; the universal meaning of Classical art desintegrated into a plurality of national and local styles. Thus, in Spain there is a consecutive development of the Visigothic, Asturian and Mozarabic styles. But when it seems that European art has reached complete desintegration, a series of religious, economic and social causes will motivate the creation of a new unitary artistic style, the Romanesque one. It will no longer be that of an empire, such as the Roman one, but of a spiritual ideal, Christianity.

The Romanesque style is born as Latin begins to break down into the Romance languages; with the disappearance of linguistic unity, a new nexus will be found, thanks to art, which along with the pilgrimmages to Santiago de Compostela and Rome, will link the European peoples. This new «universal language» will make it possible for the pilgrim or traveler to read, without need of translation, the messages expressed by a new figuration, whether it be presented in a sculptural form on the façades or capitals of the buildings, or pictorially on the walls and vaults.

Under the command of the *master masons* the buildings are constructed with architecture, sculpture and painting forming a single organic structure. This is what causes the painting, being subordinated to the architecture, to possess a decorative as well as a theological character. In general, these pictorial decorations are religious in character, although on some occasions narrations exist with a secular theme, as occurs in the oldest of the San Baudelio de Berlanga paintings (Pl. I).

Romanesque paintings are generally done in fresco, but not having perfected this technique, retouching must be done with oils or tempera. The figures which appear are submitted to a process of abstraction which is derived from the sense of creative expression characteristic of the anonymous masters who do the paintings. As a result, this painting, whose flatness and bi-dimensionality have Byzantine origins, leads in a realistic-expressionistic direction and tries, through patches of color on the faces and hands, to liven up the flat tones and discover volumetric effects which will be more fully achieved in the Gothic period.

Though Cataluña is the region on the Iberian Peninsula richest in Romanesque paintings, Castile is still not lacking in surprising examples. Thus, outstanding are the ones which are preserved *in situ* in San Isidoro de León, or those coming from San Baudelio de Berlanga (Soria) (Pl. I), and from the hermitage at Maderuelo (Segovia) (Pl. II) which have been partially or totally transferred to the Prado and which are amply discussed in the text accompanying the plates.

THE GOTHIC STYLE

The Gothic style arises as Romanesque art evolves toward more slender and spiritualized forms. A wave of tenderness has penetrated the Christian world which will be formulated literarily in the *Golden Legend* and the *Little Flowers of St. Francis*; what was before a terrifying expression will now be made lyrical. Architecture reaches for the heavens with its towers while in the interiors a «mystical space» is achieved. The predominance of openings over solid walls, in contrast to what occurred in the Romanesque period, makes for the appearance of the marvelous stained-glass windows and although the frescoes do not disappear completely, retables, many of them commissioned and paid for by the guilds (which are at this moment reaching their peak), will be the principal pictures to adorn religious buildings. These are born and are of a very small size (*retrotabula*) in the Romanesque period, for it is in the Gothic stage that they will develop, reaching, in the XVth century in Spain, proportions which can cover the altar wall in the churches and cathedrals.

The first period of Spanish Gothic painting is called Lineal or Franco-Gothic. It arises in the XIIIth century and lasts until the middle of the XIVth century. Its first examples —whether they be frontals, *retrotabulae* or mural paintings— may barely be distinguished from the Romanesque ones and some authors include them within this style. This happens with the «Guills Frontal» (C. 3.055) from the end of the century and coming from the church in the village in Gerona of the same name. But more and more the lines, due to influences coming from France and even England, become more stylized and curvilinear though the draperies preserve their sharp-edged folds. The technique of easel painting during almost the entire Gothic period will be one of *grisaille*, which is illuminated by coloring it in. But little by little half-tones and shading will begin to liven up the figures, and artistic illusion will achieve a third dimension which will model the volumes of the figures, but not the backgrounds, since perspective will only begin to interest some Italian painters in the XIVth century, and its evolution will develope in European painting throughout the XVth century. Due to this, in the *Lineal style* landscape will be flat and occupy a large part of the painting, allowing thus for the placement of many figures which will fill the surface (*horror vacui*) and which on some occasions are replaced by a neutral gilt background.

Iconographical development will also be very important at the beginning of the Gothic period; thus, besides the stories of Christ and the Virgin usual in Romanesque art, scenes from the lives of the Saints will be introduced, taken almost always from the *Golden Legend*. All these characteristics appear in an important retable, which the Prado has just added to its collection, thanks to the donation of a private individual (an example which should be followed). This retable is dedicated to the «Life of St. Christopher» and comes from La Rioja region. In it there exist reminders of Navarran mural painting from the first half of the XIVth century, but it should be dated at the end of the century, since it is related to a retable from the Monastery of San Millán de la Cogolla with scenes from the life of the titular saint and with the «first edition» of this school: the «Quejana Retable», dated 1393, which has been transferred from the Alava region to the Chicago Museum.

Chronologically the second stage of Gothic painting on the Iberian Peninsula corresponds to a stylistic trend which, proceeding from Italy, begins to substitute Gallic lineality, entering into the Gothic realm. The *Italo-Gothic* style begins in the second decade of the XIVth century, lasting until the middle of the XVth. Cataluña will be the region most quickly and strongly influenced, since the Mediterranean is in Medieval times the most ideal route of communication for linking the peoples on its shores. The stay of Simone Martini in Avignon will serve to stimulate the diffusion of the Sienese style outside of the Italian Peninsula, for there gather painters such a Ferrer Bassa (d. 1348), who will be the one to introduce the style in Spain. His masterpieces are the frescoes which decorate a chapel in the cloister of the Pedralbes Monastery (Barcelona) in which the Sienese influences are joined with Giottesque ones. To the most immediate of Giotto's followers, Tadeo Gaddi, are attributed, in the Prado, two delicate little panels with scenes from the life of St. Eloi (Pl. III). Although the Giottesque style signifies a step toward reality, since it searches for new sensations of plasticity in the figures, nevertheless the brothers Jaime and Pedro Serra, who work in the second half of the century, turn their backs on these new artistic forms, cultivating the sweet Sienese style, but interpreting it with great originality. The Prado has acquired two lateral rows from the retable which has in its center the famous «Virgin del Tobed» (c. 1373, Private Collection), a work done in collaboration although a greater participation by the head of the school, Jaime, may be perceived. In these works are represented «The Stories of Mary Magdalen and St. John» (C. 3.106-7). A delightful «Virgin of the Holy Milk» (C. 2.676) is also a work of theirs, which is a reduction of the large figure of the «Virgin del Tobed».

In Castile the Italo-Gothic style reaches, although tardily, the highest of levels. It will be a great Italian artist, Jacopo Starnina, who about 1380 will introduce it into Toledo. This Florentine who abandons his city due to social-political motives —for he is probably a *ciompi*, that is, an unflinching defender of the equality of man, basing himself on the Franciscan model— will give expression to the Giottesque forms, forging the way for the new Renaissance ideas, which his contemporaries Masolino and Massaccio will follow. This may be perceived in spite of the overpainting done by Juan de Borgoña, in the «San Eugenio Retable» in the Primate Cathedral. In the cloister of this church and in the San Blas Chapel are still conserved, in spite of their abandonment, remains of frescoes on which along with him the local painter Juan Rodríguez de Toledo also worked. This latter is the possible author of the «Retable of the Archbishop Sandro de Rojas» (circa 1420, C. 1.321), dedicated to the «Life of Jesus», which was transferred to the Church of San Román de Hornija from San Benito in Valladolid, where it was replaced by the one by Berruguete. At the feet of the «Virgin», who is in the center of the retable, are found the Toledan prelate and King Ferdinand, the one from Antequera. Even later Starninesque influences may be perceived in the «Retable of St. John and St. Catalina» (Pl. V), a work by Juan

15

de Peralta, the so-called Master of Sigüenza, but this latter is already within the *International Gothic* style.

From this third division of the Gothic style the Prado possesses important examples; possibly the most significant is the «Retable of San Felipe de la Bañeza» (Pl. IV), done by the most outstanding representative of the style in Castile: Nicolás Francés (d. 1468). His last name (Francés = Frenchman) would scarcely be an indication of his origin, if his style were not accompanied by the pictorial characteristics of *International Gothic* art. At this time, along with Italian influences arise those of the miniaturists in the European courts. And perspective begins to give a spatial and atmospheric feeling to the backgrounds, accentuating the lyricism which was delineated in the first Gothic style, as may be seen in this work by Nicolás Francés.

In the Kingdom of Aragón (including Cataluña, Valencia and the Balearic Islands), the *International* style reaches a great peak with Borrasa (C. 2.675) and Martorell. «The Virgin and Child» (C. 2.707) is possibly one of his most beautiful creations. In Aragón the Germanic and Oriental influences appear in coordination, such as in the «Retable of San Miguel» (circa 1450, C. 1.332), originating from Arguis, in which just like in the one dedicated to St. Vincent (Pl. VI), ingenuous elements appear which today seem traces of humor. This archaic feeling and the curvilinear arabesque totally disappear with the repercussion on the Peninsula of the *Flemish* style, which corresponds to the last flourishing of the Gothic period.

THE BURGUNDIAN HERITAGE

The Flemish Primitives.—To the north of the Duchy of Burgundy, in what is today Belgium and Holland, the axis of a pictorial movement appears which, if in some aspects is parallel to that which is being carried out in Italy —there are some who call it the «Nordic Renaissance»— in other aspects, it departs from it, for it searches for a Humanism different from the Italian one, based not on ideas, but on reality itself. Now these artistic and cultural movements arise at the moment when the European Gothic style has begun to take on a stereotyped meaning, similar to that which centuries before had reduced Byzantine art to pure repetition. But when it seemed that salvation could only come from Italy, a painter named Jan van Eyck (d. 1444) will give a Naturalist feeling to the painting in a large part of Europe. To do so, his style will be based on a refined technique achieved with the perfection of oil painting, with patiently applied layers of glazing. He will succeed in giving the figures a realistic character, especially in the faces and hands, for the pleats will still maintain their stiff edges, and will acquire tubular forms taken from wooden sculpture. Spain, a country he visited, has lost fundamental works by Jan van Eyck, such as the «Arnolfini Marriage Group», which today should be in the Prado, for it was stolen by Napoleonic troops from the Royal Palace in Madrid and «recovered» by the English; the National Gallery in London is not, therefore, truly its legitimate owner. Our museum only conserves a work done in collaboration with his workshop: «The Fountain of Grace» (Pl. VIII), related to his masterpiece, «The St. Bavon Retable», in Ghent. Van Eyck is a splendid portrait artist; thus, besides the «Arnolfinis», in which he succeeds in capturing an admirable homey scene and using the mirror as a foil, manages to amplify the miniscule room as Velasquez will later do in «Las

Meninas» (Pl. LXXIV), he does other portraits in which he attains a great intimacy, especially in the one of his wife Margaret. Other times he will include a portrait in a religious atmosphere, such as the Virgins in the «Canon van der Paele» and the «Chancellor Rolin»; in this last work, he introduces landscape perspective on the scene, going from an interior to an open air setting; and without neglecting spatial structures he lyrically portrays the most ingenuous little flover. By his best disciple, Petrus Christus (d. 1472-1473) —called «the Flemish Leonardo», because of the melancholy smiles which emanate from his faces— the Prado maintains a delicate «Virgin and Child» (C. 1.921) whose landscape is converted into an endless road, characteristic —as Spengler has said— of Northern painting.

There exists a series of intimately connected works, though with certain differences, done by the group of painters from Tournai, which have been assigned to the Master of Flémalle. Presently his personality has been divided into three personages: Robert Campin, his student Van der Weyden, and this latter's companion in studies Jacques Daret. Although Render's hypothesis, which attributes almost the entirety of the paintings in the group to Van der Weyden, is partially admissible, the «St. Barbara» (Pl. IX) and its companion piece, the portrait of «Heinrich Werl», along with other works, are probably paintings from Van der Weyden's early youth, for stylistically they are close to the «Scenes from the Passion», preserved in the Royal Chapel in Granada. On the other hand, they are further away from the «Annunciation» (C. 1.915) and the «Marriage of the Virgin» (C. 1.887) in which a greater Gothicism exists, as a result of which they must be earlier and thus possible works by Jacques Daret or his teacher Campin. Besides the impressive «Deposition» (Pl. X) in which there may still be perceived certain influences of Campin, the Prado preserves one of the most delicate «Pietàs» (Pl. XI) by Roger van der Weyden (d. 1465) and an enchanting «Virgin and Child» (C. 2.722) whose black background is probably the result of an unfortunate repainting. The «Cambrai Triptych» (C. 1.888-92) must be, in part, by Franck van der Stock, his student from Brussels and the one who continues with his workshop.

The fact that the important «Adoration of the Kings» by Hugo van der Goes was moved from Monforte de Lemos to the Berlin Museum has deprived our foremost museum of the possession of a masterpiece by this disturbing artist. On the other hand, the museum preserves a good piece by his teacher Dieric Bouts (d. 1475), a polyptych with scenes referring to the «Birth of Christ» (C. 1.461), a youthful work in which the chubbiness of the figures lends it a markedly popular feeling, characteristic of the Dutch painting of those times, for Bouts was born in Haarlem. Later his figures become stylized, such as in the «Emperor Oton's Judgement» (Brussels) and in the triptych in the Royal Chapel in Granada.

In the second half of the century, it is in Bruges that a new pictorial flourishing will be produced: the financial and industrial development will create a new class —the bourgeosie; it will require—in a desire to perpetuate itself— its chapels to be luxuriously decorated and its portraits to be painted with the greatest realism. This will be achieved with the settling in this city of a painter of German origin, Hans Memling (d. 1494), who in the early moments follows the line of Van der Weyden, but sweetening the forms, since he translates the vigorous language of his teacher into a style of a Romantic taste, with a feminine-like softness, very far from that which his compatriots in general were cultivating. This is perceptible in the triptych containing «The Adoration of the Kings»

(Pl. XII) in the central panel, or in the «Virgin and Child» (C. 2.543). Following him in the workshop in Bruges will be the Dutchman Gerard David, an artist impassioned with vertical forms, such as those in the «Rest on the Flight to Egypt» (C. 2.643) in which the very trees tend to exaggerate the ascendant feeling of this picture. He dies in 1523, and at this same time the Port of Bruges is closed.

In a world apart, far from the courtly or bourgeois cities, in the small town of Bois le Duc (in the south of Holland) a painter was born and lived whose fantastic originality will only be equalled in our own days. Hieronymus van Aeken (d. 1516), called in Spain Bosch, will be one of the most meticulous technicians of the painting of his times, which makes it possible for him to artistically express his protest against the life-styles of his period. Thus, with spirited and delicate coloring he achieves surprising effects, blending his tones with luminosity. Thanks to Philip II the Madrilenian Museum possesses the most important and surprising collection of his works, which are amply and well-deservedly commented upon in the explanatory texts.

The Nordic Influence in Spain.—In the second half of the XVth century Spain fully enters the Flemish sphere, rejecting, though not totally, the sweet insinuations of the Italian Renaissance. The contribution of masterpieces from Nordic painting will fertilize the field in which the style will flourish. Thus, Alfonso of Aragon possessed two Van Eycks: a triptych by the famous painter, partially preserved today in the Metropolitan in New York, was in the Carthusian Monastery of Miraflores (Burgos) and «The Fountain of Grace», which was in El Parral Monastery (Segovia) before it came to Madrid.

The first known work already within the Hispano-Flemish style and with which the «autumn» of Peninsular painting opens is the «Concellers Madonna» (1443, Cataluña Art Museum), done by Luis Dalmau after his return to Cataluña, this work is clearly of Van Eyckian inspiration. The Prado has a work by Jaime Huguet (d. 1492), the most important figure of this style in the Kingdom of Aragon. It is a «Prophet's Head» (Pl. VII) of a great expressiveness, by now removed from the style of his teacher Martorell. Now then, he never completely joins the Flemish naturalist style, bacause technically he maintains Italian reminiscences and in the forms he still remains faithful to the serpentine line of the International style, which will give his painting a delightful eclecticism. One of his closest followers is Pedro García de Benabarre, as his scenes of the «Life of SS Poylcarp and Sebastian» (C. 1.324-25) show. On the contrary, the genius and preoccupied wanderer Bartolomé Bermejo (active between 1473 and 1495), who though he is from Cordova, travels through almost all of the Kingdom of Aragon, succeeds in expressing his Flemishness with a vigor worthy of his possible teacher, the genius Nuno Gonçalves, since monumental plasticity will be his main characteristic, as his majestic «St. Dominic of Silos» (Pl. XIX) demonstrates. His style spreads at the end of the century throughout all of the Kingdom of Aragon, as we may see in Miguel Ximénez, a compatriot of Martin Bernat's by whom the Prado conserves the predella of a retable (C. 2.519).

Also in Castile, at mid-century, the Italian forms introduced by Starnina and then developed in the Renaissance in Salamanca by Nicolás Florentino, are abandoned. Early the Master of Sopetran introduced Van der Weyden's style in the central region; in some panels in which the son of the Marquis of Santillana appears (C. 2.576) his relationship to the master is so strong that it makes us think that he possibly studied in Flanders. The poet who wrote «Las Serranillas» (Santillana) will be portrayed in the «Retable of the Angels» (Duke of Medinaceli's Coll.) by the most important painter of the times: Jorge Inglés. The Prado, unfortunately, does not conserve any important work of his; a mediocre «Trinity» (C. 2.666) is doubtfully attributed to him. On the other hand, by the last great Castilian painter within this style, Fernando Gallego, there are three important works: the «Pietà» (C. 2.998), «Calvary» (C. 2.997) and, due to its qualities, especially outstanding is the «Enthroned Christ» (Pl. XX), in which there clearly exist Flemish influences while in the first two there are echoes of German or French artists from the Rhine area. They have especially strong coincidences with the style of Conrad Witz and the engravings by Schongauer, which indicates that they must be later, for as his life advances he moves toward a greater expressionism, in which the poses become more convulsive and the draperies are more elaborately twisted. Although his painting has exotic origins, it is believed —on the basis of toponomy— that he was born in the Salamanca or Zamora region between 1440-45.

It is in the times of the Catholic Monarchs that Castile will achieve its greatest artistic flourishing, to accompany its political and economic development. Not only is a large quantity of Flemish works imported, but Nordic artists will come, as well, to Spain. Two painters who work for Isabella the Catholic, Michel Sittow and Juan de Flandes, stand out among them. The former is a Russian coming from the shores of the Baltic; Juan de Flandes, on the other hand, studies along with Gerard David. Together they do the «Polyptych of the Catholic Queen», preserved in part in the Royal Palace in Madrid. Juan himself does the portrait of the Queen (El Pardo Palace) and for the Palencia Cathedral he paints the panels of its Main Retable. From the San Lázaro Church of this city come various «Scenes from the Life of Christ» (Pl. XXI).

MEDIEVAL PAINTING

BERLANGA, MASTER OF: Rabbit Hunt.

SERRA BROTHERS: Story of Mary Magdalen.

ANONYMOUS SPANIARD: Retable of St. Christopher.

GALLEGO: Pietà.

WEYDEN: Virgin and Child.

THE RENAISSANCE

III

ITS ITALIAN ORIGINS

Renaissance means *to be born again*; that is, to reawaken the Classical forms which were slumbering in the Middle Ages. For as Panofsky has demonstrated, at times Classicism was resurrected in the Medieval period. Thus in Carolingian art and at some moments of the Gothic and Romanesque stages forms originating in the Ancient world may be perceived. We might add that in Visigothic and especially in Asturian styles the Classical forms reappear, on occasions with great purity. But where the great Renaissance truly is born is in Italy and, we might say, in the city of Florence. Although its halting pictorial beginnings commence with Cavallini, Cimabue and Giotto in the XIVth century, it is a century later, in the *Quattrocento*, when it will achieve its overall structuralization. The Renaissance artist, although he wants to follow the Classical patterns and make Roman art spring up from its ruins once more, creates an original style, different from the Classical one. Humanistic curiosity which tries to capture the secrets of the world through observation, also catches hold of the artists themselves. In them, the new scientific spirit is so important that in the art of the times structures appear which have been achieved by means of a speculative activity. Thus the study of geometry and the science of numbers, developed by the Mussulman scientists, will determine *proportions* and *perspective*, the application of the infinite within a finite space, will be achieved by means of rigorous calculation. This is a novelty in the history of art, although the return to *full forms* and the search for *foreshortening* not only have antecedents in Antiquity, but also in Medieval times. On the whole, the iconography will continue to be the same as that of Medieval Christianity, though along with the figures of Christ, the Virgin and the Saints, mythological themes, very rare in the previous period, are introduced.

A painter at the crossroads of Renaissance forms and Medieval traditions is Fra Angelico (Giovanni de Fiesole, 1387-1455), whose name before taking the habit was Guidolino di Pietro. In his work the curvilinear forms of International Gothic still persist, but, nevertheless, little by little he begins to concern himself with the new luminosity and volumetric structures, as may be observed in the marvelous «Annunciation» (Pl. XXII).

There is a gap in the Prado Museum's collection when it comes to important works of the Florentine Renaissance which could have been filled in if Charles III, instead of donating his collection of paintings coming from the Farnesio family to the city of Naples (Capodimonte Museum), had brought it back to Madrid. Thus until we come to the paintings narrating the «Story of Nastagio degli Honesti» (Pl. XXIII-IV), by Sandro Botticelli (1444-1510) there is no important work from this period in the museum. If in Fra Angelico the figures are   21 expressed serenely and with a contemplative beatitude, in Botticelli the figures are restless and melancholy. His «Madonnas» lack joy and abandon themselves to a sad dreaminess, as if they were prophesying the Passion of the Son. The same thing happens in «Primavera» and the «Birth of Venus» in the Uffizi in Florence; it is accentuated even more in the «Calumny» and in his two «Depositions» and in the «Prayer in the Garden» in the Royal Chapel at Granada. Besides, Botticelli is a great portrait artist, as proved by «Lorenzo the Magnificent», «Young Man with a Medallion», or the «Portrait of a Boy», in the Cambó Collection in Barcelona.

On the other hand, our Museum conserves one of the masterpieces by the supreme representative of the School of Padua, Andrea Mantegna (1431-1506): «The Death of the Virgin» (Pl. XXV). Although he studied in the workshop of the mediocre Squarcione, his true masters are the Classical sculptors and Donatello, by whom are preserved in Padua the sculptures which decorate the main altar of the Church of San Antonio and the equestrian statue of the Condotiero Gattamelata. There only exists in the Prado a workshop replica of G. Bellini's «Virgin, Child and Saints» (C. 50) and although it is signed, the authentic original is conserved in the Academia in Venice. On the other hand, in the Madrilenian San Fernando Academy there exists a lovely «Saviour», by his hand, of which the Prado possesses a copy.

Of a Venetian air is one of the most admirable works by Antonello da Messina (d. 1479): a «Pietà» (Pl. XXVI), although we believe that it is done immediately after his trip to Venice and in his native city, since the Cathedral of Messina appears in the background. Enveloping the Flemish-like forms —picked up by Antonello in the Neopolitan court of Alfonso of Aragon, his protector— are the colorist feeling and idealism characteristic of his last years. In Venice Antonello will do some splendid portraits —in which he penetrates deeply into the psychology of the personage to a degree seldom reached in the history of painting— which will influence those done by Giovanni Bellini.

Of the *Quattrocentista* painting from central Italy the Prado has two examples: the first is a repainted «Angel», a work attributable to Melozzo da Forli (1438-1494) after comparing it to other angels he did for the Roman Church of the Holy Apostles (today in the Vatican Pinacoteca). It is interesting to note that Melozzo had contact with Pedro de Berruguete in Urbino. The other example, by Antoniazzo di Benedetto Aquili, called Romano (d. circa 1508) is an interesting triptych (C. 577 a); but also kept in the Prado is a fresco fragment representing the «Virgin and Child» (C. 577), interesting since it is the only example of this technique from the «Quattrocento» in this Museum, for in it may be perceived the importance of the drafting, which outlines the figure to make it stand out more; it comes from the Church of St. James of the Spaniards, in Rome.

The Culmination of the Cinquecento.—Around 1500 a trasformation in the Italian Renaissance takes place, although conserving its idealistic and impersonal character, which separates it from the Flemish style. Its principal novelty is derived in a gradual rejection of *anecdotal* elements, to emphasize the *content*. This change makes its acceptance possible in the other European countries, such as Spain or France, which had been more attracted to Northern painting; and even in Flanders itself the forms created by Leonardo, Raphael and Michelangelo, and later by the Venetian painters and Correggio, will have repercussions.

At the dawn of the century Florence is still the focal point where the principal artists reside. But soon they will emigrate to Rome since the Papacy, as it becomes politically vigorous, will initiate a cultural policy and will need the artists as efficient propagandists of the greatness of the Popes. Around the middle of the century the ancient seat of Roman culture will be the center of a new artistic ecumenism: the Catholicized Renaissance. A socio-artistic-cultural phenomenon it will evolve from being typically Italian to become typically European.

The first truly *Cinquecentista* painter, not only stylistically, but by temperament, although he was born and worked as an artist in the previous century, is Leonardo da Vinci (1452-1519). Gifted with a powerful intelligence, he practices not only the arts, but also scientific speculation and elaboration. He studies the human body, invents machines for ground and air travel as well as weapons of war. In spite of his impressive imagination, reason predominates in his technical and artistic projects, though few of them are carried out, due to his restlessness. In his painting light and movement are his principal discoveries, He conceives the illumination of a picture as the gradual fusion of white with black, achieving a special chiaroscuro (*sfumato*) and with *neutral*, not *tonal* colors, he succeeds in attaining soft volumes which in contrast to Michelangelo's are completely anti-sculptural. On the surface of his panels the figures are fused with the atmosphere as if a light velvet mist covered them, creating an undefined and mysterious sensation. Actually, these innovations arise as a reaction against the previous generation, specified in its master, the painter and sculptor, Verrocchio, and are motivated by Leonardo's restless and misanthropic character. From his formative Florentine years is the «Annunciation» (1472). He will move to Milan, where he will be in the service of Ludovico «the Moor». A masterpiece from this moment is the «Madonna of the Rocks» (1483) which, along with «The Last Supper» (1498), will be the culmination of this period. With the fall of Ludovico, he returns to Florence in 1505, doing the cartoon for the «Battle of Anghiari»; a year earlier he will create the famous «Mona Lisa»; and ten years later he will be called by Francis I to France, where he will end his days. The Prado has a delightful copy which is a contemporary of «La Giaconda» (C. 504). But although some critic may have considered it a second original, it is probably a copy done in the master's own workshop. Berenson formulated the hypothesis that the copyist might have been Spanish, which is admissible for in some of the details it tallies with the art of Fernando Yáñez de la Almedina, who in these moments worked in Leonardo's workshop, but the delicacy of the gray-green glazes, which soften the hands and part of the face, might have been, in our opinion, done by Da Vinci himself. Even more problematical is the «Holy Family» (C. 242) which has generally been attributed to Luini. Although today the majority of the visible surface corresponds to the style of this student of Leonardo's, in the Virgin's head and her left hand there is a technical and stylistic level surpassing that with which we are acquainted in his works. Besides, drawings exist done by the Florentine master for this or a similar composition. It was presented in Florence to Philip II as an original by Leonardo himself and was so confirmed when the picture was delivered to El Escorial (1574). Due to this we believe that it should be scrupulously analyzed since, as is known, students finished works which Leonardo had started.

The reflection of Michelangelo in this Museum is even more tenuous, only in the «Flagellation» (C. 57) may his manner of painting be perceived directly, for its author is probably Gaspar Becerra, who remained faithful to Buonarotti's creations; thus there exists in the Prado's collection a drawing by Becerra himself which is a copy of «The Last Judgement».

On the other hand, Raphael Sanzio (1483-1520) is admirably represented. He receives in Urbino, his native city, his first lessons, possibly from his father Giovanni Sanzio. Around 1500 he settles in Perusa, collaborating with Il Perugino, who influences his first style greatly. In 1504 he will move to Florence where his Peruginesque subtleties will be modified by the monumentality which he receives as a result of his contact with Fra Bartolomeo; sometimes, in his landscapes, Flemish echoes may be perceived, as may be noted in the enchanting «Holy Family with the Lamb» (Pl. XXVII), done in 1507, the year in which his productivity reaches its zenith for this second period, achieving his stylistic maturity. In autumn of the following year, called for by Julius II, he will move to Rome, where he begins to do the fresco paintings in the *Stanze* of the Vatican. The first, that of the «Segnatura» (signature) will be finished in 1511 and is a milestone in his stylistic evolution, for the spiritual impact of Michelangelo will be present in the «School of Athens» and the «Disputation Concerning the Blessed Sacrament», the main panels in this room. In the following ones he will be aided by his pupils, and he will repeatedly resort to this throughout his Roman period, cut short by his early death. Due to this, the majority of the pictures from this time conserved in the Prado are owed in great part to collaborators; he scarcely does the preparatory drawings, the roughing out and then later the retouching work. This is what occurs in the «Visitation» (C. 300), the «Holy Family» («La Perla», C. 301) and the «Madonna of the Rose» (C. 302), where his collaborators Giulio Romano, Francesco Penne and Perino del Vaga have particularly intervened. On the other hand, in the «Holy Family of the Oak» (C. 303) there may be perceived a greater participation of the master — which is even accented in the «Fall on the Road to Calvary» (C. 298). But where he achieves a true masterpiece, since there the collaboration is probably miniscule, is in one of his most harmonious pictures: «The Madonna of the Fish». Another work completely by his hand is the «Cardinal» (Pl. XXIX), in which we see his loveliest and most penetrating portrait. By his disciples, and now within Roman Mannerism, there exist excellent examples here, such as the delightful «Adoration of the Shepherds» (C. 322), by Giulio Romano.

The Mannerist Crisis.—Although the concept of Mannerism still possesses a polemical meaning, it might be considered not only an artistic form, but also an expression of a way of life, and it is one of the moments of history in which society influences art in a decisive manner. Although the artistic forms created by the masters —Leonardo, Raphael, Michelangelo, and later those of Correggio— are repeated, as Hauser has written, the artist had never possessed more liberty and originality, since the Mannerist artists and authors tend to evade reality, breaking with Renaissance norms and harmony; for if formally they are close to the Renaissance, structurally they move away from it. They also search for a new sense of space in which they set compositional and semantic elements up in the form of a «brainteaser», producing a sensation of oppression. With Mannerism it is sometimes difficult to separate the sacred and the profane, the erotic and the mystic. All of this converts it into an unpopular style only suited to courtly and intellectual minorities. In the last moments of this artistic movement it comes closer to the people through the Church. Mannerism is spiritualized and regulated within the Counter-Reformation spirit which is given to it by the Council of Trent; this is the so-called *Reformed Mannerism* and in Camón's words, the *Trentine style*. It is at this time that it is converted into the spiritual link which will join Renaissance idealism and Baroque realism. But this latter style differs essentially from Mannerism, in that although there is a sense of creative originality and desire for liberation in both, Mannerism tends toward a greater abstraction, toward a taste for more complicated forms, toward themes of a greater interpretative difficulty, and toward a lesser respect for historic reality. This style is born simultaneously in Florence and Rome around 1517, the moment at which Luther is rebelling against the Papacy. In «The Stanza dell'Incendio» (1514-1519), there already exist Mannerist forms; and in these same moments in Florence these new structures are also arising in the paintings of Pantormo and Rosso. But it will be after the Sacking of Rome, in 1527, when it spreads throughout the entire Italian Peninsula and begins to infiltrate into the European countries, such as Spain, Flanders and France (The School of Fontainebleau).

Although he is not properly a Mannerist, Andrea del Sarto (1486-1531) —only three years younger than Raphael— represents the beginning of a new stage of Florentine painting, in which is already reflected a spiritual restlessness which will be developed by painters of the following generation. It seems that he studies in the workshop of Piero de Cosimo, but his ideal masters were Fra Bartolomeo and Michelangelo, and on occasions there may be seen the influence of the painter from Urbino. The Prado conserves various works by his hand, two of them masterpieces: the portrait of his wife «Lucretia di Baccio» (Pl. XXXI) and the «Mystic Conversation» («Madonna della Scala», Pl. XXX). Another important work is the «Sacrifice of Isaac» (C. 336), of which a replica is conserved in the Dresden Museum. Other works attributed to him in the Museum's catalog are doubtful attributions. Thus, the «Holy Family» (C. 335) seems to be a Mannerist copy of the original which exists in the Borghese Gallery in Rome. One of his followers, by now completely within the Mannerist style, is Daniel de Volterra (1500-1566) by whom we have a splendid «Annunciation» (C. 522). By another important Florentine Mannerist, Jacopo Caruti, called Il Pantormo (1494-1557), the Prado possesses a delicate «Holy Family'» (C. 287). And by the great portrait artist Agnolo di Cosimo, Il Bronzino (1503-1572), the Museum conserves the delightful «Don García de Mèdici» (C. 5), a lymphatic child, the son of Cosme I and Doña Leonor de Toledo, the Duke and Duchess of Toscana; also possessing the elegant characteristics of this painter is the superb «Portrait of Alphonso II de Este» (?) (C. 69), assigned with doubts to Girolano da Carpi.

The School of La Emilia, whose central focal point is Parma will give new energy and innovations to the Mannerist evolution. Antonio Allegri, Il Correggio (C. 1489-1534) will be its creator. Although he is not properly a Mannerist, the same as Sarto, his painting anticipates this style and even the Baroque one. Of his manner of painting we shall speak when we discuss the famous «Noli me tangere» (Pl. XXXII). Besides this work, there still remains for us a delicate «Virgin and Child with the Infant St. John» (C. 112) in which he achieves an admirable sensation of penumbra though the Prado could have had a splendid series of pictures with mythological themes. Now totally within Mannerism is his immediate follower, Francisco Mazzola, known as Il Parmigianino (1503-1540) who departs from his master, excessively accentuating the elongation of his figures, giving them a peculiar rhythmical modulation. This is perceived in the well-known «Madonna with the Long Neck» in the Uffizi or in the «Holy Family» (C. 283), related to the other version of the same in the Florentine Museum; more important are the portraits of the «Count of San Segundo» (C. 279) and the one of the «Lady with Three Children» (C. 280), in which, especially in the first one, the Parmesan painter achieves an intimate psychological penetration. The Prado possesses a delicate «Viola Player» (C. 55) by a disquieting artist of this school, Nicolo dell'Abate (1509-1571) who along with Primaticio and Il Rosso is the creator of the School of Fontainebleau, developing a particular Mannerism in the Court of Francis I.

Lucca Cambiaso (1527-1585) is born near Genoa, the city where he will decorate sumptuous palaces, such as the Doria. He will come to Spain to paint in El Escorial and along with Tibaldi he will be the most important Italian artist working for Philip II; he will die in Spain. Two of his masterpieces are in the Spanish pinacoteca, his plaintive «Lucretia» and the «Holy Family» (C. 60). In them is perceived a tendency toward a cubification of the volumes and a new luminosity which later will have an influence on the creation of Tenebrism. And starting from Correggio, Federico Barocci (1526-1612) will create vibrant compositions, such as «The Birth of Christ» (C. 18) and his great «Crucifixion» (1604, C. 18 a) in which there appears a ghostly Urbino landscape.

The Venetian Colorists.—The multicolorful feeling so characteristic of the painting of the lacustrine city is due in part to a contact with the Orient; the great contrasts which appear in its paintings —where alongside delicate nudes and bacchanals, pathetic religious pictures appear— are a reflection of its complex social forms. In Venice draftsmanship desintegrates and dissolves into textures, achieved through broad brush strokes, which produce the admirable coloring in which it is difficult to differentiate tones, with which pictorial qualities are achieved which will mark the beginning of the history of modern painting. It is with .Giorgione (Giorgio de Castelfranco, 1477 or 78-1510) that this exceptional moment begins. Educated in the workshop of G. Bellini, he searches for a new pictorial style in which color is plastically formalized and naturalized. Coloring and light reach a fusion, achieving the realization —according to Fiocco— of «integral painting». Besides, Giorgione gives a tender melancholy to his painings which will produce in the spectator a sensation of profound intimacy, as may be perceived in the delicate «Virgin with Saints» (Pl. XXXIII). His known works are very few and only two are dated: «The Castelfranco Altarpiece» (1500-1505) and the so-called «Portrait of Laura» (Vienna, 1506). His premature death cuts off an artistic flow of works full of idyllic humanity and contemplative fantasy.

Titian (1490-1576), on the other hand, though he begins with a pictorial concept similar to that of Giorgione's (who was his fellow student), in a certain sense will set aside, as his life progresses, this intimate feeling in order to express the disquietudes of a courtly and grandiloquent world. And, at the end of his life, he will succeed in returning to an intimacy, but in a manner different from the one of his youth, since this latter will be achieved through expressionist means. Born in Piave di Cadore, on the slopes of the Venetian Alps, he will soon establish himself in Venice, a city which he will seldom leave and then only because of urgent calls from powerful men, especially when called for by Charles V (Bologna, 1532-33 and Augsburg, 1548 and 1550-51) for whom he will work, the same as for his son, throughout his entire life. This is the reason that the Prado preserves the most important collection of his works, representing his artistic evolution from his youthful moments —good examples of this period are «The Virgin and Child», «St. Ulfo and St. Bridget» (circa 1515, C. 434), «Worship of Venus» (C. 419) and the «Bacchanal» (Pl. XXXIV), all studied in the commentaries and of a strong Giorgionesque influence— through his last stage—such as his «Religion Saved by Spain» (C. 430), from around 1563, in which Titian has taken advantage of a picture done earlier, possibly representing the pregnant Callisto surprised by Diana and her nymphs; he changes Diana into Spain and Callisto into Religion. Being impossible to mention all of Tititan's works in the Prado, since there are close to forty of them, we will only give some examples. Thus, among the portraits, stand out those of «Federico Gonzaga, the Duke of Mantua» (circa 1525, C. 408), «Charles V» (1532-33, C. 409), painted when the Emperor is crowned, «Philip II» (C. 411), done in Augsburg in 1551 when he is proclaimed heir, the «Empress Isabel» (C. 413), and the «Knight with the Clock» (C. 412). Portraits exist in Titian's work included within a composition, such as that of the «Marquis del Vasto Addressing His Troops» (1541, C. 407), in which he allows himself to be influenced by the Mannerists («the Etruscan demons») and the fabulous work, «Charles V at Mühlberg» (Pl. XXXV). Among the other mythological pictures we can name the «Danaë» (C. 425), one of the loveliest nudes in all of universal painting, done for Philip II in 1553; «Venus and Music» (1548, C. 420 and 421); «Venus and Adonis» (1553, C. 422), and «Sisyphus» and «Tityus» (C. 426-7) finished in 1549. Among the religious ones stands out the impressive «Burial of Christ» (C. 440), a work from his last period in which he achieves an admirable synthesis and the chromatic qualities are done in a pigmentary manner, which brings him close to the final works of Rembrandt and Goya. Of it Gronau has said that «never was human pain expressed in a simpler and more artistically authentic manner».

The two other great painters of the Venetian school: Tintoretto and Veronese, are also excellently represented in the national pinacoteca. By Jacoppo Robusti, Il Tintoretto (d. 1594) there exist extremely lovely creations in which his tormented spirit and spatial preoccupation may be perceived. This latter at times gives him a scenographic feeling of Mannerist taste, such as occurs in «The Washing of the Feet» (Pl. XXXVII). Tintoretto is accustomed to repeat his themes; there exist, therefore, in our museum three «Judith and Holofernes» (C. 389-91). —one belongs to a series of «women in the Bible»— made up of «Susan and the Elders«, «Esther and Asuero», «The Queen of Sheba Before Solomon», «Joseph and the Wife of Potiphar» and «Moses Rescued from the Nile» (C. 388, 394-6) in which the perspective and foreshortening are strongly forced, since they were small pictures done to be set in the recessed panels of a ceiling, with the «Madianite Virgins» (C. 393) in the center. This gives it a great Mannerist feeling which is also perceived in «Tarquino's Violence» in which there are Michelangelesque echoes; «The Baptism of Christ» (C. 397) is one of his masterpieces with an almost Grecan spirituality. But where movement manages to become strongly convulsed is in the «Battle of the Turks and the Christians» (C. 399), reaching, in its background, a synthetic abstraction similar to that which exists in some of Boccioni's works. Stylistically less fortunate is his «Paradise»; nevertheless, it possesses iconographical interest for it is related to the immense painting which covers the great wall in the Ducal Palace in Venice. Within his portrait activity stands out the «Lady Revealing Her Bosom» (C. 382) whose gray tones anticipate those of Velasquez. Lorenzo Lotto (1484-1556) is the great creator of the local school of Bergamo; since he was born in Venice, his style is closely related to that of the painters from the lacustrine city. His preoccupation with symbology stands out in the double portrait of «Micer Marsilio and His Wife» (1523, C. 240), in which an amorino places the yoke on a betrothed couple. As Berenson has noted, the end of the tragicomedy is clear in the eyes of the spectator, for from the woman's eyes shine ambition and ill humor.

SPAIN AND THE EXPANSION OF RENAISSANCE FORMS

It is at the end af the XVth century that the influence of the Italian Renaissance will truly penetrate the Iberian Peninsula and then develop throughout the following century, passing through the various periods which we have seen follow each other on the other peninsula. Some artists take their forms directly from the Italian masters; this occurs in Yáñez de la Almedina, the Berruguetes, Luis de Varga, Machuca, Becerra and others. On some occasions Italian painters, not very important ones, and Flemish ones, are those who bring in the Renaissance structures. But *fresco* is scarcely practiced here until the end of the century, for this technique will be used for important cycles in El Escorial, the Royal Palaces and in the Palace of Don Alvaro de Bazán in El Viso del Marqués. The most frequently utilized technique in the first two-thirds of the century is oil on wood and in the final third oil will be used on canvas. Mythological themes with nudes will appear only sporadically in Spanish iconography of the times, in which «decorum» predominated, since the importance of the vigorous Spanish Catholic Church created innumerable commissions for religious paintings; under the reign of Philip II the great official portrait work begins, motivated by the desire for perpetual fame which accompanies dynasties and power.

Before the beginning of the XVIth century, in Valencia, artists appear who already begin to introduce Renaissance forms into the region. The Osonas, Paolo de San Leocadio and Francesco Pagano de Neapoli will be the precursors; to one of these last two should be attributed the enchanting «Caballero de Montesa Madonna» (C. 1335) in which in the personages and in the setting there are echoes of central Italian painting. San Leocadio and his companion worked on the retable in the Valencia Cathedral in 1472, commissioned by Alexander VI, *the Borgia Pope.* Theirs also are the two heads: «The Saviour» and «Mary» (C. 2.693 a and b). But to Rodrigo de Osona, the Younger, may be attributed the panels with the scenes of the «Passion» which are today exhibited as a loan to the Museum and in which the Italian forms are modified by an expressionism of Nordic origin.

Around 1482, Pedro de Berruguete (d. 1504), a native of Paredes de Nava, returns to Castile. He was formed within the late Flemish style; around 1475 he moves to Urbino where under the protection of Duke Federico de Montefeltro, he will do a series of pictures in which his characteristic style already appears. In it is blended a Flemish aspect, especially in the realism of the faces, with a poetic luminosity in which, although with Eyckian modifications, may be per ceived echoes of Luca Signorelli and Piero della Francesca, whom he meets in the capital of Las Marcas. The perspectivistic atmosphere of his panels is counterbalanced by the golden draperies which fill the background, following the Castilian pictorial tradition; but on some occasions, such as in the «Virgin and Child» (C. 2.709), a delicate landscape timidly appears. In his final period his style becomes more expressionistic, as may be observed in the panels which, coming from Santo Tomás in Avila, are found today in the Prado (Pl. XXVII). Meanwhile, in Toledo, Juan de Borgoña (d. circa 1535) will also introduce a style derived from Ghirlandaio, with whom he probably studied, for it is significant that he shows up in Toledo the same year the latter dies. He works dedicatedly for the Cathedral of that city (Capitular Salon, 1507-11; Mozarabic Chapel, 1514). A characteristic work of his within his first Spanish period is «Mary Magdalen with Three Dominican Saints» (C. 3.110).

But it will also be in Valencia, at the beginning of the century, that the pictorial Renaissance will continue to develop with the most vivacity, for just as in the Middle Ages, maritime communication strengthens cultural ties with the Italian Peninsula. Thus, in 1506, Yáñez de la Almedina and Hernando de Llanos return from there and begin the wings of the Cathedral retable. Formed in the Leonardesque atmosphere, though the second limits himself to uninspiredly copying the master, Yáñez will reveal to us an overflowing personality in which along with a Leonardesque influence will be perceived the influences of Giorgione's light and composition. His line has great strength, while the figures attain monumentality, as occurs in his «St. Catherine» (C. 2.902) and closely followed by «St. Damian» (C. 1.339); probably from his last period in Cuenca is the mysterious «Holy Family» (C. 2805) and possibly painted for his native Manchegan city. In the second third of the century, Raphael will be the one who stimulates Valencian painting. Spanish Raphaelism is headed by Juan Vicente Masip (d. 1549), whose masterpiece is the «Segorbe Retable» (1530); the Prado conserves by him the martyrdom of «St. Ines» (C. 843) strongly influenced by the Italian master; «The Visitation» (C. 851), in which is still perceived the influence of the Flemish painters in the landscape and a «Christ Shouldering the Cross» (C. 849), possibly based on a work by Sebastian del Piombo. His son Juan de Juanes (d. 1579), in spite of being better known, does not attain the technical quality of his father. «The Last Supper» (C. 846) is his most popular work, and though it follows somewhat the one by Leonardo, the forms are cloyingly sweet, except in the delicate and realistic still life on the table, in which, according to tradition, the Holy Grail stands out among the objects. His scenes from the «Story of St. Stephen» (C. 838-842) are possibly his most lovely creations: in the «Burial of the Saint», he portrays himself and in the «Leading of St. Stephen to His Martyrdom», the figure of St. Paul has the features of Cosme di Mèdici, recalling the portraits done of him by Il Bronzino. The supposed «Portrait of Don Luis de Castellá» (C. 855), if it is a work by either one, probably corresponds to the father for it possesses great technical and psychological vigor.

To the introducer of the Renaissance in Seville, Alejo Fernández (d. 1545-46), Angulo wisely assigns the «Flagellation» (C. 1925) in which there exist strong echoes of Germanic painting which confirms the hypothesis that Alejo was of Germanic origin. Better represented is the work of the Toledan Pedro Machuca (d. 1550) which will evolve in Italy and Granada. From the earliest moment and related to Beccaffumi's art is the «Madonna of Suffrage» (C. 2.579) dated 1517, which makes the author of Charles's Palace in Granada one of the first Mannerists. From a Hungarian collection comes the «Descent from the Cross» (C. 3.017), done by then in the region of Granada for although Italian forms persist, there are very Spanish realistic details, such as the child with the bandaged toothache, not to mention the Spanish inscription.

Standing out in the second Mannerist stage of Spanish painting is Luis de Morales (1520-1576), from Extremadura. We shall describe his style in the commentary on his tender «Virgin and Child» (Pl. XLIII). On many occasions he will succeed in expressing mysticism through an ascetic refinement such as occurs in the «St. Stephen» (C. 948 a). An example of delicate composition is the «Presentation» (C. 943) and his capacity as a portrait artist stands out in the «St. Juan de Ribera» (C. 947), for is represents his protector with a markedly nostalgic character; Ribera was the Bishop of Badajoz, later he would be Archbishop of Valencia, where he acquires works by El Greco. At the end of his life, Morales, poor and almost blind, dedicates himself to painting miniatures, while Philip II is surrounded by mediocre painters. Of the artists whom he sends for to decorate El Escorial, among the Spaniards, the only one worth mentioning is Juan Fernández Navarrete, «the Mute» (d. 1579), who introduces the Venetian influence into Spain, but the Prado only has a single and youthful work of his, the «Baptism of Christ» (C. 1.012) in which he appears as a Raphaelite and it serves as a «model» to enable him to get the contract for El Escorial. In the last third of the century, painters appear who are dedicated almost entirely to painting portraits. The first of them is Alonso Sánchez Coello (d. 1568); although from Valencia, he is considered Portuguese due to his residence in the neighboring country. He owes his style to a great extent to his teacher, Antonio Moro (whom we shall discuss later) and he is then influenced by Titian, through the paintings by him kept in the Royal Palaces, and although technically he does not succeed in equalling either of them, his portraits possess a markedly realistic tone which presages Velasquez, which becomes patent in the portraits of «Isabel Clara Eugenia» and «Catalina Micaela», the daughters of Philip II (C. 1.137 to 1.139). Nevertheless, in the one of «Prince Don Carlos» (C. 1.136) he prefers to idealize the traces of mental imbalance, giving his face an agreeable expression. The «Mystic Marriage of St. Catherine» (C. 1.144) is an example of the academic coolness used in the treatment of religious painting, of which abundant examples exist in El Escorial. His most important follower is Juan Pantoja de la Cruz (1553-1608) who also begins as a painter of religious narratives; it will be after the death of his teacher when he begins his cycles of portraits. Around 1600 he paints enchanting feminine figures in which stiff, ornate costumes frame the faces. On the other hand, the portraits of «Philip III» (C. 2.562) and of his wife «Doña Margarita» (C. 2.563) —done in 1606— achieve a unitary feeling by means of the lighting effects.

A Festival of Lights: Domenico Greco.—The somber panorama of Spanish Renaissance painting, only sprinkled with minimal flickers, will suddenly be flooded with light by a luminous flash from Eastern Europe; as so often happens in history, «from the East came a light». Domenico Theotocopuli (or Theotocopulos) (1541-1614), called during his lifetime in Spain, Domenico Greco, and later El Greco, is born in Candia (Crete) were he begins his studies in the icon workshops; at twenty he moves to Venice where he learns with Titian the

Venetian techniques and from the Bassanos he takes his luminism. In Rome (though later he will affirm «that Michelangelo was a good man who did not know how to paint») he will accept this latter's sculptural forms which he will later apply in his painting.

But it is in Spain where he will achieve the true transformation which will make him one of the most formidable geniuses in universal painting, maintaining his artistic independence and refusing to let himself be regimented in any way. Now then, without Toledo —as Marañón indicates— it is impossible for us to understand El Greco's greatness. His mystic nature makes him accept the ideas of the exalted Castilian religious atmosphere at the end of the century. He becomes the personal friend of poets and mystics, such as the Beatus Juan de Avila, Il Paravicino, St. Juan de Ribera, etc. That and his contact with the sculptures of Alonso de Berruguete make the mystical tension in his painting increase and his personages as they become more spiritualized will also dematerialize, being converted into winged, almost ethereal, forms which have been compared to Bizantine models he must have seen in his youth. Although a good part of the convulsive postures of his personages are derived from Mannerist forms, he breaks with the lines and anatomical proportions of the Italians; and although his coloring has a Venetian origin, it finally dissolves into truly palpitating flashes, achieved by dipping cloths in the pigments or by direct application with the fingers. This feeling of technical convulsion brings him at times to clean his brushes by running them directly along the margins of the canvas.

Somewhat forgotten in the past two centuries, it was at the beginning of this one that he was rediscovered by Bartolomé Cossío, his first great biographer. This work has been continued antithetically by Camón and by Wethey; for if the former maintains a criterion of valiant «openness», in which sharp esthetic perceptions abound, the American critic has, perhaps to an excessive degree, pruned out the catalog of his works. The Prado only possesses one painting in Greco's Italian style: «The Annunciation» (C. 827) which due to its strong Mannerist character, should be thought to have been done in Rome in spite of the fact the background recalls the Teatro Olimpico in Vicenza, a work by the Venetian architect Palladio. From his first Spanish moments is the Retable of Santo Domingo el Antiguo (1577, Pl. XXXIX). After having done a series of masterpieces such as «El Expolio» (1578), the «Martyrdom of St. Maurice» (1580) and above all «The Burial of the Count of Orgaz» (1586), around the end of the century he gets contracts for several retables; outstanding are the ones for San José, in Toledo; the Hospital de la Caridad, in Illescas, and the Colegio de Doña María de Aragón, in Madrid (1596-1600), from which will come the pathetic «Baptism of Christ», whose flickering tones give the figure a ghostly form. Probably done right afterwards are the «Crucifixion» (C. 823) and the «Resurrection» (C. 825); the «Pentecost» (C. 828) must be from the following decade since the face of the third apostle on the Virgin's right offers us the portrait of an already older El Greco. The superb «St. Andrew and St. Francis» (C. 2.819) was probably done in the last decade of the century, a moment at which he also does the «Coronation of the Virgin» (C. 2.645) —very close to the one at Illescas— and the prodigious «St. Sebastian» (C. 3.002), for although Wethey sees the participation of the workshop in it, its fluttering, palpitating technique certifies it as by El Greco's hand, but now mutilated, since due to their elongation the legs were 31 cut off—possibly as the result of an 18th-century estheticism. The «Adoration of the Shepherds» (Pl. XLII), along with the «Assumption» (Santa Cruz Museum in Toledo), are the works in which Domenico' Greco's painting culminates.

El Greco was also a portrait artist of the first order as the portraits appearing in «The Burial of the Count of Orgaz» show. He had already done important pieces in his Italian period («Julio Clovio»). In the Prado the unfolding evolution of his Spanish portrait work may be followed, for ten examples exist. The series begins with the «Nobleman with His Hand on His Chest» (Pl. XL) and there are others just as important, such as «Doctor Rodríguez de la Fuente» (circa 1580; C. 807), «Don Rodrigo Vázquez», President of the Council of Castile (circa 1600; C. 808), «Bachiller Jerónimo de Ceballos» (circa 1608; C. 812) and above all, the mysterious «Unknown Gentleman» (circa 1610; Pl. XLI) and the impressively realistic «Trinitarian Friar» (C. 2.644), done with the technique of his final years. The portrait of «Julian Romero, 'of the Heroic Deeds'» merits separate mention, due to its peculiar composition, since is shows him praying, as if the painting were a sculpture, and being presented by his patron Saint to God. This iconographic rarity is another symptom of the great spirituality which El Greco attains in Spain, for as his epitaph Brother Hortensio Paravicino, his friend and contemporary, will write at his death: «Crete gave him his life and brushes; / Toledo a better fatherland where he begins / to achieve in his death eternity».

Idealism and Realism in Flemish Renaissance Painting.—With the disappearance of commercial and artistic life in Bruges, the workshops are moved to Antwerp, the new seat of Flemish industry and banking, and as the city straitens its mercantile ties with Italy, it will cause the Nordic Renaissance to flourish there.

It is very significant that a painter who possibly studied in Bruges, Joachim Patinir (d. 1524), the most important landscape artist of his times, would at the end of his life settle in this city. His landscapes, although they have Gothic origins, such as in the displacement of the horizon into the distance —to make possible the situation of multiple scenes in his panels— already begin to reflect a preoccupation with an approximation to nature, for they bristle with spires similar to the ones which exist in the proximities of Dinant, though some writers see in these backgrounds the influence of Leonardo. Possibly the best collection of his works is the one which belongs to the Prado. «Charon Crossing the Styx» (Pl. XLIX), the «Temptations of St. Anthony» (C. 1.615), with figures by Quentin Matsys, and the «Penitent St. Jerome» (C. 1.614) are among the loveliest of his productions.

In Antwerp Jan Gossaert (1465-1533), called Mabuse, is the first one —as Van Mander, the biographer of the Flemish painters of his time, says— «to introduce the true manner of ordering and composing scenes with nude figures and a poetic feeling». He accompanies Philip of Burgundy to Rome (1508) and there he sketches the Classical monuments which he will use in the architectural backgrounds of his works. Even so, he will not abandon the Flemish technical tradition and, besides, he bases himself on some of the Classics from the previous century; thus he does freely adapated copies of the figures in «Christ, the Virgin and St. John the Baptist» (C. 1.510) from the St. Bavon Retable in Ghent. His masterpiece conserved in the Prado is a «Virgin and Child» (Pl. XLV). The «Virgin of Louvain» (C. 1.536) could be a youthful work of Bernard van Orley

(1492-1542), from Brussels, who also receives his formation in Rome. Other works of his on the same theme are conserved in the Prado, such as «The Virgin of the Holy Milk» (C. 1.920), still inspired by a work of the Master of Flémalle. A very important work is «The Holy Family» (1522, C. 2.692) of a strongly Raphaelesque taste. Elías Tormo thought that on St. Joseph's beard Dürer himself might have collaborated; we consider that the marine landscape that may be observed through a window is painted by Patinir in his last period. A style of painting loaded with social satire is developing in Antwerp, as well. Its creator is Quentin Metsys or Matsys (1465-1530); born in Louvain, he soon moves to the commercial emporium, where he lets himself be influenced by the traditional and the Italianate painters, besides capturing the spirit of Erasmus of Rotterdam. He uses satire in a symbological manner, as he does in the «Old Woman Tearing Her Hair» (C. 3.074), probably an allegory on envy or anger, and especially in his pathetic «Christ Before the People» (Pl. XLVI). The social criticism is continued by Marinus Claeszon van Reymerswaele (d. 1567), such as in «The Money-Changer and His Wife» (Pl. XLVII); the Prado has, as well, two dramatic «St. Jeromes» (C. 2.100 and 2.653) and an expressive «Virgin of the Holy Milk» (C. 2.101), with an apocryphal anagram of Dürer's. Other artists go on cultivating the style created by Matsys thus Pieter Coecke van Aelst (1502-1550), a Humanist in spirit— he translates Vitrubio and Serlio— cultivates architecture and sculpture in Brussels (such as a «Baby Jesus», discovered by us, today in the Toledo Museum). Charles V names him an artist of the Royal Court; for this reason his works are very abundant in Spain. The Prado conserves two complete triptychs (C. 2.223 and 2.703), as well as two wings, one with impressive ladies in mourning (C. 1.610). But his major greatness originates from the fact that he was the master of Pieter Bruegel, the Elder (1529? - 1569), who goes to Italy after his teacher dies. After his return (1554), he creates a style in which the popular element is converted into an extremely lovely artistic expression and in which landscape takes on a new meaning. The Prado, besides a grisaille in very unsatisfactory condition which represents the «Adoration of the Kings» (C. 2.470), possesses one of his captial works: «The Triumph of Death» (Pl. XLVIII). His style is continued by his son Pieter, the Younger, such as in the «Landscape with Snow» (C. 2.816), in which he faithfully copies a picture of his father's which has been lost. When he on some occasions departs from his father's style, as in his mythological themes («The Rape of Proserpine», C. 1.454), he loses his vivacity. Another of Bruegels' followers in landscape painting is Lucas van Valckenborch (d. 1597, Frankfurt) by whom the Prado conserves interesting works.

In the last years of the century Michel Coxie (1499-1592) works within the style of Romanism or Reformed Mannerism, and especially for Philip II, for whom he copies Van der Weyden's «Deposition» (El Escorial). But his masterpiece in the Prado is the great triptych with «The Life of the Virgin» (C. 1.468-70), painted for St. Gudule in Brussels. The central scene with the death of Mary is enveloped by a Romanist architectural setting. On the other hand, the portrait artist most highly valued by Philip II is Antonio Moro (Anton van Dashort Mor) (1519?-1576); born in Utrecht, he studies in Antwerp and travels to Spain to paint personages of the Court, and then he goes to England to portray «Mary» (Pl. LIV), the second wife of the Prudent King. Among his most energetic portraits is the one of «Metgen», his wife (C. 2.114), as well as the one just cited. Of great expressive force is also the one of «Doña Juana of Austria» 33

(C. 2.112), the mother of King Sebastian of Portugal, and the one of «Emperor Maximilian II» (1550, C. 2.111). In the one of the «Buffoon Parejón» (C. 2.107), may be intuited those which Velasquez will do of similar beings. Moro and Titian are the ones who will break the trail for the great Spanish portrait painting.

Holland.—Although Holland, along with Belgium, in the XVIth century was still joined to a unified Flanders under the Spanish Crown, due to ethnological and social reasons, its art begins to take on a character different from the states to the south, since in it there are expressionist forms which bring it close to those to the north of the Rhineland. Some artists are close to the group at Antwerp; thus Jan van Scorel (1495-1562) also travels in Italy and allows himself to be influenced by the Romanist school and by the Venetian painters. The Prado possesses an important «Portrait of a Humanist» (C. 2.580), pointing out the Tower of Babel; this makes it iconographically close to another work of his, «The Universal Flood» (C. 1.515), in which the forms take on a Mannerist exaltation, with anamorphosis being applied to some of the figures.

It is in Jan Mostaert (d. 1555) that tradition and the new ideals are blended. Born in what is now Holland (Haarlem), he gives a new poetic meaning to reality, as the painters of the second generation will do. This may be noted in the sensitive portrait of «The Young Gentleman» (C. 3.209) who may have been a member of the Austria Family, a work recently acquired by the Prado. The figure who introduces Mannerist forms in Haarlem, due to the proximity of Antwerp, is Cornelis Cornelisz (1562-1638), by whom the Prado conserves in its collection a lovely and important mythological work: «The Judgement of Apollo» (C. 2.088).

Germany.—The representation of Medieval German painting in the Prado is almost nil and as far as Renaissance painting goes, in contrast with the Flemish, it is deficient. This seems strange, since the political and social contacts between the two peoples were very close, especially in the XVIth century. And although in the palace inventories the Germanic paintings cited are scarce, and many of these were lost in consecutive fires, a great number of German engravings came to the workshops of our painters, and these, on many occasions, were then copied (Gallego, Master of La Sisla, etc.). It is necessary to recognize a certain enmity, if not of the people —for German works existed in monasteries and churches— at least of the Spanish aristocracy, toward Teutonic expressionism. In spite of all this, the Prado has an excellent representation of the work of Albrecht Dürer (1471-1528) in which stand out the splendid «Self-portrait» (Pl. LII), his «Adam and Eve» (Pl. L and LI), and a stupendous «Portrait of an Old Man» (1525, C. 2.180), thought until not long ago to be by Hans Himhoff. By another important painter of the times, Lucas Cranach, the Elder (1472-1553), are preserved two scenes of hunts in honor of the Emperor Charles V, given by Frederick of Saxony near the castle of Torgau (1554, C. 2.175-76); four years later he would be the Emperor's prisoner in Mühlberg. Besides, the Prado possesses a superb portrait by Holbein, the Younger (1497-1543, Pl. LIII), which is amply commented upon. By a follower of the style of this painter, Christoph Amberger (d. 1561 or 1562), is conserved the possible portrait of the goldsmith from Augsburg «Jög Zorer» (C. 2.183) and that of his wife (C. 2.184), which were painted in 1531.

RENAISSANCE PAINTING

BOTTICELLI: Story of Nastagio degli Honesti. Panel I.

BOTTICELLI: Story of Nastagio degli Honesti. Panel III.

MELOZZO DA FORLI: Angelic Musician.

LUINI: The Holy Family.

RAPHAEL: Fall on the Road to Calvary.

VERONESE: Jesus and the Centurion.

TITIAN: Danaë Receiving the Shower of Gold.

TINTORETTO: Lady Revealing Her Bosom.

LOTTO: Micer Marsilio and His Wife.

BASSANO: Adoration of the Shepherds.

ANONYMOUS SPANIARD: XVth Century. Caballero de Montesa Madonna.

BERRUGUETE: Virgin and Child.

MACHUCA: Deposition.

YAÑEZ DE LA ALMEDINA: St. Catherine.

JUANES: St. Stephen Led to His Martyrdom.

CORREA: The Annunciation.

SANCHEZ COELLO: The Infanta Isabel Clara Eugenia.

MOSTAERT: Portait of a Gentleman.

PANTOJA: Margaret of Austria.

THE BAROQUE STYLE

IV

ITALY AND ITS ORIGINS

Originally the term *Baroque* has a negative connotation, for it comes from its symbolic similarity with the barrueca» pearl, a term given in Portugal to one with deformities. When the word was introduced into France (*baroque*), it soon took on the meaning of eccentric or strange, and was especially used to designate artistic forms which were considered extravagant. In the XVIIIth century it will be applied first to the plastic arts and later to literature and music. Although in the following century the deprecatory aspect begins to lessen, for the Romantics on some occasions defend the works of the XVIIth century, it is around 1900 that thanks to Wölfflin its true recovery begins. Eugenio D'Ors comes to consider the Baroque style a current in history, and even defines it as an artistic manifestation which appears at the zenith of all civilizations. But generally this apellative is applied to the period in the history of art which falls between Mannerism and Neoclassicism; that is, more or less in the period from 1600 to 1750. In Spain the latter date is specifically 1752, when the San Fernando Academy is created as the organization formed to seek out and destroy the anti-Classical «monstrosities».

Baroque painting, the same as sculpture, begins by being realistic but an exacerbated tendency toward a search for movement, brings it, above all in the XVIIIth century, to the theatrical and sensational. Its preoccupation with open forms and vision of depth ends up by breaking the formal and compositional balance, achieving fantastic representations. The Baroque style tends, besides, toward a search for an unlimited perspective, possibly based on the contemporary philosophical preoccupations with managing to define the infinite. In this period, religious themes multiply since it is necessary to spread the stories of the new saints and perpetuate those of the ancient ones.

Tenebrism and Classicism in Italy.—In the first moments of the Italian Baroque style, the same as in the rest of the European regions, there exists a preoccupation with the search for reality, which joined with the attainment of new lighting effects, whose origins were found in Mannerism and the Bassanos, will essentially achieve the change in style. The first one to break the trail is Michelangelo Merisi, *Il Caravaggio* (1573-1610), achieving an illumination of natural derivation in which the shadows violently dissipate in zones illuminated by a single gleam coming from an elevated and exterior source —the so-called «cellar lighting». With this skylight illumination, at the artist's convenience faces, arms, torsos are made to stand out... leaving in darkness or shadows the rest of the painting, with which a sensation of mystery is achieved; because of this, this style has received the name of *Tenebrism*. But Caravaggio, before achieving this innovation in his period of maturity, which begins in 1598, does paintings in which the figures and objects are enveloped in tenuously vaporous atmosphere with lyrical shading, in which there only exists a preoccupation with volumes and in which the objects are substantial beings, whose qualities are esteemed, that is, whose materials are emphasized. For, as Martín González has said, «a cloth, some fruit open up a whole sensorial world for the spectator».

In the *Tenebrist* period, not only is the plastic intensity accentuated, but limiting the poetic sense the artist stresses realistic values. Thus, in Caravaggio's religious pictures the attributes of the saints disappear, and he relieves them of their halos, changing them into purely human beings, which on some occasions causes ecclesiastical protests, which prohibit the hanging of his works in churches. Nevertheless, Merisi's art is in accordance with the mandates of the Council of Trent, for besides not painting any female nudes, he departs from the false gaudiness which in years past had often decorated churches and cathedrals. His life is in concordance with his effervescent art, which brings him to be pursued by the law and to carry out his impressive work in mid-flight. Born, near Bergamo, in the town which gives him his nickname, he receives his formation in Milan; possibly in Genoa he becomes acquainted with Cambiaso's luminism and in Venice with that of the Bassanos. Later he stays for a time in Rome. Appearing among his first Tenebrist paintings is his «David, Victor over Goliath» (C. 65); rediscovered by Longhi, a cleaning has revitalized its qualities and tones, allowing us to see that it is an indubitable and extremely beautiful work of his.

The Prado has important samples of Caravaggio's followers; thus we will cite «The Holy Doctors Cosme and Damian» (C. 2.759), by Giovanni B. Caracciolo, «Battistello» (1570-1635) and an important series within the style: «The Story of the Baptist» (C. 256-8 and 291), the work of Massimo Stanzione (1585-1656), to whom is owed the well-composed «Sacrifice to Bacchus» (C. 259), painted for the Buen Retiro Palace in 1634.

Echoes of Tenebrism are still maintained, through Ribera in the later Neopolitan painters, Preti and Cavallino, for example. Mattia Preti (1613-1699) is one of the most important masters of the painting of his times. To him is owed the exquisite «Gloria» (C. 3.146), in which is perceived a contact with Luca Giordano; it is painted shortly after he moves to Malta in 1660, where he will remain until his death. His strict contemporary is Bernardo Cavallino (1616-1656), whose work was cut short due to the plague which put an end to his life at the beginning of his mature period. In his painting there is such an exquisiteness, at times a bit sophisticated, that it makes him one of the precursors of the *Rococo* style. The fundamental characteristics of his style are distilled in his «Cure of Tobias» (C. 3.151) and «The Wedding Banns» (C. 3.152), by this same artist, a recent and lucky acquisition. Important pieces exist by the eclectic Andrea Vaccaro (d. 1670). We shall discuss Giordano's work within the last period of the Baroque style in Spain, due to his stay in this country and the influences which he exercised here.

Tenebrism also develops, though ephemerally, in other regions of Italy, since Caravaggio traveled over almost the entire Peninsula. Thus, the Tuscan Orazio Gentileschi (1563-1639) allows himself to be influenced in Rome by the Tenebrist style, which will dissipate when he moves to France and later to England, where he dies. From this last period comes his decorativism, as in «Moses Rescued from the Waters» (C. 147), but it will be another pictorial center which will gradually eclipse the forms of Caravaggism: Bologna and its Classicism. It is in Bologna, that for the first time the first Academy of Fine Arts will be established, where painters will acquire a formation which is at once artistic, historical, literary... in short, academic. Members of the Carracci Family will be the promoters of an eclectic academicism; its founder Ludovico (1555-1619) will achieve paintings of high quality, such as his «St. Francis of Assisi» (C. 70) and his «Prayer in the Garden» (C. 74). The one to spread the style —in which within a strong personality are melded the forms of Raphael, Michelangelo and Il Correggio, along with Venetian coloring— is Annibale, his cousin. Among his most beautiful productions is «Venus, Adonis and a Satyr» (C. 2.631) in which he has let himself be carried away by the Venetian element, departing from academicism. Annibale is also the creator of a type of idealized landscape which will lead to the ones by «Le Lorrain» (Pl. LXXXI) and Poussin (Pl. LXXX). A charming version belongs to the Prado (C. 132), which is described in the inventory of the painter Maratta's collection as with «figure che si bagnano»; it formed part of a series whose three remaining pictures Wellington took to London, when he «recovered» the paintings which Joseph Bonaparte had in his luggage. Later, the Bolognese school will be headed up by Guido Reni (1575-1642), who will achieve great fame; in spite of this, in his youth he succumbs to Caravaggesque «dissipations», as may be seen in his delightful «Hippomenes and Atalanta» (C. 3.090), discovered by Pérez Sánchez; the evolution of his style will be studied when we comment upon his «Cleopatra» (Pl. LXI). Connected with this school is Gian Francesco Barbieri, Il Guercino (1591-1666); in 1618 he travels to Venice, as a result of which he will fortify his coloring, departing from academic rigidity and achieving a strong monumentality which would impress Velasquez, who in 1631 visits him in Cento, his native city. His influence is visible in the «St. Thomas» (Cathedral Museum in Orihuela) by this Andalusian painter. Standing out among the other pictures in the Prado is the impressive «Susan and the Elders» (C. 201) done in Guercino's Roman period as commissioned by the powerful Cardinal Ludovisi. In this latter painting he is far from the eclecticism of his first moments, which is perceived in the «St. Peter Freed by an Angel» (C. 200); within a more personal style is his «St. Augustine» (C. 202). Extremely succulent is the «Adoration of the Shepherds» (1614, C. 95), by Giacomo Cavedone (d. 1660). On the other hand, in Rome Andrea Sacchi (d. 1661) and his student Carlo Maratta (d. 1713) are creating important works, such as the life-like portrait which the latter does of his teacher (C. 327) or the one which Sacchi paints of Francesco Albano (C. 326), a painter of sensual «mythologies».

FLEMISH REALISM

Rubens and His Circle.—Just as in order to have an acquaintance with the stylistic evolution of the European painting of the first generation of the century, it is necessary to know Caravaggio's work, the second generation is based upon Rubens. He is the principal exponent of the artistic ideas of the Counter-Reformation, for when Holland becomes independent and turns Protestant, Belgium continues to remain under the Spanish Crown and stays Catholic. The pictorial school of this region is, to a great extent, the school of Rubens, and just like the Spanish one, it will exalt the Catholic faith. Meanwhile, in Holland, only some scenes from the Old Testament and the life of Christ will be narrated, with artists dedicating themselves almost entirely to genre and portrait painting, which in Flanders will be cultivated on a smaller scale.

The work of Peter Paul Rubens. (1577-1640), which embraces all genres, is prodigiously represented in the Prado Museum, where his entire development may be followed, since from the time he was young he works for the Spanish Court, finally becoming an ambassador for the King of Spain. On the other hand, his birth contrasts with his Hispanicism, somewhat paradoxically, though it is a symbol of his times, for his father was a rebel and was in exile when Peter Paul first saw the light of day. This takes place near Cologne, not far from Antwerp, the native city of his family, where he will move at the age of ten, along with his devoted mother. There he recieves his formation within an Italianate artistic atmosphere. From 1600 on he will stay in Italy for more than eight years; though he resides in Mantua, he will travel to Florence, Rome and Venice, soaking up not only Venetian coloring, but also the Michelangelesque forms, though he will accept only sporadically Il Caravaggio's luminous innovations. In 1603 he arrives in Spain as part of an artistic legation, painting in Valladolid, when he is only twenty-three, his majestic equestrian portrait of the Duke of Lerma (C. 3.137), thanks to a commission from this powerful *valido* (Prime Minister), and the series of the «Apostles» (C. 1.646-57), in which there may still be seen a Tenebrist influence in the light, and in the poses, Mannerist postures. Back in Antwerp, in 1609, he does the gigantic «Adoration of the Magi» (C. 1.638) for the Salon of the States in this city's Town Hall. Later, during his second stay in Madrid (1628), Rubens will expand this piece in which the influence of Titian and Michalangelo in his work may be felt. Still from the artist's youthful period is the dynamic «St. George and the Dragon» (C. 1.644). But it is in the cartoons for the tapestries on Eucharistic themes commissioned by Isabel Clara Eugenia for the Barefoot Carmelites in Madrid that religious allegory achieves its true vigor. A large part of the definitive versions are conserved in the Prado where they stand out plastically and iconographically. The rapid sketches, meanwhile, are found in Cambridge. In «The Triumph of the Church» (C. 1.698), that of «The Eucharist over Idolatry» (C. 1.699), and that of «Faith over Philosophy» (C. 1.701), the combative spirit of the Counter-Reformation Church is expressed and, at the same time, the forms take on a convulsive feeling. The important commission, finished in 1628, meant the important amount of 30,000 florins for Rubens.

At the same time the artist profusely cultivates mythological themes, among which stand out «The Three Graces» (Pl. LVI), «The Judgement of Paris» (C. 1.669), «The Rape of Prosperine» (C. 1.659), «Andromeda Freed by Perseus» (C. 1.663), and «The Nymphs Surprised by Fauns» (C. 1.665), in which he succeeds in capturing movement in action, in such a life-like fashion that it will only be equalled, throughout the XVIIth century, by another picture by Rubens himself, his «Peasants' Dance» (C. 1.691). In this tiny panel, which he will keep during his lifetime, he idylically narrates, like Titian, the joy of living. This theme again appears, though in a more reposed and courtly manner, in the prodigious «Garden of Love» (C. 1.690), in which he portrays himself in his mansion in Antwerp in the company of beloved friends. In landscape, as well, he achieves

40

an expressiveness of movement, dramatizing it by giving it a disquieting depth, such as occurs in his «Atalanta and Meleager Hunting the Calydonian Boar» (C. 1.662).

His portrait activity merits separate mention and, as we have seen, it begins in his youthful years. One of his loveliest portraits is the one of «Maria Mèdici» (Pl. LV). It is interesting to compare the portrait of the «Cardinal Infante Don Fernando», the victor at Nordlingen (1636, C. 1.687) with the one of the «Duke of Lerma» (1603) to observe the evolution toward an exalted Baroqueness, with the emblematic representation in the heavens of a winged victory and the Eagle of the Austria Family. The artist maintains this unbridled feeling until the end of his days, for just before he dies he does his fabulous «Andromeda, Freed by Perseus» (C. 1.663), which is finished by his student Jordaens.

Jacob Jordaens (1593-1678) is the painter who best interprets the expressive Rubenesque feeling; but instead of being a fervent Catholic like his teacher, he converts to Protestantism and is a supporter of the House of Orange, even secretly suggesting in some of his works anti-Catholic allegories. For this reason, he attempts to evade religious themes, though he cultivates versatility, as his mythological scenes show, and in which on some occasions he is ironical, as well. Among these scenes we can cite the «Offering to Pomona» (C. 1.547). His character, sarcastic and loquacious, brings him to do *genre scenes*, among which stands out «The King Drinks», which he repeats successively and in which is satirized Flemish gluttony. In others, he reflects the exaltation of popular life, such as in the admirable «Itinerant Musicians» (C. 1.550) in which two singers accompanied by a recorder are represented with a seldom equalled realistic forcefulness. In «The Jordaens Family» (C. 1.549) the painter presents us with a scene of extremely lovely intimacy which is very close to Dutch painting.

Anthony van Dyck (1599-1641) departs somewhat from Rubens' painting, tending toward a greater elegance, in some cases bordering on affectation. This is understandable, since he is not exactly a student, but rather a collaborator of the famous artist's, and even this for a short time (1618-1619), since he leaves for England, and a year later on November 20, 1621, goes to Italy, where he will remain for six years. In Genoa he portrays the city's aristocracy, with the elegant noblewomen standing out. One of the first portraits he does is that of «Doña Policena Spinola, Marchioness of Leganés» (C. 1.493), who soberly dresses in the Spanish fashion. These noblewomen contrast with the ones he will later represent in his second English period, when they will appear dressed up in rich cloth and with plunging necklines, as we see in the portrait of his wife «Maria Ruthwen» (C. 1.495), identified by the oak leaves which adorn her hair. Among the other portraits done at this time are the one of the «Countess of Oxford» (C. 1.481), the «Count of Arundel with His Grandson» (C. 2.526), the delicate «Self-portrait with Sir Endymion Porter» (Pl. LVII) and the portraits of «Charles I»; the Prado preserves a delightful sketch of an equestrian one (C. 1.484). Also in the parenthesis in Antwerp he expressively captures personages such as the «Prince of Orange» (1628, C. 1.482), the painter «Martin Ryckaert» (C. 1.479) and the «Musician Liberti» (C. 1.490). Without matching Ruben's productivity, Van Dyck's work is extensive, and he also cultivates religious themes, especially in his youthful years. His «Seizure of Christ» (C. 1.477), «Crown of Thorns» (C. 1.474) and «Serpent of Bronze» (C. 1.637) are youthful works in which may still be perceived Rubens' influence and, nevertheless, alongside it there exist mellow forms of an Italian origin.

The artist from Brussels Jan Bruegel de Velours (1568-1625) translates into the Baroque style the *genre scenes* which his ancestor, Bruegel, the Elder, initiated; in them, instead of the painter being an actor, such as occurs in Holland, he is converted into a mere spectator. We shall pursue this in the commentary upon Plate LIX (Teniers) and it may be seen in the «Peasant Dance Before the Archduke and Duchess Albert and Isabel Clara Eugenia» (C. 1.439) and in its companion piece, «The Wedding Banquet» (C. 1.438), painted in 1623. Bruegel will also be the initiator of the *cabinets d'amateurs*, as his early «Allegory on Sight» (Pl. LVIII) demonstrates. His paintings of *flowers* (C. 1.419 to 1.426) will find great acceptance; on some occasions he will decorate paintings by his esteemed Rubens with them, such as in the «Virgin and Child» (C. 1.417); other times he will add landscapes, such as in the portraits of «The Archduke and Duchess» (C. 1.683-1.684). But the ones who will generalize the *genre scenes* are the Teniers. By «the Elder» (d. 1649) the Prado possesses only his «Story of Reinaldo and Armida» (C. 1.825-1.836); by his son (1610-1690) there exists, on the other hand, a copious representation. Among his most characteristic works are his «Rural Festivities» (C. 1.785 to 1.790); in «Le Roi Boit» («The King Drinks», C. 1.797), he will do a burlesque interpretation of Jordaens' favorite theme, while in the «Monkeys» which carry out human tasks (C. 1.805 to 1.810), he uses a sense of irony. He also represents military scenes, such as «The Bivuoac» (C. 1.811) and «The Guard Post» (C. 1.812), which recalls works of Wouwermans'. But he enters most fully into the picaresque world in his *drinkers* (C. 1.791 to 1.796) and in the «Old Man and the Maid» (Pl. LIX), which we have selected as a sample of his art. Adriaen Brouwer (d. 1638), on the other hand, is the one who penetrates the true life of «les misérables», as Van Ostade, who studied with him in Frans Hals' workshop, is doing at the time in Holland. His realism would bring him to paint the most sordid elements of popular life, such as «The Lice Hunters» (C. 2.731) or «The Peasants» (C. 1.391-1.392), with their uncouth diversions.

The same as in Holland, the *still-life* and *animal paintings* will possess a great importance in Flanders, and especially in Antwerp. But here forms will become exhuberant, for which a great space will be necessary. Within an almost Dutch simplicity, Clara Peeters (1589?-1676) does *still-lifes* in which dishes and foods-tuffs are harmoniously structured. The Prado possesses three of them signed in 1611, and in one of them (C. 1.621) in the luminous reflections on the metallic pieces miniscule self-portraits appear. In this same line is the delicate «Still-life» (C. 1.606) by Osias Beet (1622-1679?). Frans Snyders (1579-1657) will be the one who applies Rubenesque opulence to the genre, and though he does impressive still-lifes, such as the «Fruit Vendor» (C. 1.757), he stands out when he paints animals in movement, a genre of which the Prado possesses a copious collection. His best students are his brother-in-law Paul de Vos (1590-1678) and Jan Fyt (1611-1661), of whom the Madrilenian Museum also has an excellent representation; in their works the fluidity of the teacher will be converted into impasto. This is accentuated in another important still-life painter from Antwerp: Peeter Boel (1622-1674) whose *cupboards* and *still-lifes* show the stylistic evolution of the school.

HOLLAND

Realism and Intimacy.—During the XVIth century —as we have already indicated— the northern Low Countries, although until the end of the century they remain under the Spanish Crown, start to move away, not only sociologically, but also artistically from the southern states, what is today Belgium. The war, followed by independence and peace (1609), makes their painting follow different paths. In Holland Puritanism causes religious painting to scarcely be practiced —except for some Biblical scenes— and nudes are strictly forbidden, the only one who ignores this is the genial figure of Rembrandt, who has as an antecedent the painters of Utrecht who in Rome had been in contact with Catholic circles. Therefore the themes handled will be especially those of «genre painting» —which extend from Biblical subjects to tavern scenes— landscapes, portraits, still-lifes and even animal paintings.

The battle for independence produces enmities during the XVIIth century, which makes understandable the scarcity of Dutch painting possessed by the Prado. In spite of this, the delicate Gerard Terborch (d. 1662) visits the Peninsula during these times; souvenirs of his trip are some of his delicate little portraits which may be considered «micro-versions» of those by Velasquez; but only one work of his is known to be in Spain (Alcázar in Seville).

While in some Dutch cities Mannerism is still maintained, in Utrecht a center of Italianism is developed; it is founded by Abraham Bloemaert (1569-1651). Without visiting Italy, he develops in his work the aesthetic ideals of this country; his greatest merit stems from having brought together a group of students whom he will encourage to get to know Italy and among whom Dutch Tenebrism will be formed. Standing out among them are Terbrugghen (d. 1625) and Honthorst (d. 1626) and to whom has been attributed the stupendous «Incredulity of St. Thomas» (C. 1.963), surely a work of Mathias Stomer's (d. after 1650), who finds himself in Rome in 1630, from where he will go to Naples and Sicily; this gives us an explanation of the existence of works of his in Spanish collections. Although his style originates from Honthorst's, his painting possesses a markedly personal accent; it is more violent and restless, due to the fact that he is influenced by the «savageness» of Caravaggio's Sicilian period.

Dutch portrait painting opens in the Prado with an idealized pair by Michiel Janszoon van Mierevelt (1567-1641), who in Delft, where he resides, becomes the portrait artist most respected by the bourgeosie in that region. Although he lacks originality, he is, on the other hand, meticulous in the study of the physiognomy of the personages. This may be noted in the «Portrait of a Gentleman» (C. 2.977) in which there appear the physionomic traces of a syphilitic: a nose with a «saddle shape», early baldness, reddish blotches on his face...; the one of his wife is that of a bored and insipid aristocrat.

Although it is not exactly a portrait, but rather a composition with a historical basis, the «Artemisa» (Pl. LX) by Rembrandt Harmensz van Rijn (1606-1669), since it represents the likeness of Saskia, the artist's wife, may be included within this genre. This is the loveliest and most important of all the works of this school which exist in the Prado. Is is done immediately after he leaves his native city, Leyden, and settles in Amsterdam, where he contracts marriage (1634). On the other hand, the «Self-portrait» (C. 2.808) is a doubtful attribution. The gigantic figure that was Rembrandt precludes any further commentary here. 43

His style was already imitated from its first moments; thus, the year after he does the «Artemisa», Salomon C. Konnick (1609-1656) does a «Philosopher» (C. 2.974) in which he vulgarizes a study by the master, though it is still not lacking in skill of execution, such as in his use of *sgraffito* (scratching) in the whiskers, allowing the ground to show through, a method which was used in polychromed sculptures. Within this style is found the «Adoration of the Shepherds», a work by Benjamin G. Cuyp (1612-1652). In 1954 the Prado acquired the work as a possible Rembrandt, based not only on the resemblance of the styles, but also on the existence at that time of an apocryphal anagram. There is another version in Bordeaux by Van Rijn and in it the personages are similar to those by Van Ostade.

Adrien van Ostade (1610-1684) spends his entire life in Haarlem, where he receives the influence of the Flemish painter Brouwer and of Frans Hals. He does a great number of small pictures in which he portrays the sordid life of the craftsmen of the city; but in them there also exists a gaiety —especially that achieved through wine— as may be seen in the pictures of his in the Prado (C. 2.121-23 and 2.126). The works conserved in Spain by other great minor masters who cultivate genre scenes, are very rare. Therefore we will only cite a «Scene of Soldierly Gallantry» (C. 2.586) by Palamades (d. Delft, 1673), an «Old Woman» (C. 2.136) by Brekelencam (d. Leyden, 1668) and the «Skaters» (C. 2.079), a delightful work by Drooshsloot (d. 1666). It is a shame that we have none of Leonard Bramer's (1596-1674) «witchcraft» pictures, but we do possess a mythological painting, «Hecuba's Suffering» (C. 2.069) and another one which is religious, «Abraham and the Angel» (C. 2.070). Neither do we have any of the street scenes which made Gabriel Metsu (1629-1667) famous, but rather his «Dead Rooster» (C. 2.103), one of the most interesting examples of Dutch still-life painting, in which objects are handled with complete veracity.

The Prado preserves important examples of the two creators of Dutch «still-life» painting: Pieter Claesz (d. 1671) and Williem Heda (1594-c. 1681). By the former there is a lovely «Bodegon» (C. 2.753), with his characteristic golden browns; by the latter there are three lovely «Tables» (C. 2.754-56) which may be considered antecedents of those by the painter Jan Davidsz de Heem (1606-1684), born in Utrecht. This latter, though, when he moves to Antwerp in 1636, makes the forms more Baroque and gives his pictures a colorist feeling, departing from Heda's gray tones.

One of the basic genres of Dutch painting is that of landscape, which in the Prado begins with one of its earliest examples, done by Gilles van Coninxloo (1544-1607); Carel van Mander —the first biographer of Northern painting— considers him to be the initiator of the theme. This work, not yet on display, although small in size, possesses a great beauty. The memory of Bruegel may still be perceived although lessened by the Mannerist diagonals. It probably comes from his period in Antwerp, from where he was expelled due to his anti-Spanish sentiments. He moved to Frankfurt and there he allows himself to be influenced by Adam Elsheimer (d. 1610), who spends a long time in Rome, where they call him «Adamo Tedesco». His «Ceres in the House of Becuba» (C. 2.181) is found in the Prado. Until Hercules Seghers (d. 1638) his genial disciple, he will not be outdone in Dutch landscape painting. The influence of Seghers and the mellow feeling found in Rembrandt («landscape», Duchess of Alba's Coll.) are picked up by Jan Van Goyen (1596-1656), a small, but enchanting sample of whose art is maintained by the Prado, in which he synthesizes and simplifies even more the tones which Seghers used. He reduces them to golden earthen shades and greenish grays tonally unified by the atmosphere. Thus it is possible to date this «Landscape» (C. 2.978) between the years 1630 and 1640.

In the Prado two small pictures are attributed, with doubts, to Jacob van Ruisdael (1628-9-1682). The first, a «Beech Forest» (C. 1.729), although signed, is within the style of his teacher Cornelis Vroon (d. 1671); if it is not by this latter, it could have been done by the young Ruisdale in the teacher's workshop. On the other hand, the lovely —though impoverished by old varnishes— «Fox Hunt» (C. 1.728) is, as far as we are concerned, an indisputable work of Ruisdael's and related to his German period (C. 1650), when he traveled through the sylvan regions of Westphalia and Hannover. The whitish touches in the little figures of the hunters and animals correspond to those which appear in other paintings from this period, such as one in the Uffizi Gallery. The «Landscape» by Hobbema (C. 2.860) is of doubtful attribution.

The genre of *battle scenes* was cultivated in great abundance by Philips Wouwerman (1619-1668), who from his native city of Haarlem sends works, first, all over Holland and later they will be spread throughout the European Courts.

SPAIN

Paradoxically, when in the XVIIth century Spanish political and economic decadence begins, one of the most magnificent stages in universal painting will develop. Valencia and Toledo will be the sites of the first centers, in which realism will arise, a style which will later be developed in Madrid and Seville. In part it is due to the rapid arrival of Caravaggio's works to the Iberian Peninsula, but the existence of a chiaroscuro tradition in Spanish painting should also be noted. Pedro de Campaña had already introduced a taste for luminous contrasts in Andalusia, and later El Greco, Luca Cambiasso and Navarrete will do so in the center of the Peninsula. It might possibly be the revival of an Oriental feeling, of popular origin, which considered light the expression of good and darkness that of evil. If good is separated from evil, but in continuous battle, then light and shadows are contrasted in painting. Therefore, in Spanish Tenebrism a battle is enjoined between light and darkness, similar to the struggle of a flame against the black of night, which makes the figures painted similar, as Camón has said, to retable sculptures lit by votive candles.

The most direct precursor of *Spanish Tenebrism* is Frair Juan Sánchez Cotán (d. 1627), who after studying in Toledo, spends the last years of his life in the Carthusian Monastery in Granada. In his «still-lifes», without being acquainted with Caravaggio, he offers us an original Tenebrism, impregnated with a great spirituality. Only a semblance of his style exists in the Prado, in the «Bodegón» (C. 2.808) by his follower Felipe Ramírez, but here Ramírez pairs up the austere Cotanesque thistle with a delicate lily in a golden glass, a luxury which is lacking in the still-lifes by the Carthusian monk. In Toledo itself, influenced by El Greco, although dirtying his coloring with brown earthen tones, may be found Luis Tristán (d. 1624). By him is the pair of pictures formed by «St. Monica and a Companion» (C. 2.836 and 2.837) which come from one of his capital groups, the Yepes Retable, signed in 1616. The portrait of «El Calabrés» (C. 1.276), 45 «favorito e mezzo spia» of Philip II's, according to what a Venetian ambassador wrote, demonstrates Tristán's admirable portrait activity. Pedro de Orente (1588-1645), from Murcia, will move at a very young age to Toledo, where he perfects his *luminism* with El Greco and Tristán. To this he adds his formal and ico-nographical admiration for the Bassanos, whom he imitates, though he replaces the ardent coloring with earthen tones, very typical of the Spanish taste of the times. This is obvious in the «Travels of Lot's Family» (C. 1.017) or in the «Sheep Roundup» (C. 1.020) which the Prado preserves, among other works of his. With him, the bridge between Toledan and Valencian painting is establis-hed, since he moves to this latter region, where he will do the majority of his work. And there he will come into contact with Francisco Ribalta (1565-1628), the true initiator of Spanish *Tenebrism*. Having studied in El Escorial, the contact with Cambiasso and Navarrete will intiate him into *luminism*, as may be noticed in his earliest work, «Christ Nailed to the Cross», done in 1582, and conserved in L'Ermitage in Leningrad. Later in Italy where he becomes acqua-inted with and copies Caravaggio's work, he is preoccupied with the truly Te-nebrist problems. He will apply them to his two magnificent works: «Christ Embracing St. Bernard» (Pl. LXII) and «The Appearance of the Lamb to St. Francis» (C. 1.062) in which the mystical sense is Hispanically transformed into an ascetic one; in the latter, the luminous effect emanated from a candle held by a monk who appears in the background is admirable.

Surely Jusepe Ribera (1591-1652) studies at first in Valencia alongside Ribalta. Born in Játiva, he moves when very young to Italy, where he will soon follow in Caravaggio's footsteps, not only imitating him stylistically, but, during his youthful years, also in his picaresque life. After his exciting Roman period, he will go to Naples around 1616, fleeing from the law, but there love, followed by marriage, and professional success, give him a certain serenity which will make it possible for him to develop a style of his own. Although his roots are Cara-vaggiesque, Ribera will achieve a more relaxed technique than that of his spiritual teacher. The brushwork will attain a greater agility, becoming broader and thicker. Thanks to his powerful artistic merits, he will obtain the protection of the Viceroys, the Duke of Osuna and Count of Monterrey, and he will also receive important commissions from the Spanish Court. His pictures slowly begin to put aside the Tenebrist shadows, searching for a new coloring in which there are Correggian and Venetian infusions, as may be observed in the «Trinity» (C. 1.069), so close to the one by El Greco. But where he achieves a greater originality in these moments is in the «St. John in the Desert» (C. 1.108), «Jacob and Isaac» (C. 1.118), from 1637, and «Jacob's Dream» (C. 1.117), done two years later. Where he demonstrates his powerful knowledge of light, form and color-ing is, above all, in his «Martyrdom of St. Bartholomew» (Pl. LXIV), done this same year; all the personages in these pictures are taken from real life, plastically expressing the character of the Neopolitan people. It is a shame that of another masterpiece, «The Triumph of Bacchus», there only remain two fragments, a «Head of a Woman» (C. 1.122) and another of «Silenus» (C. 1.123), for the picture was destroyed in the fire of 1734. Iconographically very interesting is the «Women's Combat» (C. 1.124) in which is recalled a duel fought a century before, when two women disputed the love of a young gallant. At the end of Ribera's life, it is possibly a personal disgrace —the seduction of his daughter, at the age of seventeen, by Don Juan José de Austria, who comes to Naples to smother

Masianello's popular rebellion— which makes him return to Tenebrism. A peak work from this moment, done the very year of his death, is the pathetic «Penitent St. Jerome» (C. 1.098), which might have been a psychological self-portrait.

The century begins shakily in Seville, for the principal painters are Pacheco and Roelas. At the same time, Francisco Pacheco (1574-1653) is more interesting as a theoretician than as a painter (his *Art of Painting*, 1649, offers extremely important data about art in Andalusia). His style is very dry, as may be seen in his «Saints» (C. 1.022 to 1.025); his Christs with four nails, served as a model for his son-in-law, Velasquez. Nevertheless, Juan de las Roelas (d. 1625) introduces an ephemeral Venetianism of a still Renaissance character into the city on the Guadalquivir. The most personal artist is, nonetheless, Francisco de Herrera, the Elder (d. 1656); younger than the previous two, he is the true introducer of realism in the southern region. Of an irascible character, his life is as restless as that of Caravaggio: he even counterfeits money, but is freed from jail by Philip IV, who admires his political bravado, which causes him to move to Madrid, where he dies. The «St. Bonaventure Receiving the Franciscan Habit» (C. 2.491 a) which, along with other works of his and Zurbarán's, formed part of a group done for the Sevillian convent of St. Bonaventure, is a painting very characteristic of his first style, in which toasted tones predominate and along with splendid heads full of realism, other poorly drawn ones appear, typical of his unstable character, which will bring him to botch his work. On the other hand, in the «Pope Leon I, the Magnificent» (C. 832 a) an airiness arises which foretells the works of the following generation, as a result of which the picture was attributed to his son. Terrible and life-like is his «Head of a Decapitated Saint» (C. 3.058).

Francisco de Zurbarán (1598-1664) will be the principal exponent of *Andalusian Tenebrism*, even cultivating this style when his companions in Pacheco's workshop, Velasquez and Cano had abandoned it, as well as the city. Although he studied in Seville, he was born in the south of Extremadura (Fuente de Cantos), a region economically and socially dependent upon the Andalusian capital. He is married twice in Llerena, where he works for some ten years, and he returns to Seville under the auspices of its Town Council. To this Sevillian period belongs the pair of pictures the «Vision of St. Peter Nolasco» (C. 1.236) and the «Appearance of St. Peter to His Saintly Namesake» (C. 1.237), painted in 1629 for the cloister of the Merced Convent. These are very important within Zurbarán's work for in the pictures some of the most elevated moments of the soul, even attaining contemplative ecstasy, are represented without any rhetoric; here the drapery is illuminated with the soft Tenebrist shading of the master, in which a white and diaphanous light, tinted with a pale sunset pinkishness, emphasizes the corporeal forms. In the following decade, in triumph, he moves to Madrid where he does the works which we discuss with the plates. Besides being a painter of monks, he creates enchanting «Immaculate Conceptions» (C. 2.992) and young female saints (Pl. LXVII and C. 3.148). But where he achieves an abstract concreteness in the volumes and textures of things is in his *still-lifes* (Pl. LXV and C. 2.888); whether they represent ceramic ware, fruit or flowers, in them he expresses his great love for everyday reality.

As the century advances, political centralization causes Madrid to become the tentacled focal point which will attract the provincial painters, which will make the local areas weaken. Thus, the Dominican Frair Juan Bautista Maino   47

(1558-1648) —though of Italian origin (he is born in Pastrana) he will do his early studies in Toledo— will do one of the Spanish victories, his «Reconquest of Bahia» (C. 885), for the Monarchs' Salon of the Buen Retiro Palace, where other artists will also work. In this painting the Tenebrism is brightened up, achieving formal and luminous effects comparable to those attained by contemporary Dutch painters. Vicente Carducho (1557-1638), arrives from Italy as a child, accompanied by his brother Bartolomé, a painter at El Escorial. Throughout his entire life he will maintain his eclectic style, not exempt from Tenebrist touches. A clear example of this is his series on the history of the Carthusians done for the Monastery of El Paular (1626), examples of which exist in the Prado (C. 639, 639 a, and 2.501-2.502), where on occasion, such as in the «Death of Odon de Novara» (C. 639), his activity as a portrait artist comes to the surface. Here he shows Odon's figure, in clerical vestments and with a biretta in his hand, and behind him appears the profile of Lope de Vega, an old man by that time. He will also paint battle scenes for the Monarchs' Salon, the same as Eugenio Cajés (1574-1634), by whom is an important «Virgin and Child» (C. 3.120) which possesses the monumental feeling of the Bolognese classicists. Although of a later generation, Frair Juan Rizi (d. 1685?) still remains within the Tenebrist style, doing works of a great religious intimacy, such as in «St. Benedict's Dinner» (C. 2.600) and the «Saint Blessing Bread» (C. 2.510).

The Singularity of Velasquez.—Besides being the most important Spanish painter of his century, Diego Rodríguez de Silva Velasquez (1599-1660) is the first one to move from Tenebrist painting toward the forms of a luminous realism. Although he does not go as far as Rubens' Baroqueness or universality, for neither does movement in action interest him, nor does passion move him in the execution of his pictures, as Berenson has noted, his style, just as that of Piero della Francesca's, is within the field of «non-eloquence». Now then, he is a Baroque painter, especially from the time he settles in Madrid, since he searches for spatial depth, achieving what according to Wölfflin is the principal characteristic of the Rococo style, «the creation of the unattainable», and, besides, in his figures the lines disappear, a characteristic, according to Lafuente Ferrari, of the Baroque style. But, in contrast, if his personages remain static, in their faces the personality of each individual is emphasized, as is the singularity of his objects —as Pita has said— thanks to his manner of being and the calmness which is derived from the fact that he does not have to paint to make his living. We comment at length (Pl. LXXIV-V) upon his creative sense of space: we have already stated that the conceptualization of space is one of the most typical characteristics of the Baroque style. This takes place in the portrait of the actor «Palbo de Valladolid» (C. 1.198) in which with all architectural reference lacking, as in «The Fifer» by Manet, the figure is situated within an unspecified space, to which only a brief shadow gives consistency. Velasquez also is preoccupied with the meticulous technical elaboration of his works, and for this reason he executes them slowly. First he has «the idea»; then he does compositional studies, basing himself on engravings and real life; he does sketches, and without a previous outlining, he directly attacks the execution of the picture, by means of which he achieves his particular spontaneity. This will bring him to make frequent «corrections» and at times he will repaint the picture almost entirely, whether it be immediately after he has finished it, or after several years have gone by, if it remains close at hand in the Palace. Thus we see, for example, how in «Las Lanzas» (Pl. LXXI) he has changed the stance of the horse several times, or in the equestrian portrait of Philip IV (C. 1.178) he repaints various times the two back legs of the horse, changing it, as Gaya has said, into a hippogriff. And the portrait of Philip IV, from 1624, which was believed lost, may be found, as X-rays plainly show, hidden beneath another portrait done in 1628. The same thing occurs with the portrait of his wife Isabel de Borbón, done in 1628 and redone in 1631.

Velasquez forms part of the generation which is born along with the century and to which belong Bernini and Van Dyck. In the literary field, he is a contemporary of Calderón's with whom his compositions share a similarity. A Sevillian by birth, his father is of Portuguese origin and his mother of a Sevillian family, from which he takes the last name for his signature. It is almost certain that he begins his apprenticeship with the violent Herrera, the Elder, unquestionable echoes of whom remain in his early style. At the age of twelve he works in Pacheco's workshop. This latter will not only teach him pictorial techniques, but also iconographical and literary knowledge. His father-in-law's admiration is what makes him give the hand of his daughter, Juana, to Velasquez. With references from his father-in-law for the influential Sevillians at Court, Velasquez arrives, for the first time, in Madrid in 1622. But he will not be definitively introduced at Court until the following year, thanks then to the poet Rioja and the Count-Duke of Olivares. A portrait of Philip IV makes him famous and he is appointed a royal painter by the monarch. Later he will be First Chamberlain and «personal painter to the King». When, in 1628, Rubens visits the Spanish Court, Velasquez not only receives his advice, but will accompany him in visits to the Royal Collections and El Escorial. It is possibly the Flemish painter who urges him to travel to Italy, and in 1629 he embarks at the monarch's expense and carrying letters of introduction to his ambassadors. After having visited the principal cities, he returns at the end of a year and a half, commencing a new period in which his style is more fluid. He accompanies the sovereign on his trips, such as those he makes during the War of Cataluña (1644). He returns to Italy once again in 1649, this time as an already famous artist, and is received by the Pope himself, of whom Velasquez paints the astonishing portrait in reds and golds. There «the cavalier Velasquez» acquires statues and pictures which will decorate the new rooms in the Palace. The sovereign, restless due to the artist's delay, sends for him several times and strictly orders him to return. In 1651 the artist is once again in Madrid, where, so he won't leave again, Philip IV names him his chamberlain, which will take away from the painter's time but will allow him to do laborious works such as «The Spinners» or «Las Lanzas». His devastating success makes the King concede him the title of Knight of St. James in 1658. And two years later Velasquez will arrange the decorations for the royal wedding on the Isle of Faisanes in the Bidasoa River. The intensive work undermines his health, with the result that when he returns to Madrid a little less than a month of life is left to him.

From his Sevillian period there only exists in the Prado Museum the «Adoration of the Kings» (Pl. LXIX) and possibly a portrait of «Pacheco» (C. 1.209); his bold «Sor Jerónima de la Fuente» (C. 2.873) is a work done after his first trip to Madrid. If it hadn't been for French pillaging and Wellington's «diplomacy», the «Water Carrier of Seville» (Wellington Museum, London) would today be in the Prado. As we have said, from Velasquez's first moments in Madrid is the portrait of «Philip IV» (hidden beneath another one); similar to it is the one of the «Infante Don Carlos». In 1627 he does his first historical composition of large format: «The Expulsion of the Moriscos», which is lost today; we only conserved a memory of it in a sketch by Cajés. «The Drunkards» (C. 1.170), begun in 1628, is a picture in which the mythological theme is interpreted in a human manner; the lack of harmony between the composition and the atmosphere is due to the fact that at first it was done as an interior scene, and then after Velasquez's first trip to Italy he places the personages against a landscape. Among the works painted during his first trip to Italy stands out «Vulcan's Forge» (C. 1.171), in which he now achieves a great harmony between the figures and the atmosphere. In it, in a Calderonian manner, the artist presents us with the scene of the cuckolded husband with the greatest subtlety, for although he coarsely seeks vengeance, each one of the personages expresses himself psychologically in a different manner. In the work, the nude acquires a new meaning in Spanish paintings, possibly to surprise the Italians, who criticized the lack of this genre on the Iberian Peninsula. Its companion piece, «Joseph's Tunic», is preserved in El Escorial. In 1632 Velasquez would do his «Christ» (C. 1.167), with four nails, in accordance with the iconography established by Pacheco. It is an expiatory crucifix and is supposed to be related to the «secret sins» of the monarch, who donates it to the San Plácido Monastery. From this epoch must be the «Buffoons» (Pl. LXXIII) and the «Coronation of the Virgen» (C. 1.168), a work in which, due to the influence of El Greco, Velasquez spiritualizes the tones. It is possible that the two landscapes of the «Villa Mèdici» (Pl. LXX, C. 1.211) are from the first Italian trip. From the second, the masterpieces are the portraits of «Innocent X» and the «Rokeby Venus», where he will achieve textures which surpass the Venetian masters. Upon his return, Velasquez's palette becomes even more airy, dissolving the forms and achieving prodigious subtleties, such as happens in the 'crazy' «Don Juan de Austria» (C. 1.200), in which the artist gives an ironic view of the history of Spain, possibly representing in the background the Battle of Lepanto. Standing out in this final period is a series of portraits such as the austere one of «Doña Mariana de Austria» (C. 1.191) and the one of «Philip IV» (C. 1.185) in which the physical and psychological decadence of the monarch may already be seen. On the other hand, in the one of «Doña Margarita» (C. 1.192) there is a prodigious colorist feeling in which the carmines and pinks resound with the whites and silvers in a true chromatic symphony; it is a shame that when it remained unfinished, Velasquez's son-in-law Mazo put in some rather coarse reddish drapes. The masterpieces of his final moments, besides the prodigious «Mercury and Argos» (C. 1.175) —which indicates with its sketchy and impasted brushwork how Velasquez had been able to change his technique throughout his life— are «Las Meninas»» (Pl. LXXIV and LXXV) and «The Spinners» (Pl. LXVI).

The Madrilenian Generation Related to Velasquez.—As we have seen, Velasquez leaves a very small number of paintings behind, due to his desire for perfection; for contrary to Rubens or even Zurbarán, he was incapable of industrializing his art, which he loved so fervently. Velasquez limits himself to having two or three helpers around to grind his colors, stretch the canvases or do copies of the royal portraits ordered by important Spanish families or by foreign sovereigns. But in spite of this, he exercises a certain influence over the Madrilenian painters of his times, not only among his few disciples —among whom stand out the Sevillian mulatto Juan de Pareja, author of the reposed «Calling of St. Matthew» (1661, C. 1.041), the Gallician Antonio Puga, to whom is attributed the «Painter's Mother» (C. 3.004) and especially outstanding is Juan B. Martínez del Mazo (d. 1667) who, as we have seen, finishes a painting or two of Velasquez's and paints his «Family» (Vienna Museum), inspired by «Las Meninas». The «View of Zaragoza» (C. 889), technically related to the «Hunters on Scaffolding» (C. 2.571), is possibly his, except for some glazes in the background done by Velasquez. In these two pictures the delightful figures in the foreground were already highly praised in the artist's own time. Mazo's stay in Rome is documented and this confirms the attribution of «Titus' Arch» (C. 1.212) which forms part of series of Italianate landscapes (C. 1.215 to 1.218). A certain contact with Velasquez may also be perceived in some works by the artist from Calatayud Jusepe Leonardo (1600-1656); a disquieting figure, his flaming temperament leads him to insanity, which causes him to abandon painting from 1648 on; he will die in Zaragoza. In the style of Velasquez, to a certain degree, is the «Birth of the Virgin» (C. 860) and his «St. Sebastian» (C. 67). For the Monarchs' Salon Velasquez commissions him to do the «Surrender of Juliers» (C. 858) and the «Capture of Brisach (C. 859), in which he demonstrates his compositional skill. His contemporary from Valladolid, Antonio de Pereda (d. 1678), famous for his paintings of still-lifes and allegories on vanity, will cultivate a style which evolves from an austerity at the beginning of the century to a Flemish-like airiness. It is also for the Monarchs' Salon that he paints his «Help for Genoa»» from the Marquis of Santa Cruz (1634, C. 1.317 a). His artistic evolution may be followed in the Prado with the «Anunciation» (1637, C. 2.555), «Christ» (1641, C. 1.047), «St. Jerome» (1643, C. 1.046), «St. Peter Freed by an Angel» (1644, C. 1.340) and the «Appearance of the Virgin to St. Felix Cantalicio» (1665, C. 1.317 b), in which his technique has become more airy.

Painting at the Court of the Last Austria.—It is during the reign of Charles II that a series of painters, setting aside the style of Velasquez, will follow the trails blazed by Rubens and Van Dyck, although they will accept the coloring of the Venetian artists. As Spain leaps over the social and political precipice, a series of excellent artists will appear at the Court; they not only paint on canvas, but also cultivate the fresco genre, possibly influenced by Italian Baroque art, which will convert Madrid into one of the main colorist centers of Europe. This period begins with Juan Carreño de Miranda and Francisco Rizi, both born in 1614; Carreño (d. 1685), an Asturian from Avilés who studied in Valladolid, will move while he is still young to Madrid, where in 1669 Charles II will designate him «royal painter». He has been one of the greatest Spanish portrait artists, as is demonstrated by his likenesses of «Doña Mariana» (C. 644), the Regent Queen, and of her absurd son, «Charles II» (C. 642 and 648), in which influences from Velasquez may still be noted. In the one of the Russian ambassador «Pedro Ivanowitz» (1681, C. 645) the majesty and coloring approximate him to Rubens; the «Duke of Pastrana» (C. 650) is more Van Dyckian. Carreño will also paint a deformed being: the «Monster», dressed (C. 646) and nude (C. 2.800), crowned with leaves and bunches of grapes, changing her into a youthful Bacchus. In his «St. Ann Instructing the Virgin» (C. 651) and in the sketch of «Herod's

Banquet» (C. 3.088), in preparation for the now lost picture done for the Madrilenian San Juan Church, he shows himself to be a great colorist. Francisco Rizi (d. 1685) —the brother of Frair Juan Rizi— although he also cultivates the portrait genre, a worthy example is his «Artillery General» (C. 1.127), above all, is a spirited decorator, applying to his canvases the broad strokes of a fresco painter, in his «Immaculate Conceptions» (C. 1.130 a), or in scenes related to the «Birth of Christ» (C. 1.128 to 1.130, 2.962 and 3.136)). The «Auto-da-fe» (1683, C. 1.126) reproduces the one held in the Plaza Mayor of Madrid on June 30, 1680, and is a work of greater historical than artistic interest.

A Radiant Sunset.—Claudio Coello is generally considered the artist in whom Madrilenian Baroque painting culminates; now then, if Fate had given long lives to three painters born in the decade from 1625 to 1635, this artist would not be the last of the great painters from our golden age, for Mateo Cerezo (1626-1666), Juan Antonio Escalante (1633-1670) and José Antolínez (1635-1675) would have been very close to Coello's style since they made up the most advanced group of the leading Baroque painters. If Juan Carreño de Miranda took a step forward in Baroque line, they reached the maximum exaltation of forms and color. In Cerezo, from Burgos, his Van Dyckism will be absorbed by his own strong personality as his production advances. If in the «Mystic Marriage of St. Catherine» (1660, C. 559) and the «Assumption» (C. 659) Flemish and Venetian influences may still be seen, at the end of Cerezo's life the chromatic pigments envelope the forms which are impregnated with a strong ascetic-mystical spirit, such as occurs in the delicate «Soul's Judgement» (C. 623). The Cordovan Juan Antonio Escalante, in his early moments lets himself be influenced by Giordano and Francisco Rizi, with whom he collaborates, as is shown by his youthful «Andromeda and the Dragon» (Prado Trust). Later his painting becomes more fluid and exciting —at times with his works even being confused with those by Italians of this moment; thus his «Elias and the Angel» (Berlin Museum) has been attributed to the Venetian Francesco Maffei. A similar version has recently been incorporated by the Prado; it forms part of a series, along with other Eucharistic allegories, proceeding from the Merced Convent in Madrid. In the «St. Rose of Viterbo» (C. 3.046), he paves the way for the Rococo style; although at times he neglects the drafsmanship, the new tonalities used by him, especially in his pinks and blues, cause these works to be considered among the most original ones from the Spanish painting of his century. Antolínez, the same as Escalante, searches for diagonal movement in his pictures, to which he applies effervescent coloring, such as occurs in the «Death of Mary Magdalen» (C. 559); he becomes famous, above all, for his unusual typology of the «Immaculate Conception» (C. 2.443); he is, besides, an original portrait artist, as two delicate *children's heads* (C. 1.227-28) show, in which Escalante asserted that he stained the cheeks with pink.

The long life of Claudio Coello (1642-1693) and his prodigious technical knowledge, as well as his careful compositional sense, make him the culminating figure in the painting of his times. His eclectic formation will bring him to reconsider Spanish pictorial traditions, and he returns to the past of Velasquez without abandoning the contacts with Flemish and Venetian painting. In a period when haste predominates, just as today, he scrupulously elaborates his works; but this does not cause him to ignore fresco painting, which he practices with agility, although his favorite genres are the portrait and religious compositons. His earliest picture in the Prado within this last genre is «Jesus at the Temple Door» (C. 2.583), in which at the age of eighteen he does an important work. Now then, within the eclecticism of the Carracis, still under their influence during his stay in Rome, four years later he will do his «Triumph of St. Augustine» (C. 664), already under the Rubensian influence, in which Baroque theatricality triumphs. Thus, in the lower section he places the head of Seneca as a symbol of the victory of the Church over the Classics. In the «St. Dominic of Guzmán» (Pl. LXXVII) and in the «St Rose of Lima» (C. 662-63), which form a pair, he reminds us of sculptures. From his portrait activity are the phantasmagoric «Charles II» (C. 2.504) and the realistic «Father Cavanillas» (C. 992).

The arrival in Spain (1692) of the Neopolitan Luca Giordano (1632-1705) causes a change in the style in use here at that time. He achieves such prestige in the atmosphere of the Court of Charles II, that while he is still alive his name will be hispanicized to become Lucas Jordán. His formation begins in contact with Ribera's art and alongside his father, a mediocre painter, but who according to tradition by obligating him to paint rapidly, makes him attain his facility of execution; from this he acquires his nickname of «Fa presto» (do it quickly). While very young he goes to Rome where he acquires his knowledge of frescoes and his decorative style, thanks to Pietro de Cortona, though he will never abandon the memory of Ribera. He not only attains a vertiginous execution in his works whether they are large frescoes or compositions in oils, but his imagination will create original structures, though sometimes haste will cause him to use prefabricated molds. Thus certain foreshortened positions are repeated in many of his figures, which sometimes proceed from Florentine Mannerism —he stayed in this city for two years— or from the Venetian painters. During the ten years he spends in Spain (he leaves in 1702) he does not only large and fantastic frescoes in the Royal Palaces (thus in the Buen Retiro Palace, today an integral part of the Prado Museum, he paints the «Story of the Golden Fleece»), El Escorial and, above all, the extremely lovely one in the Sacristy of the Toledo Cathedral, but a great number of oil paintings, of which the Prado has more than thirty, which run from small sketches for his large fresco compositions —such as the five for the «Battle of San Quintín» (C. 184-188) which he paints for the monumental stairway at El Escorial— to the large compositions such as «Rubens Painting the Allegory on Peace» (C. 190), in which he expresses admiration for the Flemish painter, certain influences of whom may be perceived in Giordano's Spanish period. He also cultivates the portrait, such as the ones of «Charles II» and his wife «Mariana on Horseback» (C. 197-198) of which there exist various replicas.

To a large extent it is to Giordano that we owe the development of Spanish fresco in the XVIIIth century, from Palomino to Goya. Thus, Acisclo Antonio Palomino (1655-1726) who was born in Bujalance and studied in Cordova and then Madrid with Claudio Coello, when Giordano arrives will rapidly adopt his style in his numerous decorations in fresco. In the Prado Museum there exists an «Immaculate Conception» (C. 1.026) in which he still remains within the Madrilenian tradition of the XVIIth century. On the other hand, his allegories on «Fire» (C. 3.186) and «Air» (C. 3.187) are more within Roman classic decorativism. In his «St. Ines» (C. 3.161) there are finally echoes of the Neopolitan artist.

Andalusia and Granada.—Meanwhile the Granadan school is focused around Alonso Cano (1601-1667), who after having studied in Seville and having spent a prolonged period in Madrid, will finish out his days in his native city. Although of a passionate character —suspicions exist that he murdered his second wife— his temperament is not reflected in his work, for he takes minute care in his compositions, doing previous sketches for them, managing to formulate his ideal of beauty within a rigid structure, perfectly geometrical, and with rounded forms. In it his types attain a definite personality, standing out against neutral backgrounds or, later, after arriving in Madrid in 1636, against airy landscapes. This may be perceived in «Christ and the Angel» (C. 629) which he later repeats (Pl. LXVIII), but especially in the «Miracle at the Well» (C. 2.806) in which the silvery tones of the first period disappear to open the way for a greater chromatic use, for the sense of color will triumph in his Granadan period when he does his masterpiece, the «Stories of the Virgin» for the cathedral, of which he will be a prebendary (1657). There he creates a type of Virgin which will obtain extensive diffusion, such as the one which appears with the «Child» (C. 627). Also conserved here are some of the «Kings of Spain» (C. 632 and 633) which he would do for the Royal Palace. His principal Granadan followers are Juan de Sevilla («Lazarus and Epulon», C. 2.508) and Pedro Atanasio Bocanegra («The Virgin and Child with Saints», C. 629).

Seville.—With the death of Zurbarán and the departure of Velasquez and Alonso Cano, only two important painters remain in the Andalusian capital in the second half of the century, Murillo and Valdés Leal. Removed from the Madrilenian style they will develop strong personalities of their own. Bartolomé Esteban Murillo (1618-1682) thanks to his talent and personal amiability will obtain an extensive clientele. At the age of twenty-five he achieves the commission for the group of paintings, today split up, for the cloister of the San Francisco Convent. The commissions multiply and in this first period he does works in which a certain contact with Zurbarán's Tenebrism may be noticed; he has still not departed from it when he paints the «Galician Woman with the Coin» (C. 1.002) and the «Old Woman Spinning» (C. 1.001) in which there also exist reminiscences of Velasquez's first period. Still Tenebrist are «St. Jerome» (C. 987) and his «Anunciation» (C. 969) which he will later repeat in different versions. In his famous «Holy Family with the Little Bird» (c. 1650, C. 960) chiaroscuro shading still exists. Years later when he does the two pictures for the church of Santa María la Blanca (1665), «The Patrician's Dream» (C. 994) and the «Revelation of the Dream» (C. 995), his technique has become more airy, placing white on a white background in the landscape before Malevich does it in his famous abstract painting. His «Immaculate Conceptions» will be his most popular works; in the Prado we have a series of them, among which stands out the famous so-called «Soult» one (C. 2.809), since it was taken to France by this Napoleonic general. With his varied themes in the representations of the «Virgin as a Child» or of the «Baby Jesus», he achieves a fortunate success, such as in the «Good Shepherd» (Pl. LXXVIII). Other very successful pieces are his «beggar-boys», no example of which exists in the Prado. On the other hand, we possess three of his lovely landscapes, among which one stands out with jagged mountains and a woman on a donkey with a child in her arms, followed by a peasant; it could, therefore, represent the «Flight into Egypt» (C. 3.008). In it is foreseen what will later be

Romantic landscape painting. From his rare activity as a portrait artist we have two good examples, the portrait of «Nicolas Ozamur» (C.3.060) and the one of the «Gentleman of the Collar» (C. 2.845), one of the most important portraits in all of Spanish painting.

A personality totally different from that of Murillo's is that of Valdés Leal (1622-1690), for his psychopathic temperament is reflected in his nervous and convulsive style, cultivating «ugliness», and delighting in the repugnant and the macabre. The same as Herrera, the Elder, on occasion he will neglect the draftsmanship, but, on the other hand, he always handles color with great ease, achieving an open technique. After spending his youth in Cordova, where he studies, he moves to Seville at the age of thirty-five and there spends the rest of his life. The Prado Museum has in its collection two of the works done for the Santa Isabel Convent in this city, the «St. Jerome» (C. 2.593) and a «Martyr from the Hieronymite Order» (C. 2.527) in which the vibrant colorist feeling of the Sevillian painter may be appreciated. But in spite of the dirty condition which muddies their tones, it is in «Jesus Among the Doctors» (1686, C. 1.161) and the «Presentation of the Virgin» (C. 1.160) that his expressive feeling becomes clear in its entirety.

FRANCE

By around 1600, the wars with Spain and internal discord had eventually impoverished the European country best endowed by Nature. With political and religious balance reestablished, Maria Mèdici has Rubens and his collaborators decorate the Gallery of the Luxembourg Palace (1622-25). Meanwhile, certain French painters travel in Italy discovering the Tenebrist style. Among the earliest is Louis Finsonius (d. 1632) who, though born in Bruges, upon his return settles in Aix-en-Provence, painting portraits and above all religious pictures, such as an «Annunciation» (C. 3.075), in which Mannerism and Tenebrism join symbiotically. There does not exist a single example in Madrid of the most personal artist in the group, Georges La Tour, for works known to be his are very rare. There is, however, something by Le Valentin (Jean de Boullogne, 1594-1632), to whom Voss attributes the «Martyrdom of St. Lawrence« (C. 2.346), possibly painted in Rome, and according to Masuret, perhaps in collaboration with Nicolas Tournier (d. 1634), another of the early Gallic Tenebrists. Baroque realism will reach its extreme in this country with the Le Nain Brothers, and the *vanitas* themes (C. 3.049) by Jacques Linard (d. 1645): the version in the Prado is a simplification of another famous one dated 1644.

While Tenebrism triumphs in the popular and bourgeois media, in the Court and among the aristocracy, in general, this style is looked down on, with a preference for cheerful tones and the allegorical subjects which the Italian Classicists were cultivating. Due to this, Simon Vouet (1590-1646) will have a brilliant, precocious career: at the age of fourteen he was painting portraits in England; then he travels to Constantinople and on his return establishes himself in Italy, achieving triumph in Rome. Although he does not reject the strong shadows of Tenebrism, his composition and coloring are inspired by the Bolognese artists. This eclectic style will be accepted by the Court of France and Louis XIII will name him a royal painter. The Prado, besides a «Mystic Conversation» (C. 539), possesses one of his most important works: «Time Vanquished by Youth and

Beauty» (C. 2.987), signed in Rome in 1627, it is a perfect example of his style, in which color and composition are knowledgeably blended.

During Louis XIII's reign the signal figure will be Nicolas Poussin (1594-1665), with whom Classicism fully triumphs in France. His major preoccupation is consecutive arrangement, based on optic and geometrical studies, besides that of following themes from Classical Antiquity. A characteristic example is «Parnassus» (Pl. LXXIX), done in Rome, where he spends many years. In this work, as in the majority of his production, the figures are placed harmoniously and even in his «Bacchanal» (C. 2.312) and Meleager's Hunt» (?) (C. 2.320), themes which suggest compositional fantasy, he follows his rigid pattern. In his landscapes (Pl. LXXX), the same Classicist harmony reigns. Now then, Claude Lorrain (Claude Gellée, 1600-1682) will be the true creator of French landscape art, though until Turner and the Barbizon school, his innovations would not again be taken advantage of. These innovations are rooted especially in the magic of the luminosity, thus he captures solar, sunset and nocturnal effects and reflections on the ocean and rivers (C. 2.553, 2.555, 2.557, 2.558 and 2.261); outstanding is «The Embarkation of St. Paula Romana at Ostia»» (P. LXXXI).

Since the XVIth century, portrait painting has been somewhat forgotten in France, from the time when Corneille de Lyon and François Clouet had done versions full of personality and enchantment. In the first half of the XVIIth century it will be the Belgians such as Rubens and Frans Pourbus, the Younger (d. in Paris 1622), who will do the official portraits. By this latter we have the one of «Maria Mèdici» (1617, C. 1.624), a commission from the Court, stiff and stereotyped, while in the one of Philip IV's wife «Isabel» (C. 1.625) there is a greater feeling of intimacy, for she appears playing with a little dog. Also of Flemish origin, from Brussels, is the great renovator of French portrait art, Philippe de Champaigne (1602-1674); his paintings will be characterized by the delicacy of his gray tones and the realism of the person portrayed. Thus it occurs in the «Louis XIII» (1655, C. 2.240), who is dressed in military fashion, but where his personality stands out is in the «Christian Soul Accepting Its Cross» (C. 2.365), inspired by the ascetic meditations of the XVIIth century, which gives it a somewhat unrealistic character. Sebastian Bourdon (1616-1671) is also an excellent portrait artist, as the «Queen Christina of Sweden on Horseback» (1653-54, C. 1.503), a masterpiece done for Philip IV, shows. In the Court of Louis XIV, the ostentation and etiquette are reflected in the majestic feeling of the portrait artists, among whom stands out the Catalán Jacinto Rigaud (1659-1743), who upon moving to Paris will achieve splendid success, even establishing a workshop in which collaborators do the torsos and backgrounds, while he, except on important commissions, limits himself to doing the faces. An excellent example of his style is the portrait of the «Sun King» (C. 2.343), whose battle in the background was painted by a specialist in this field, Parrocel (d. 1752); in the one of Philip V (C. 2.337), from 1701, this king appears dressed in Spanish fashion for the first time. Rigaud admired and collected works by Antoine Coypel (d. 1722), a fervent Reubensian by whom we have a «Susan Accused of Adultery» (C. 2.247). Very preoccupied with reality is Jean B. Jouvenet (1644-1717), whose «Magnificat» (C. 2.272) is a good example of his religious compositions.

BAROQUE PAINTING

CARAVAGGIO: David over Goliath.

GUIDO RENI: Hippomenes and Atalanta.

GUERCINO: Susan and the Elders.

GENTILESCHI: Moses Rescued from the Waters of the Nile.

PRETI: Gloria.

LUCA GIORDANO: Bethsabe in Her Bath.

RUBENS: The Duke of Lerma.

RUBENS: The Triumph of the Church.

RUBENS: Peasants' Dance.

RUBENS: The Garden of Love.

VAN DYCK: The Seizure of Christ.

JORDAENS: The Jordaens Family in a Garden.

STOMER: The Incredulity of St. Thomas.

OSTADE: Rustic Concert.

METSU: Dead Rooster.

HEEM: Table.

ZURBARAN: The Vision of St. Peter Nolasco.

CANO: St. Bernard and The Virgin.

PEREDA: Help for Genoa.

MAINO. Reconquest of Bahia Brazil.

VELASQUEZ: Crucified Christ.

VELASQUEZ: The Count-Duke of Olivares.

VELASQUEZ: The Infanta Margarita.

VELASQUEZ: Vulcan's Forge.

MURILLO: The «Soult» Immaculate Conception.

MURILLO: Gentleman of the Collar.

CARREÑO: The Duke of Pastrana.

MATEO CEREZO: Soul's Judgment.

BOURDON: Christina of Sweden, on Horseback.

CLAUDIO COELLO: The Triumph of St. Augustine.

ESCALANTE. The Prudent Abigail.

LINARD: Vanitas.

THE XVIIIth CENTURY

V

ROCOCO AND ACADEMICISM

France.—During the XVIIIth century France will be the center of artistic attraction for the European Courts. At the same time that it imposes the style of dress and dining, it will make a great number of painters submit to its artistic norms. It is during the time of Louis XV that the reaction begins against the style of arid equilibrium of the previous reign. Decorators and painters will react searching for an assymetry and even disorder, with style books spreading among the workshops in which Rococo triumphs. Cold colors will be dropped in favor of tonalities of a Flemish and Dutch taste, following Coypel's precedent, and sensationalism will be sought after. In spite of being a strict contemporary of Rigaud's within the new style we may include Nicolas Largillière (1656-1746), who cultivates portraits of a decorative and amiable type which pave the way for the Rococo style. Such occurs with the daughter of Philip V, the future wife of Joseph I of Portugal, «María Ana Victoria de Borbón» (1724, C. 2.277), elegantly dressed in pearl gray and phosphorescent blue tones. The figure who truly commences this new style is the sickly Jean-Antoine Watteau (1684-1721), a visionary with a sarcastic spirit, whom society will require to camouflage his preoccupation beneath the silks and satins, under which the hidden satire often appears, such as in his «Marriage Contract» (Pl. LXXXII). On the other hand, in his pair «Festivity in a Park» (C. 2.354), he limits himself to melancholily presenting us with a scene of gallantry.

The favorite painter at the Court of Louis XV is François Boucher (1704-1770) who eroticizes gods and young women. Within his style we possess only two pictures with *amorinos* (C. 2.854-55). Jean B. Greuze (1725-1805), although he practices «moralizing fables», at times also gives his art erotic connotations, such as may be observed in the «Young Girl from the Back» («La pudeur agaçanté», C. 2.590 a). The Prado is totally lacking in any example of the genial observationist Fragonard; in the San Fernando Academy there exists a youthful work: «The Sacrifice of Coresus» and a sensational portrait is preserved in the Cambó Collection (Barcelona). Jean Marc Mattier (1685-1766) also cultivates the Rococo portrait with great originality, as is demonstrated by the one of «Maria Leczinska» (C. 2.591), dressed in the radiant blues characteristic of his palette.

Our principal museum lacks a worthy collection of French Neoclassical painting, which is born as a counter-reaction against the artistic «excesses of the Rococo style. Not only Rome, but Greece is also taken as an example. The Prado only has a series of estimable *Italian landscapes* by Claude Josep Vernet (1714-1789) in which he vacillates between Rococo and the new artistic style, and, above all, a masterpiece by Hubert Robert (1733-1808), in which «The Colosseum» (C. 2.883) is represented. In it appears the influence of the Italian Pannini, somewhat abbreviated by the poetry of Fragonard.

French Painters in the Court of Philip V.—Philip V and his policy of «afrancesamiento» in Spain, attracts to the Peninsula a certain number of artists among whom there are painters of certain importance, such as Jean Ranc (1674-1735), as is demonstrated by the works conserved in the Prado or the Oriente Palace. A lovely example is the picture of «Charles III, as a Child» (C. 2.334), of delicate tonalities and in which he appears classifying flowers with their Latin names; (later he will be the one who creates the Prado as a Natural Science Museum). The sketch for «The Family of Philip V» (1733, C. 2.376) makes us think that the final picture, lost today, was better than the one on the same theme (1743, C. 2.283) done by Louis Michel van Loo (1707-1771), this last one being ostentatious and of a large size and whose main interest lies in the iconography, for it represents a reunion of the Royal Family. Now then, we must recognize that his portraits «are well done». The most personal artist in the group is Michel-Ange Houasse (1680-1730), who works for Philip V between 1717 and 1730. His «Holy Family» (1726, C. 2.264) is beautifully done and in it he expresses his acquaintance with Italian painting. Inspired by Poussin are the «Bacchanal» (1717, C. 2.267) and the «Sacrifice to Bacchus» (1720, C. 2.268) in which a realistic feeling of Flemish and Dutch origin is added; thus, a child throws up the wine he has liberally consumed. Besides, he is a sensitive landscape artist, standing out with his «View of El Escorial» (C. 2.269) in which he paves the way for Romantic landscapes. He is also an excellent portrait artist: the delicate grays of the ill-fated «Louis I» (1717, C. 2.387) anticipate the ones that Goya will use around 1800.

Italy and Its Pictorial Relations with Spain.—In the middle of the XVIIIth century the decorative genius of Venetian painting once again wakens, especially in the incandescent work of Giovanni Battista Tiepolo (1696-1770). Although there exist two excellent precursors in Venice, Piezzetta and Pittoni, he will be the one who makes the splendor of large frescoes spring up once again, not only on Venetian «terra ferma», but even in the lacustrine city itself. Starting in 1751 he will spend three years painting in the Wüzburg Residence. After an intermission in Venice, during which he decorates the Labia Palace (1757), in 1761 he settles in Madrid —sent for by Charles III— where he remains until his death. He does some of his loveliest and most splendorous frescoes in the Royal Palace, helped by his sons, and culminating in the one which in the Throne Room represents the «Apotheosis of the Spanish Monarchy», dominating the four corners of the world. In it, his coloring is purified and crystalized, daring to fill a large space with a sky in which over white tones he applies, wtih an irresistible force, indigo blue and pure green, counter-pointing it almost musically, such as in «The Four Seasons» by Vivaldi. Instead of notes he will use reds, oranges, cobalts... which will arouse the stupor and even hate of the «prudent» Neoclassical artists. The Prado preserves a preparatory sketch representing the «Olympus» (C. 365) connected with his decorations in the Halberdiers' Salon. Meanwhile he paints large pictures for other palace groups, with the retables for the San Pascual Church in Aranjuez (Pl. LXXXIII) standing out.

Since the XVIIth century, Italian fresco painters had already come to work in Spain; thus Velasquez brought Mittelli and Colonna to decorate the Buen Retiro Palace. Still conserved is the large Monarchs' Salon; (a carefully executed sketch for it exists in the Prado). In the epoch of Charles II, in the final moments of this reign (1747), the important Neapolitan artist Jacopo Amiconi (1675-1752) will be sent for; besides decorating some of the ceilings at La Granja, he does some portraits such as the one of the «Infanta María Teresa Antonia» (C. 2.392) who married the Dauphin of France, the son of Louis XIV and that of the «Infanta María Isabel» (C. 14). Better than this one is the arrogant «Marquis of La Ensenada» (C. 2.939). When he dies, another Neapolitan comes to Madrid to replace him, Corrado Giaquinto (1700-1765), a delightful composer of scenographies worthy of Giordano. In the Oriente Palace he paints the «Birth of the Sun, with the Triumph of Bacchus» («Salon of the Columns»), whose very careful sketch is in the Prado (C. 103), as well as the one of the «Battle of Clavijo» (C. 106). Lovely Baroque-like compositions of cheerful tones are the ones of «Justice» and «Peace» (C. 104 and 582), one of them painted for the Junta Salon of the Academy. He also cultivates scenes with religious or mythological motifs; some important examples of which are here. Although other Neapolitan painters do not come to Spain, they send their works to this country, commissioned by Charles III. Thus, by Giovanni Paolo Pannini (1691-1765) are conserved in our famous museum some of the famous «Ruins» (C. 273, 275 and 276), in which reality is mixed with fantasy. There are also two religious paintings of his: «Jesus Disputing with the Doctors» (C. 277) and with the «Money Changers in the Temple» (C. 278), both sketches for larger compositions. And the «Turkish Legation in Naples» (C. 54) is an important work by Giuseppe Bonito (1707-1789). There also exist examples of other XVIIIth century Italian schools, with a landscape by the Genovese painter Alessandro Magnasco (1677-1749) standing out; in it within a luxuriant and tempestuous vegetation —chromatic pigments glitter— a «Christ Waited On By Angels» (C. 3.124) appears. Another work which may be included in the Italian school is the «View of Venice from San Giorgio Island» (C. 475), one of the loveliest and most characteristic works of Gaspare van Viteli (van Vittel, 1693-1737), for although he was born in Utrecht, he spent part of his life in Italy taking part in the creation of Venetian landscape painting and he influences Giovanni Antonio Canal, «Canaletto» (d. 1768).

Mengs and Spanish Academicism.—When the San Fernando Academy of Fine Arts was founded (1752), its principal objective was that of the «purification» of the arts —just as the Academy of Language had been born to «refine» the Spanish language —and the organization attempts by all the means within its power to free of Baroque trappings not only Spanish buildings, but also sculptural and pictorial works. The arrival in Spain of Anton Raffael Mengs (1728-1779), a Czechoslovakian artist born in Aussig, sets a new course for Hispanic painting, for the Academy will oblige Spanish painters to follow his example, imitating the Graeco-Roman style which he theoretically considers the only practicable one, though at times he departs somewhat from his principles. With excellent qualities as a draftsman and vast technical knowledge, his compositions are at times cold, such as occurs in his «Adoration of the Shepherds» (C. 2.204), done in Rome in 1770 and in which the influence of Correggio is perceived. On the other hand, many of his portraits are excellent; this is true of the study for the one of «Maria Luisa de Parma» (Pl. LXXXVI) as well as for his self-portrait (C. 2.197), similar to another version in Munich. Luckily for Spanish painting, 63

Mengs' pontificate was fleeting; for although some artists would follow the Neoclassical norms set by him, others gradually abandon them.

At mid-century the group of courtly decorators, made up by the González Velasquez Brothers and their circle, will maintain an eclectic style, which will become more Neoclassical at the time in question. The unruly Luis Paret y Alcázar (1747-1799) breaks away from it, for his temperament and ideas do not agree with those of his companions in the Academy. Possibly influencing in the formation of his style is the painter Charles François de la Traverse (d. 1789) —in the Prado a «Hunt» (C. 2.496) of his is exhibited— but there is no doubt that he knows the work of Fragonard and Boucher from their engravings and that he had in front of him the delightful little pictures of Houasse. But he does not limit himself to facile copying, but rather, with an admirable originality and gracefulness, offers us amiable chronicles, in which many times is hidden his irony toward the Spanish courtly society under the reign of Charles III. Among the works of this type stand out: «The Royal Couples» (C. 1.044), a typical festival celebrated in Aranjuez in 1773 the «Masked Ball» (C. 2.875), in the Príncipe Theater; the «Swearing In of Ferdinand VII as the Prince of Asturias» (C. 1.045), on September 23, 1789, in the Jerónimos Church; and, above all, «Charles III, Lunching with His Court»» (Pl. LXXXVIII). Besides he is a good painter of «Flowers» (C. 1.042-43) and an excellent landscape artist, but, nevertheless, an inconsistent religious painter.

Luis Eugenio Meléndez or Menéndez (1716-1780) begins his career with some religious scenes in which pigmented textures exist —the «Virgin and Child», for example, done in 1739 (Prado Trust, Casa de Colón, Las Palmas). Now then, he will come to be the best Spanish bodegón painter of his times (P. LXXXVII). Francisco Bayeu y Subias (1734-1795), summoned from his native city of Zaragoza, would achieve the protection of the omnipotent Mengs, who offers him important decorative commissions in the Royal Palaces, for which there exist studies in the Prado as well as numerous religious and mythological compositions of his. Nevertheless, what interest us in his art are his popular scenes, expressed in cartoons for the tapestries which he does for the Royal Factory, directed by him (C. 605-607 and 2.520). Also interesting are his portraits, such as that of his daughter «Feliciana» (C. 740 h). His brother Ramón (1746-1793) and José del Castillo (1737-1793) collaborate with him in the creation of these cartoons, but the genius and unmatchable gracefulness of Goya stands out over them. On the other hand, outstanding in this genre is the Valencian Agustín Esteve (1753-1820), who will collaborate on some occasions with Goya. He almost always maintains a Neoclassical feeling, although he is not ignorant of English painting, as is denoted in the portrait in white of «Doña Joaquina Téllez de Girón» (C. 2.581), daughter of the Duke of Osuna. The true heir of decorative paintings, begun by Giordano and continued by Giaquinto, is Mariano Salvador Maella (1739-1819); only Goya will surpass his fresco decorations. His style will little by little diverge toward Neoclassicism. Thus in four panels representing the *seasons* (C. 2.497-2.500) he changes these, within the classicist ideal, into Flora, Ceres and Bacchus; winter is an exception and he will personify it in two old men. His «Seascapes» (C. 873-75) will achieve great success, and neither will he neglect the portrait, such as the one of the enigmatic Infanta «Carlota Joaquina» (C. 2.440), who will be Queen of Portugal.

GOYA

The work of Goya represents a whole chapter of the history of Spain, at a time when the political darkness is sometimes illuminated by the passionate desire for liberty of the Spanish people. His production is immense: some five hundred paintings are known; a thousand drawings; some two hundred and seventy-five watercolors and lithographs. Because of this, here we can only treat very briefly his stylistic evolution in conjunction with his biography, leaving somewhat disjointed the structural development of his life and production, although complemented somewhat by the commentaries to the plates.

Francisco de Goya y Lucientes is born in the impoverished Aragonese town of Fuendetodos, on March 30, 1746, to a modest family. His father left no will «because he had no reason to». He has his first lesson with a not very learned monk and then he moves on to the workshop of José Luzán, who was formed in the Neopolitan school. After twice failing in the biennial contests of the San Fernando Royal Academy, he goes to Italy in 1770, where he wins a second prize given out by the Academy at Parma. This trip will open doors for him in Zaragoza, for he is commissioned to paint the choir vault of the Pilar Cathedral. And four years later, when he is married to the daughter and sister of the Bayeu family, he joins the group of painters who work for the Royal Tapestry Factory (Pl. XC). Although the first cartoons are weak, little by little, he develops a style in which his personality will be defined. And meanwhile the growth of his clientele among the aristocracy and intellectuals begins. By the age of forty he has done religious paintings, popular scenes, portraits and decorations with elliptical structures and rapid brush strokes. Around this time he gains the friendship of the Duke and Duchess of Osuna, the Infante Don Luis and the Duchess of Alba. The sovereign himself, Charles III, poses for him and names him «royal painter»; his son Charles IV, in 1789, will make him first among the royal painters. Years earlier, in 1780, he had been elected to the Academy, when he presented his «Christ on the Cross» (C. 745) with its cold Neoclassical feeling.

At the height of success he suffers an illness which endangers his life and changes his life-style and his art forever. Upon becoming deaf, he isolates himself from the world and withdraws within himself. After a year of total inactivity (1792), he begins to prepare the engravings of «Los Caprichos» (whose sketches belong to the Prado), penetrating into a world of monsters, witches, murderers, robbers, prostitutes; but underneath it all the problems he brings to light are eternal ones. Besides they possess a symbolic value, with which he will attack the socio-political structure of the times. At the same time, he does paintings of popular pastimes (1793, San Fernando Academy). Somewhat recovered, in 1795 he holds the position of director of painting in the Academy and paints the posthumous portrait of his brother-in-law Francisco Bayeu, shaded with the grays characteristic of this period, and also the one of the melancholy Duke of Alba (C. 2.449), leafing through songs by Haydn. At the same time he will paint one of the Duchess, whom he will later paint in his prodigious portrait in black tones (Hispanic Society, N.Y., See Pl. XCI) and a year later he does the frescoes in San Antonio de la Florida. In 1800, after he does other portraits of friends and the Royal Family, he does one of the most surprising works in universal painting: «The Family of Charles IV» (Pl. XCII). The «Majas»

(Pl. XCI, C. 742) are probably inmediately previous, for in the nude one there still remain Neoclassical traces. Before the Napoleonic invasion he continues to execute elegant portraits such as the one of the actor Máiquez (C. 1.807), one of his most animated masculine portraits, in which with a nervous style he manages to emphasize the sensitive intelligence in the face of his friend, giving him a faintly Romantic feeling. In it the grays and ochres are handled with almost musical modulation, revolutionizing the pictorial technique of his times.

Napoleon decides upon the occupation of Spain, believing that the corruption and mistakes of Charles IV's reign would make it a case of simple military deployment; to achieve it, he confides in the collaboration of Godoy, several times portrayed by Goya. Nevertheless, when everything seems settled —with the monarchs in Bayonne and Joseph Bonaparte designated to occupy the throne— the Madrilenian people rebel on the Second of May, and this will be the torch which sets off the tinderbox of Spain. As so many times has happened, the Iberian soil is covered with bloody ruins, where famished spirits swarm. Goya reflects this Apocalyptic world in the «Disasters of War», «The Colossus», and in the two famous paintings: «The Second of May», and «The Executions of the Third of May» (Pl. XCIII). During the war he portrays personages from the two fighting camps; thus he does the usurper «Joseph I», in the Madrid Town Hall, his collaborator Mayor «Don Francisco Silvela» (1809, C. 2.450), «General Palafox» (C. 725) and Lord Wellington. He does an effigy of Ferdinand VII himself a little before his French exile in 1808, and upon his return. In this time of neediness, he sends his friends succulent tidbits, but painted ones done by himself as Christmas greetings; among them stands out the «Slice of Salmon» (Oskar Reinhart Foundation, Winterthur, Switzerland) and in the Prado two other «Christmas cards» exist: a «Dead Turkey» and «Chickens and Roosters» (C. 751-52).

With the war ended, he does a self-portrait (C. 723) and paints personages of the times, doing religious paintings, among which stands out the «Last Communion of St. José de Calasanz» (Escuelas Pías, Madrid). With the reinstatement of Absolutism in Spain, Goya, an old liberal, has to seek refuge in his villa, the Quinta del Sordo, where confronting the world around him with his own manner of being, he does in his «Black Paintings» (Pl. XCV and Pl. XCIV) the most pathetic pictorial representation of all time until we come to Edvard Munch. Only in his «Disparates» (Insanities) will he manage to penetrate so profoundly into the depths of the subconscious.

Fearing that his life might end on the gallows which Calomarde had raised in the Cebada Plaza, he asks to move —with Royal permission— to France, to «visit medicinal baths»; but instead of being at the baths, in July of 1824 he can be found in Paris, «weak and not knowing a word of French» (Moratín), but he is able to contemplate «Les Massacres de Scio» by Delacroix in the Salon. Established in September in Bordeaux in the company of Doña Leocadia Weiss, the companion of his final years, he begins to prepare his lithographs —«he is still learning» the new method of engraving— «The Bulls in Bordeaux». In 1826 he makes a quick trip to Madrid, and is painted by Vicente López (C. 864, Casón del Buen Retiro). The following year Goya returns, doing a darling portrait of his grandson and when he goes back to Bordeaux, the one of Juan Bautista Muguiro (1827, C. 2.898) «at the age of eighty-four», of a great plastic beauty and which complements his impressive final portrait, the one of Don Pío de Molina (Reinhart Coll.), an authentic symphony in gray tones. Also, from a few months before his death —he dies on April 16, 1828— must be the graceful «Milkmaid of Bordeaux» (C. 2.899), in which with bluish and gray tones, as well as soft greens, he succeeds in harmoniously representing youthful melancholy. With these last pictures Goya moves toward a new conception of painting.

THE ENGLISH SCHOOL

Although in England, since the XVIth century, some important painters had existed in an isolated fashion, such as the miniaturist Hilliard, the creation of a true pictorial school is only achieved in the Neoclassical period. Now then, while European painting is cooled down by the resurrection of forms taken from Roman and Greek painting and sculpture, in England a style arises in which there exists complete liberty and independence with respect to the painting of other European countries. The portrait is especially emphasized with a mark of elegance and distinction, characteristics which are the offspring of the English character itself, though contributing to the formation of this style is the portrait work done in Great Britain by Holbein and especially Van Dyck, in whose art the British aristocrats see their aesthetic ideals realized. Without these painters, the development of English portrait art in the XVIIIth century could not be explained. Very significant is Gainsborough's deathbed farewell to Reynolds, when he tells him: «Good-bye, I hope we'll meet in eternity, with Van Dyck for company».

Only in recent years has the Prado Museum managed to assemble a certain number of English paintings from this period; today, in conjunction with the collection maintained in the Lázaro Galdiano Museum, the evolution of the English portrait may be followed. The generation of 1725 is headed up by the two afore-mentoned painters, with the precedent of Hogarth, the true creator of the school. Sir Joshua Reynolds (1723-1792), born of a modest family, will soon scale the social heights, achieving the successes which bring him to create the Royal Academy, of which he will be President for life. A great admirer of Murillo, with whom he is acquainted thanks to the great number of his works preserved in England, and a trip to the Mediterranean which he begins in 1749. He will also let himself be influenced by Italian and ·Flemish painting; nonetheless, he will achieve an indisputable originality, in which elegance plays the most important part. Very erudite, he will also cultivate the mythological genre and landscapes. But where his personality shines most brilliantly is in the portrait, to which he applies a refined technique: although he produces a sensation of spontaneity, the execution has been done mindfully In the Prado exist the portrait of an «Ecclesiastic» (Pl. LXXXIV) and the one of «Mr. James Bourdieu» (C. 2.986). On the other hand, the artistic career of Thomas Gainsborough (1727-1788) will be slower, although at the mid-point of his life he will already be established in the extremely elegant neighborhood of Pall Mall, in London, and George III will open the doors of the Court to him. Although less cultured than Reynolds, his temperament is more genial. Lacking the yearn for travel of his companion, in his work he follows the English tradition. Therefore in his painting, which originates in Van Dyck, he achieves chromatic effects in which by using a single color, he develops multiple variations, especially of blues. Thus a good example of this is the portrait of «Doctor Sequeira» (Pl. LXXXV); of poorer quality is the one of «Mr. Robert Butcher of Walt-tamstan» (C. 2.990).

By the third important painter in England at this moment, George Romney (1734-1802), there exists in the Prado a «Portrait of an English Gentleman» (C. 2.584) and the delightful one of «Master Ward« (C. 3.013) in which is represented a typical English «little rich boy», portrayed alongside his dog, where it seems Romanticism may already be sensed. Romney was of a passionate character, as his burning love for Lady Hamilton demonstrates; this love was shared by .Nelson and this almost drove Romney crazy. In the numerous portraits of this ardent woman he changes the poses, some of which are taken from Classical sculpture, which denotes his passion for things Italian, for on some occasions influences from the Bolognese classicists may also be perceived.

At the beginning of the XIXth century this tradition of elegance in the portrait still continues, with Thomas Lawrence (1769-1830) standing out. A child prodigy, at the age of ten he already successfully exhibits a series of two-toned portraits done with pastels. At a very young age he becomes the idol of British aristocracy, especially among the ladies, of whom he does beautiful portraits, in which the clothing and hairdos are as important as the faces, differentiating himself in this from the majority of his contemporaries who left these details in the hands of collaborators. The technical execution of his works is of a vibrant realization, although on occasion it reaches the level of rhetoric, such as in the portrait of the «Count of Westmoreland» (C. 3.001), who appears leaning against the pedestal of a column, wearing the Court uniform characteristic of the Lords, red with ermite trimming and lined with white silk, and beneath this mantle, a velvet dress coat and white stockings; the «coup de vent» hair style, used by the dandies of George IV's epoch, adds a Romantic, though also pedantic, touch. Nevertheless, in the delightful portrait of «Marthe Carr» (C. 3.012) he achieves a great intimacy and some extremely delicate chromatic effects in its whites and pinks, making it one of his most important masterpieces, in which he departs from the academic and courtly feeling which he generally employs. Also by his hand is the picture of a «Noblewoman of the Storer Family» (C. 3.011), other members of this family vere portrayed (C. 3.000 and 3.014), by Martin Shee (1769-1860), whose main interest stems from the fact he represents personages of the British bourgeosie who had contact wtih Spain. Shee was a student of Reynolds' and his successor at Court.

Somewhat younger than Lawrence and the most important Scotch painter of the times, is Henry Raeburn (1756-1823), who is formed in the Neoclassical style, but his personages possess a markedly realistic character. A good example of this is the painting of «Mrs. Maclean of Kinlochaline» (C. 3.116), one of the three sisters Samuel Johnson praises for their beauty in his *Tour of the Hebrides*. The continuer of his style in Edinburgh is John Wattson (1790-1864); an important work of his is the «Portrait of a Gentleman» (C. 3.003). A representation of the three most important landscape artists of British painting, Constable, Turner and Bonnington, only exists in the Lázaro Galdiano Museum. As a sample of this moment, in the Prado there exist two small sketches of Seville (C. 2.852-53) done by the indefatigable traveler and engraver, David Roberts (1796-1864).

XVIIIth CENTURY PAINTING

HOUASSE: Louis I.

VAN LOO: The Family of Philip V.

MAELLA: Seascape.

F. BAYEU: Picnic in the Country.

MAGNASCO: Landscape: Christ
Waited On By Angels.

LAWRENCE: Miss Marthe Carr.

PANINI: Ruins with St. Paul (?)
Preaching.

GOYA. The Painter Francisco Bayeu.

GOYA. The Dummy.

GOYA. Ferdinand VII.

GOYA. The Dressed Maja.

GOYA: Duel with Clubs.

GOYA: The Colossus, or Panic.

GOYA: The Second of May, 1808.

GOYA: The Disasters of War, drawing.

SCULPTURE

VI

The collection of sculpture in the Prado generally goes unnoticed by the visitor since it is swallowed up by the fabulous gallery of pictures. Now then, there are other museums in Spain which offer a vision of Spanish sculpture: the National Sculpture M. in Valladolid, the Catalán Art M. and Marés. M. in Barcelona, and in Madrid the National Archaeology M. The Prado conserves an important collection of Classical works; the majority comes from the Royal Collections; the most ancient have been donated by Don Mariano de Zayas. The sculpture in the Prado begins chronologically with a magnificent Sumerian head, one of the largest known, which might be the portrait of «Gudea» (2300 B.C.), the famous «patesi» (governor) of Lagash; an Egyptian «Falcon» from the Saïtic Empire is also exhibited. Older than this is a delightful «Kouros» (youth) from the beginning of the VIth century, similar to ones found in the Acropolis in Athens. Now then, continuing with Greek sculpture, by the earliest great sculptor of this century, Myron, is the «Athena» which formed part of a group with the satyr Marsyas; in this Roman copy are perceived the forms of Classical realism which fully triumphs with Phidias, to whom is owed the «Athena Parthenos» (438 B.C.); a copy, although of reduced size and from the Roman period, picks up the expression of the Phidian ideal. The «Centauromaquia» (battle of the gods and centaurs) which decorated the sandals of the gigantic statue is copied on the lower part of an amphora (1st century A.D.) conserved in the Museum. One of the loveliest versions of Polyclitus' (the third great sculptor of this century) «Diadumeno» (Pl. XCVII) exists here. From among the representations conceived in the following century stands out the «Satyr in Repose», for it is in contact with the style of Praxiteles, and was restored by the great Baroque sculptor Bernini, according to the inventories. But, above all, an impressive «Head» in bronze (Pl. XCVIII) stands out; it falls within the style of Lysippus who, along with Scopas, completes the great trilogy of the moment. The typology of the «Hypnos» has been related to this latter or Praxiteles; in a marvelous Roman version the advance of sleep is plastically expressed.

The Prado possesses important sculptural works in which the Hellenistic forms have been Romanized. Among them we may cite the «Venus with the Dolphin» (1st century A.D.), which although derived from a type created by the followers of Praxiteles and related to the «Capitolina» and «Mèdici Venuses», the hair is especially of Roman taste; it was discovered by Christina of Sweden. This is also true of the «Venus of the Apple», the one «of Madrid», and the one «of the Shell», or the series of the «Muses» coming from Hadrian's Villa in Tivoli and the «Bacchantes», for although they derive from an original by Kalimakos, they possess a certain academic coolness characteristic of Roman art.

Possibly the most original piece from this moment is the «Neptune» done by the sculptors who in Hadrian's epoch were working in Aphrodisia de Caria (Asia Minor); it was discovered in Corinth in the XVIIIth century. The «Rape of Ganymede» is also of a Hellenic-like taste. Along with historical relief (the Museum conserves a magnificent sarcophagus) the portrait is the most personal genre in Roman art, for although Greek antecedents exist —there are good copies of Hellenistic originals here— in the Empire it will undergo uncommon development. The Prado possesses stupendous versions of Augustus, Anthony Pius, Trajan, Hadrian, Drussus the Younger... within the characteristic realism; but in some cases, such as in Hadrian's favorite, the Bithynian Antinoo, the features are idealized due to a Hellenistic influence. Very interesting iconographically is the possible portrait of Hannibal.

From the Medieval period there are few representations. The earliest is a lovely Romanesque «Seated Virgin», from the XIIth century, in the Maderuelo Chapel. On the other hand, standing out within the Gothic style are: a German «Christ» (XIVth century), in the chapel cited; two extremely lovely Flemish versions of «angels», which may be dated in the mid-XVth century and a charming «Virgin and Child», from the same school, but done at the end of the century, for it is similar to versions which exist in the region of Burgos.

Neither does the Prado have an authentic Renaissance collection, but there are exquisite productions, such as the fragments with relief work coming from the funeral monument for Gaston de Foix, the work of Agostino Busti, «Il Bamballa», whose famous seated statue is preserved in the Sforzesco Castle in Milan. In the same case [Room 83], another delicate relief represents an «Allegory of Francesco Mèdici», the work of Giambologna (Jean de Douai, 1524-1608); possibly his is a small equestrian statue of Philip III, done before the one which may be admired in the Plaza Mayor in Madrid. The «Charles V Conquering Anger», a work by Leon Leoni (1509-1590), from Arezzo and who studied in Milan, stands out; the pieces of armor may be dismantled to show the Emperor nude as if the statue were the portrait of a hero of Antiquity. Commissioned in 1549, it was probably finished in 1555. Along with his son Pompeyo, Leon does a great number of portraits of the Emperor, of his son and relatives, of which the Prado possesses a wide selection. Some other portraits of the Hispanic Caesar are owed to other Italian authors, and outstanding is the one done by Bandinelli (C. 284), Michelangelo's Florentine rival. Within the orbit of this latter is a delicate bust of «Christ» [Room 6], attributed to Begarelli (Mòdena, c. 1500-1565). The Renaissance culminates in two rare sculptures by El Greco: «Epimethus and Pandora», whose iconography, as Xavier de Salas has obviously shown, is taken from Erasmus' *Adages*.

Within the scarce representation of Baroque sculpture stand out the small equestrian portraits of royalty, such as the one of Louis XIV, owed to François Girardon [Room 34; 1628-1713] and the one of Charles II of Spain, which though Berninesque, is the work of Giovanni B. Foggini (1652-1725), today in the Juntas Salon. Standing out due to its grace and delicacy is the «Group of Children [Room 39], done in marble by the most important Sicilian sculptor of the Baroque period: Giacomo Serpotta (Palermo, 1656-1732) with the serpents which allude to his last name; here he moves away from the stucco which he commonly used.

SCULPTURE

SAÏTIC ART: Falcon.

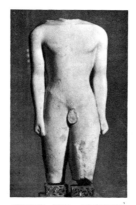

GREEK ART, ARCHAIC:
Kouros (youth).

PHIDIAS. Copy of Athena.

ROMAN ART: Venus
with the Dolphin.

ROMAN ART: Hyp-
nos (sleep).

ROMAN ART: Hadrian.

ROMANESQUE ART:
Seated Virgin.

GOTHIC ART, FLEMISH:
Virgin and Child.

POMPEYO LEONI: Char-
les V and Anger.

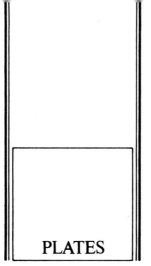

PLATES

MASTER OF BERLANGA.
Paintings from San Baudelio de Berlanga: Hunting Scene (Detail) (c. 1100). Fresco retouched with oils, transferred to canvas, 185 × 360 cm.

Romanesque painting in Castile opens with the paintings by the first Master of Berlanga. Their strong Mozarabic characteristics must fix their date earlier than the accepted one, as Camón Aznar has pointed out. According to him, there is «such an Oriental atmosphere in them that we do not find a single possible reference to compare in all of European art».

These paintings come from a unique building: the Mozarabic church in Casillas de Berlanga. It was built in the XIth century on the southern bank of the Duero River where it passes through the region of Soria. The date of the building's construction may be fixed between the time of Alfonso VI's conquest of this zone and its repopulation by Alfonso the Warrior (1108). Since this building was built in an uncertain and dangerous period, the hypothesis that it was a hunting palace before being consecrated as a church is not far-fetched. It remained undiscovered until 1907; after its existence became publicized, the greed of some and the neglect of others let these paintings be exported to the United States, where the whole was split up and distributed among various collections. Luckily, an important part has returned to Spain, thanks to an unlimited loan offered by the Metropolitan Museum (N.Y.), although in exchange the Spanish government has in turn «loaned out» the apse of the Fuentidueñas Church (Segovia).

Two groups of paintings exist which come from this hermitage: those which we may designate as by the first Master of Berlanga are the more Orientalized of the two and are the ones done in the lower part of the hermitage; and the second Master would be the one who paints the religious scenes, in the upper part, and all of whose work done in this church still remains in the United States. Here we are interested in considering just the first Master, since he is the only one represented in the Prado Museum. All his known work is of a secular theme, representing in the panels which he did, battle and hunting scenes. Just so in the one reproduced here; there appears a fragment from a rabit hunt, in which a knight with a trident pursues two hares with his pack of hounds. In another scene, an archer appears shooting an arrow at a deer which has already been wounded; then we have a white elephant carrying a castle-like structure, and a soldier with a lance and buckler; a bear and a camel remain in America. There is represented, as well, a Byzantine-type tapestry with eagles in it. In all of it the Mozarabic character is so strong that, as we said earlier, it makes one doubt that these paintings were done in the XIIth century. In the Master of Berlanga's work there exists a preoccupation with realism, show in an attempt to express movement and proportions. His spirit of observation has caused him to capture important details in treating animals, which since prehistoric times had no greater representation in the history of Spanish art. These frescoes have been in the Prado since 1957.

PLATE I

MASTER OF MADERUELO.

Original Sin. Paintings from the Maderuelo Hermitage: 1st third of the XIIth century.
Wall fresco and tempera, transferred to canvas, 498 × 540 cm.

The anonymous artist from Maderuelo expresses for us here one of his best done scenes, the moment in which Adam raises his hand to his throat with a worried look after having eaten the forbidden fruit. Meanwhile, a very feminine Eve continues to flirt with the serpent. Here the representation of human forms shows a strongly Romanesque character, since the artist limits himself to merely outlining the components of the human body. But the greatness of his art is rooted in the expressionist sensibility with which he executes this compositon, thanks to draftsmanship which as Post has said possesses «impressive and powerful lines». Next to it and on the spectator's left, the Creation of Man appears. The trees give a sense of landscape to the atmosphere. On one of the sections alongside the entrance only the head of a dog remains which has been related to the shepherds, while these latter appear facing it, in an important spot, for Maderuelo is in a pastoral area.

This detail forms part of the paintings which used to adorn the chapel of Santa Cruz de Maderuelo (Segovia), today in the Prado, where they have been carefully reconstructed. On the vault a Christ in His Majesty («*Maiestas Domini*», and not a «*Pantocrator*») appears surrounded by four angels, because the Evangelists («*Tetramorfos*») appear on the lateral walls above a representation of the Apostles, with seraphim and a feminine figure which could be either the Virgin or a saint. The artist based this scene on the *Apocalypse.* On the altar wall, Mary Magdalene is washing Christ's feet on one side; on the other, is an Epiphany scene; and in the center there is a Mystic Lamb.

This work is done with a technique which is very characteristic of the Romanesque style: combining fresco with tempera retouches. The palette is very somber with the figures outlined in a dark ochre, almost black. They are colored in only with reds, blues, whites and earthen tones. Cook, supported by Gudiol, thinks that this work may be by the same master who decorated the Church of Santa María de Tahull. But it should be taken into consideration that schools of painters existed which cultivated a similar style and which is very difficult to differentiate.

PLATE II

Taddeo Gaddi (Circle of).
St. Eloi in His Goldsmith's Shop (1350-1380).
Tempera on wood, 35 × 39 cm.   C. 2.842

There are still lovely works from the Italian Proto-Renaisance whose authors are unknown or subject to controversy. This is the case of two small panels preserved in the Prado, showing St. Eloi appearing before King Chlotar and the saint in his workshop. Due to their themes and format, they must have belonged to a «pala» (small retable) dedicated to the Patron of the gold and silversmiths. This was usual in those times since the retables of the guilds, not only served to decorate the church, but also gave a sense of power to the various groups of artisans since they had begun to compete with the nobility in the decoration of the important places of worship.

But who did this work? Due to its style of a Giottesque derivation we know that it was painted in Florence in the second half of the XIVth century. In the last century these two panels had already been attributed to Taddeo Gaddi (1300-1366). Berenson thought that they were close to the style of Jacopo di Cione (Orcagna); Donati (1966) also believes that they might be by this artist. The sensitive art historian Enzo Carli (*La pittura gotica*, 1965) goes back to the original attribution to Gaddi.

The scene which is reproduced here represents the daily activity of a Florentine goldsmith's shop in the XIVth century. The work was done in full view of the public, as is still the custom today in some Italian cities. On the bench is a series of jewels which are being given the finishing touches by St. Eloi, aided by two other artisans. The saint finishes the work on a saddle for King Chlotar, while his companions work on a cross and a repoussé panel. In a domestic scene in the background a woman stirs up the fire in an oven with a small bellows and a young man pounds with a hammer. In the meantime, the saint's client, King Chlotar, along with his companions, admires the young artisan's work.

The same as in the companion piece, the composition is very harmonius here; a great preoccupation with perspective, although it is not successfully achieved in the bench, manages to create a surprising effect in the workshop's vaulting where groin vaults appear between transverse arches. The spatial effect is attained by a graduated chiaroscuro technique. In this small work there also exists a search for volumes and colors which is within the best Giottesque tradition. Thus the figures, dressed in luxurious clothing, give a sensation of corporality. On the other hand, the gold background, which covers the spaces not filled by architectural forms is of a markedly Gothic characater.

In 1883 these panels were listed in the catalog of the auction of the Toscanelli Collection, in Pisa. They were transferred to the Spiridon Collection by 1898. Acquired by the illustrious politician and patron of the arts, Francisco de Asís Cambó, they were donated by him to the Prado in 1941.

PLATE III

NICOLÁS FRANCÉS.
Retable with the Lives of the Virgin and St. Francis. Central Panel (1445-60).
Tempera modeled with oil, on wood, 557 × 558 cm.   C. 2.545

This retable is a well-preserved work and comes from a chapel on a farm near La Bañeza (León), called Estepa de las Delicias, belonging to the Marquis of the same name. Since this painter worked in the Cathedral at León and for the King of Castile, it is surprising that he would condescend to do such an important work for such an insignificant place. The relationship of this piece with the León retable is very close; though it is less ostentatious in form and composition, it is less carefully done, except for the panel which we show here. It is possibly painted after the retable of the León Cathedral, which is shown by its more intense coloring and greater mastery in the oil glazes; for in Spain, even earlier than in Italy, colors dissolved in oil are used for retouching the tempera.

The complete retable is formed by nine panels, plus the nineteen on the predella, with alternate depictions of apostles and prophets. The central panel, illustrated here, shows the «Virgin and Child». Mary has two large angelical musicians at her side and two other smaller ones in the lower part of the picture; the instruments they have are a lute, a harp, a citar and a hand organ. The Virgin and Child are placed under a ciborium whose style recalls a religious building, and Mary in turn is seated on a throne on which there is a lovely red damask cushion. She wears a blue tunic and the Child, semi-nude wearing a coral amulet against evil spirits, plays with a little bird; in the background are remainders of the gilding.

Above this panel, an incomplete one, «The Assumption of the Virgin», is found, over which, like a spire, there rises the Crucified Christ, wounded by Longinos and accompanied by the Virgin, St. John and the three Maries. In the right-hand section, the lower panel represents the Annunciation, in which an angel, not a servant girl as Sánchez Cantón says, waters the sweet basil plants with water which he draws from a well and God the Father, with a pontifical tiara, exhales the Holy Spirit out through His mouth. Above, we have the «Nativity» and «Christ's Presentation at the Temple» in the upper panel of the section. In the left-hand section appear stories from the life of St. Francis. «St. Francis Before the Sultan of Baylonia» is the scene represented in the lower panel; in the next one we have «The Canonical Approbation of the Franciscan Order», by Pope Innocent III (1216), and in the last one, «The Saint with Stigmata».

In all these panels, a great preoccupation with perspective exists. Although it may be stylistically included within the International Gothic movement, certain Italian influences exist which may possibly come from the Circle of Dello Delli (Nicolas Florentino), who at this time worked in Salamanca. But this influence is more visible in the Santa Clara Retable in Tordesillas. The work entered the Prado in 1931.

82

PLATE IV

JUAN DE PERALTA (Master of Sigüenza).
Retable of St. John the Baptist and St. Catalina: Salome's Dance. (Middle of the XVth century).
Tempera on wood, 64 × 135 cm.   C. 1.336

The panel which is reproduced has been attributed to the «Master of Sigüenza», the name which was given to an anonymous artist, since this painting along with others by his hand come from Los Arces Chapel, today a sacristy, in the cathedral at Sigüenza. Still there are the frontal and upper section which would complete this piece. Meanwhile in the Prado, besides this panel, we have the central one with the two saints who give the retable its name and whose heads were repainted in the XVIth century, and the lateral sections in which are represented «The Beheading of St. John the Baptist», «St. Catalina with the Wheels of Martyrdom», and «The Decapitation of St. Catalina».

In the same cathedral there exists another retable which is, so it seems, by the same hand; it is dedicated to St. Andrew and one of the Deacon Saints. Another St. Andrew (Private Collection, Paris) is signed: Johns Peraltis, which has made possible the identification of this Master as Juan de Peralta. The style of all these panels is uniform and is derived from that of Rodríguez de Toledo, a painter who studied with Gerardo Starnina (an important Italian artist from the end of the XIVth century who comes to Spain, bringing an evolved Giottesque style which presages Masaccio's art —the Chapel of St. Eugene and St. Blas in the Primate Cathedral). But here in Juan de Peralta's painting the facial characteristics lose the soft Florentine modeling, becoming sharper and deformed, at times reaching Expressionist forms. Although Post tried to identify this painter as Juan Arnaldi, active in Zaragoza in 1433, Gudiol has wisely considered Juan de Peralta to be one in the same with Juan de Sevilla, which would clear up the formation and evolution of his work. Thus he may be considered an Andalusian painter, but who studied in Castile, where his art evolved from a first Starninesque moment in the triptych in the Lázaro Galdiano Museum (Madrid) in which a certain blandness exists in the forms, to a harsher and more pathetic style, within the currents of the International Gothic style.

In the scene which is reproduced, the moment in which Salome chastely dances before her step-father Herod is somewhat ingenuously represented. Herod wears a royal crown. On a table there are dishes and food, in a prelude to the later Spanish still-lifes. Although at first glance it seems that a superficial narrative predominates, with some observation we see the preoccupation with the perspective in the floors and ceilings which makes this work a diachronic precedent of the painting of the Spanish Renaissance.

The panels were acquired by the Patrons of Artistic Treasures and the Prado Museum in 1930; they had belonged to the Retana Collection.

PLATE V

ANONYMOUS SPANISH ARTIST FROM LEVANTE.
The Martyrdom of St. Vincent (c. 1460).
Entire wing, oil and tempera on wood, 250 × 84 cm.   C. 2.670

This «Martyrdom of St. Vincent» is an integral part of one wing of a retable which is possibly dedicated to this saint's torture and death. Also preserved in the Prado Museum is another section of this retable. In the upper
scene, above the panel illustrated, the saint appears on the pyre, kneeling on
the grid, and in the lower panel, this one, he has been thrown in the water
with a millstone around his neck by three bailiffs, although they look more
like children, since all these scenes are narrated with a primitive ingenuity.
The action unfolds here; in the foreground St. Vincent appears dead, after
his body has been washed ashore by the waves in spite of the enormous
weight of the stone wheel. In the background, some ships, among them a
caravel, are represented. On the coast, on the spectator's right, a fortress
reminds us of Bellver Castle in Majorca.

The atmosphere of the scene and its representation of the sea, which
greatly reminds us of the Mediterranean, make us think it is by an Aragonese master from around 1460, who works within the Hispano-Flemish
style. His Levantine origin is clarified by the use of gold relief work on the
clothing of the figures and in the halo around the saint's head. In spite of
its ingenuous primitive touch, there exist certain preoccupations with perspective, and these, as well as some details like the flatness of the tones,
make us think of tendencies of an Italian origin besides the above-mentioned Northern ones. From the chromatic point of view, it is interesting
to point out the delicate blue shades of the water, against which the flesh
tones of the child-like executioners stand out.

In the upper scene, the companion section shows the saint as he is beaten
while bound to an x-shaped cross. In the lower section we find the dead
saint, on the bank of a river, surrounded by crows, a peacock, dogs and
other animals. In the background is a city which peasants are entering.

This retable is a delightful example of popular art which, anonymous
like the folk ballads, merits, due to its spontaneity and sensitivity, the honor
of being exhibited in the Prado from the time astute collector Pablo Bosch
donated it in 1915.

PLATE VI

JAIME HUGUET.
A Prophet (c. 1435).
Tempera on wood, 30 × 26 cm.   C. 2.683

This small fragment from a *sub-predella* (typical of the Kingdom of Aragon) is a lovely representation of the style of Jaime Huguet, the great Catalonian painter from the XVth century, by whom the Prado has only this one delightful example. Though it is miniscule in size, the quality is wonderful and the extremely lively expression of the subject portrayed possesses a look of naturalness which is surprising considering the time at which it was done; besides, its great technique of draftsmanship recalls some contemporary artists from Northern Italy who were accustomed to working in the demanding medium of fresco. According to Ainaud de Lasarte, the typology of this face with slanted eyes and an oblique glance may be linked to some of the figures in the dismantled San Jorge retable. This fragment should, therefore, be considered among the youthful works of the painter from Valls, done at a time when his technique is more careful, before his collaboration with a workshop which will reduce the quality of much of his production.

In spite of a fragmentary sentence on a *filacteria* (small banner inscribed with a prophesy which generally accompanied the figures of the prophets), we cannot definitely identify the prophet here represented. The primary origin of the work is also unknown; it was donated to the Prado Museum by the illustrious patron of the arts, Don Pablo Bosch.

PLATE VII

Jan Van Eyck and Collaborator.
The Fountain of Grace (c. 1423-1429).
Oil and tempera on wood, 116 × 181 cm.   C. 1.511

The attribution of this work to Jan Van Eyck has been questioned, even to the point of believing it to be a copy of a lost original, a hypothesis which may be rejected, considering the quality of some of the figures. The «Fountain of Grace» is very closely related to the famous «Adoration of the Lamb» (1425-29) in St. Bavon in Ghent, but the symbolism and its technique make us think that it must have been done prior to the «Adoration» and even before Van Eyck's trip to Spain since there exist no motives or decoration with Spanish characteristics, contrary to what happens in later works. Van Eyck comes to Spain on two occasions, accompanying diplomatic legations searching for a wife for the Duke of Burgundy, Philip the Good, who became a widower in 1425. The first legation went to Valencia in 1427; when it failed, in 1428 the legation returns to the Peninsula, to ask for the hand of his daughter Isabel from the King of Portugal John I; on this occasion Van Eyck makes a pilgrimmage to Santiago, visits John II and the King of Granada.

It is possible that the triptych of which this piece was the central panel was not directly commissioned —according to César Pemán— but merely acquired by John II from the painter, having been done previous to these trips, or in any case as Kämmerer suggests (1898) between the two. The same as his masterpiece, this is also an exaltation of the Eucharist. An enthroned and blessing Christ presides over the scene, surrounded by the symbols of the four Evangelists (*Tetramorfos*); at his feet is the Mystic Lamb and on the sides the Virgin and St. John (*Deesis*); in the Gothic dais which shelters the Savior, the Prophets are sculpturally represented. On an intermediate level we find a field with angelical musicians of Germanic typology. And in the lower section, on both sides of the Eucharistic Font on whose waters float Sacred Hosts, the Church and the Synagogue appear. In the former are a number of figures which are real-life portraits, such as those of the Emperor Segismundo, Pope Martin V (d. 1431), the King of France Charles VII, if it is not as Pemán affirms, John II of Castille—if this were true, the date of «The Fountain of Grace» would only have to be changed to around 1430, before the death of the Pope who is portrayed, and on the end, so it seems, Jan Van Eyck himself. As we said earlier, some of them are of such a high quality that it is impossible to attribute them to a disciple or a copyist, but rather they must necessarily be considered the work of the Flemish master himself, done in his youth, with the collaboration of a master from the Rhine area, as Bruyn indicates; though the date which Post gives (1420) seems premature. The panel comes from the sacristy of El Parral Monastery (Segovia); as Pemán has demonstrated, the one described by Ponz in the Palencia sacristy is the one found today in the Oberlin (Ohio) Museum. The original was taken to the Trinidad Museum in 1838 and moved to the Prado in 1872.

PLATE VIII

MASTER OF FLÉMALLE (Attributed to).
St. Barbara (1438).
Oil on wood, 47 × 101 cm.   C. 1.514

The name of Master of Flémalle, or Merode, has been given to a group of paintings which critics today attempt to divide among Robert Campin, Roger Van der Weyden's master and another student of his called Jacques Daret. And even more, recently the hypothesis, not at all extreme, has been offered that some of these works are by Van der Weyden himself, at a young age, shortly after he leaves Campin's workshop where he is documented in 1427.

The close relationship which exists between this «St. Barbara» and the «Virgin and Child» (Prado) by Van der Weyden, makes this hypothesis possible. This panel, along with the one in which appears the Franciscan «Heinrich Werl with St. John the Baptist», forms part of the triptych whose central panel is now lost. At the foot of the Franciscan's portrait there is an inscription in which it says that the work was done in 1438, the year in which the subject, as a professor at the University of Cologne, attends the Council of Basil (1431-1439).

St. Barbara appears here in a superbly elegant room in which the smallest details have been faithfully recorded. She is seated on a reversible bench and reading with her back to a roaring fireplace. The light from the fire is reflected against the objects, producing flickering shadows which contrast with the static ones cast by the daylight; this is one of the most interesting achievements by the Flemish painter who did this picture, especially since in the other pictures attributed to the Master of Flémalle if there are shadows, they are inert. This occurs in the other works which are kept in the Prado under his name («The Marriage of the Virgin» and «The Annunciation») in which the International Gothic style is more noticeable than in the «St. Barbara» and its companion piece.

This picture is one of the precursors, along with the «Arnolfini Marriage Group», by Van Eyck (which was in the Royal Spanish Collection), of Dutch interior painting. If it were not for the tower (which may be seen in the background through the window) a fundamental symbol of the saint, since her father locked her in it before beheading her— this could be an example of a Flemish interior, with a young girl in her study, or, in any event, the Virgin Mary, since the attributes of the saint's purity: the lily, the water jug and basin; are also Marian Symbols.

The other side of the panel was also painted, and below a thick layer of covering paint two halos may be seen. X-ray studies have discovered nothing, but Renders believes that the drawing of the Virgin with Chid, in Dresden, attributed to Van der Wyden might have been a preparatory sketch for this side of the piece. It was in Aranjuez until 1827. We know that it was acquired by Charles V.

PLATE IX

ROGER VAN DER WEYDEN.
Deposition (1436-1437).
Oil on wood, 262 × 220 cm. C. 2.825

Without a doubt, this «Deposition» is one of the most important and beautiful pictures from Medieval Flemish painting. It was done between 1436 and 1437 for the Chapel of the Crossbowmen's Guild in the Church of Notre Dame des Victoires, in Lǫuvain.

The composition, just like in certain sculptural reliefs of the period, is arranged vertically, since the upright of the cross divides it in half, balancing it in an admirable fashion. There is thus a group of three people on the right and also an almost identical one on the other side. The verticality of the cross is mitigated by a diagonal which goes from the head of the young man who has removed the nails from Christ's body to the Virgin and St. John's right foot, also touching the Saviour's and Nicodemus' heads. The entire composition in general is comprised within an oval, and a perfectly clear, undulating line, forming an «s», gives a syncopated feeling to the whole central part of the painting, reminding us of musical compositions, of the period, since its structure corresponds to four points, with a quaternary rhythm, exactly the same as the four-four time of the «Stabat Mater Dolorosa» by the Franco-Flemish composer G. Dufay (d. c. 1470). This undulating line begins with St. John's right foot (*Sta-*), which is equal to a half-note; it continues with Adam's skull (*-bat*) and the Virgin's right hand (*Ma-*), for two quarter-notes; followed by a half-note, the Evangelist's left foot (*-ter*); the blue mantle is the same as a long series of quarter rests; two more quarter-notes are formed by the Virgin's left hand (*Do-*) and Christ's right hand (*-lo-*); His left one and His navel represent a dotted half-note, (*-ro-*), and Christ's crossed feet (*-sa*) form the last note of this phrase, a whole one. Panofsky had already intuitively perceived the painter's intention when he said that this painting was not oriented toward action, nor toward «drama, but rather in the direction of the essential problem of concentrating a maximum of passion in a form as rigorously structured as a Shakespearian sonnet». Now, more than a sonnet, as we have seen, it is related to a musical composition.

Von Simson (Art Bull. 1935) has carefully studied the theological criteria pertinent to this picture relating them to the «Compasio», the pain which Mary shares with her Son, affirmed by the parallelism of the two figures. His idea is derived from Bernardo de Claraval. Also the gilded background, besides emphasizing the delicate chromatic tones, possibly is meant to give an intemporal feeling to the action which is shown—for Van der Weyden, influenced by the mysticism of his times, probably wants to express to us that Christ's body is being taken down from the cross, not on Golgotha only, but at every moment in the lives of all men.

PLATE X

ROGER VAN DER WEYDEN.
Pietà (1440-1450).
Oil on wood, 35 × 47 cm.   C. 2.540

This «Pietà» is the loveliest version in a series of works on the same theme which are attributed to Roger van der Weyden or his disciples. On the left is a group in which stands out the Virgin holding the inert body of her Son, with evident spiritual suffering. The dramatic expression of the mother is softened a little by the infinite tenderness which flows from her face; next to her St. John helps to support the weight of Christ's body. Meanwhile, on the other side appears the figure of Broers, a citizen of Malinas, who was the donor of this small but masterful work; he is kneeling and piously contemplating the scene, expressing a sincere but not overly dramatic emotion. Van der Weyden's ability to portray religious sentiments with a profound emotional intensity is what brings him to do a great number of works related to the Passion of Christ, in which the divine becomes human.

Thus in this «Pietà» the tragedy takes place in a setting appropriate for men; in the background, on the horizon of a typically Flemish plain, a Gothic city may barely be seen; and almost half of the painting is devoted to the sky, a rare thing among the Flemish primitives. Against this sky with vague, slowly moving clouds and circling swallows, an immense cross stands out as a symbol of salvation. Roger van der Wyden's (or in French, Roger de la Pasture) naturalist technique causes him to paint the hairs on Christ's legs one by one; as we see, this admirable Flemish painter joins realism and an idealistic sense which is parallel to the Florentine «quattrocento».

The ancient origin of this painting is unknown today and we only know that in the XIXth century it belonged to the Duke of Mandas.

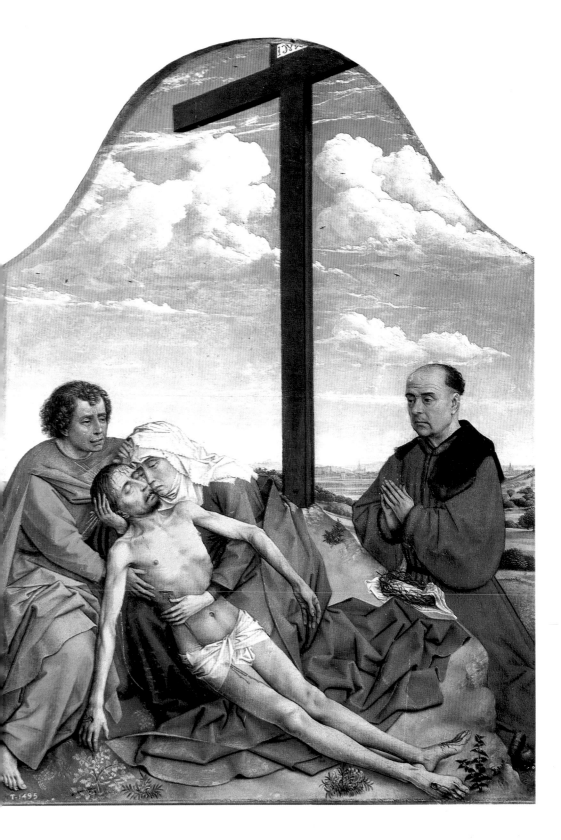

HANS MEMLING.
Adoration of the Kings (c. 1470).
Oil on wood, 145 × 95 cm. (Total.)   C. 1.557

This «Epiphany» is the central part of a triptych in the Prado Museum, completed with a «Presentation in the Temple» and an «Adoration of the Baby Jesus by Angels and the Virgin». Memling bases this work on a master piece by Roger van der Weyden (possibly his teacher), the retable from Santa Columba in Cologne, today in the Pinacoteca in Munich, in whose central panel the same theme appears handled in a similar manner, but Memling has spaced out and simplified the scene. Thus St. Joseph, on the right, is not involved in the action and the donor has been placed to one side, for he is the clean-shaven figure on the far left, while in Van der Weyden he appeared in the center of the composition. A kneeling king kisses Jesus' feet with a certain timid affection, in contrast to the one in Van der Weyden's painting, who kisses his hand fervently. It has been thought that two of the kings may be portraits of Charles the Bold and Philip the Good.

The heroic feeling characteristic of Van der Weyden has disappeared in this work. The forms are softer and the figures express a lyricism very typical of Memling's art. In opposition to the master's strong vibrant lines, the student offers homogeneous, softer surfaces and sometimes uses iridescent tones in the clothing of the elongated, almost Mannerist, figures.

Before doing this «Adoration», Memling did a version which is more faithful to Van der Weyden's original, which is also in the Prado Museum. Later, in 1479, he did a replica for Jan Floreins, today in the Hospital of St. John at Bruges, in which the forms are even more stylized.

In the «Presentation at the Temple», behind the figure of Simeon, there appears a face which is reminiscent of Memling's hypothetical self-portrait. This triptych belonged to Charles V and was in the Castle of Aceca, in the Township of Villaseca de la Sagra (Toledo). It entered the Prado in 1847.

HIERONYMUS BOSCH.
Table of the Seven Deadly Sins (1480-1490).
Oil on wood, 150 × 120 cm.   C. 2.822

This table, which represents the seven deadly sins, is possibly one of the earliest works by Bosch which is conserved, as may be seen by the dense brushwork and a certain rigidity of a Gothic feeling. In the center of the table are three concentric circles, like a large eye, that of God, since in the pupil the figure of Christ appears, displaying the wounds from the Crucifixion, suffered to achieve the redemption of mankind; below this there is an inscription which reads, «Careful, careful, God is watching you». But men senselessly let themselves be carried away by their passions and continue to sin. On various filacterias the words of Moses appear: «It is a nation which has lost its common sense; there is no intelligence among them. If they were prudent they would understand and think about what was going to happen to them».

The outer part of the eye is divided into seven parts, in which appear the seven deadly sins. Each one of them has an inscription in Latin with the corresponding designation. «Gluttony», the last in the series, is represented by a man who anxiously devours some meat and drinks at the same time. On the table other succulent dishes await. Another diner is avidly drinking, spilling the liquid all over himself; he has a chicken leg sticking out of his pouch and underneath a fine gauze on his leg may be seen an open syphilitic sore, as will also appear in other of Bosch's works. Meanwhile a woman brings in a roast chicken and a large sausage is also being roasted over the fire.

In the four corners, inside of circles, appear: the Death of the Sinner; the Last Judgement; Hell; and Heaven. In Hell, the glutton no longer devours delicious foods, but is rather damned to eat what is laid out on a table: a frog, a serpent and a large lizard. As Isabel Mateos indicates, the importance of this table-top, apart from its beauty, is especially founded «on the fact that it constitutes the starting point for anyone who is interested in the interpretation of Bosch's pictures», since many of its iconographic motifs are later repeated in his other paintings.

According to Carmen Bernis, by studying the dress of the figures it may be dated around 1480-1490. In has been disputed whether this piece was originally a table-top or a panel to be hung on a wall; in the inventories of Philip II, it appears as the former. In 1574 it was in El Escorial and Father Sigüenza says that it was «an excellent painting and tablet».

HIERONYMUS BOSCH.
Epiphany (c. 1510).
Oil on wood, 33 × 72 × 138 cm.   C. 2.048

This «Epiphany» must be a work from Bosch's later years, with its greatly
harmonious equilibrium, possibly a reflection of a spiritual serenity. The
closed triptych represents the Mass of St. Gregory with donors (?), in which
scenes of the Passion are portrayed in grisaille around an Ecce-Homo. But
a surprising event takes place when we open the triptych, for one of Bosch's
most lovely works in the formal aspect appears before us.

The landscape which fills the background of the three panels unifies the
whole: the scenes of the central panel with the lateral ones in which other
donors appear along with their patron saints, St. Peter and St. Ines. This
landscape is one of the most lovely ones in the Flemish painting of the time.
The shimmering light of the summer's end is prodigiously captured here;
in the background among golden fields, an imaginary Jerusalem rises with
a mixture of buildings—some Flemish, like the windmill, and others, such
as some Oriental towers which recall *ziggurats*. In the center, above the city,
the Star of the East appears, and on the left there is a lagoon with silvery
waters. While Herod's army searches for the new-born Babe, tragedy is not
lacking—on the left-hand panel a bear devours a traveler and a woman
flees from a wolf; on the right, some peasants do a happy dance.

In the central scene the Magi, whose rich clothing is embroidered with
allegorical motifs, worship the Baby Jesus, Who appears in the arms of His
mother in the traditional manner. The King who offers Him a tray with
incense or myrrh has the visit of the Queen of Sheba to Salomon embroidered on his cloak; the offering of gold, with the goldsmith's representation of the sacrifice of Isaac, has been placed on the ground. There are
some strange figures which look out from the stable in ruins, encased in a
glass tube; Brand-Philip, referring to Hebrew texts, believes that he is the
False Messiah; Comb thinks that the figures are the evil shepherds, and one
of them the False Messiah; their clothing has motifs taken from the Baby-
lonian Talmud. The true shepherds look on from outside, one of them
with an envious expression. In the meantime, St. Joseph appears to one side,
drying the Child's swaddling clothes over a fire.

Baldass dates the work 1490; Friedländer, 1495; and Tolnay, 1510, a time
which fits the clothing worn. On the wings of the triptych, appear the
coats of arms of the Bronckhorst and Bosschuyse Families and the slogan
«een voer al» (one for all). This work belonged to Jan de Casembroot, Lord
of Backerzeele, a supporter of William of Orange. As punishment, Philip II
confiscated the work and gave it a place of honor in his oratory at El Escorial.

PLATE XIV

HIERONYMUS BOSCH.
The Garden of Delights (1500-1510).
Triptych. Oil on wood, 195 × 220 cm. (Total).   C. 2.823

This painting is possibly one of the most extensively studied pictures in
the Prado Museum in recent years. A great number of articles and even
an ingenious monograph (Fraenger, *The Millenium of H. Bosch*) have been
written about it. According to this last author, Bosch was a member of
an Adamite sect, that of the *Brothers of the Free Spirit*, and therefore the
«Garden» would be an illustrated explanation of the sect's doctrines, in
which sexual liberty, through illumination from the Holy Ghost, would
be one of the paths leading to the salvation of the soul, that is, to a return
to the original innocence described in Genesis. Clothing and marriage were
the fruits of sin. Now, many of Fraenger's interpretations are not convinc-
ing. For example, he does not follow the logical thematic order of the triptych: Creation, the World and Hell. Explaining it, rather, with an Adamite
criterion, it would go in this order: creation, purification (Hell is not eternal
punishment, but purification), and in the central panel instead of a sinful
world there appears the *millenium*, a state of perfection in which there are
only pleasures, without sin. Combe and Gauffreteau-Sévy, among others,
believe, on the other hand, that although Bosch might have been acquainted
with these doctrines, his object, nevertheless, was to condem them, just as
much as he condemned carnal sins. Father Sigüenza, in his *History of the
Order of St. Jerome* (1605), was the first to give us a moralistic interpretation of this triptych, opposing the accusations of those who condemned
Bosch's paintings as heretical. As his principal argument, he puts forth
«the great consideration which his work merits from King Philip II, who
if he would have seen any indication of heresy, would not have permitted
these pictures to have reached his rooms». But his moralistic arguments
interest us more today, and thus he says of these pictures: «they are skillful
and prudent texts..., a painted satire on the sins and aberrations of men».
He also adds that these latter become beasts, which throws light on Bosch's
symbolism. More recent critics are returning once again to a moralizing
interpretation, basing themselves on Father Sigüenza, who called this
triptych, the *madroña-berry* triptych, because this fruit's «delicate fragrance
may barely be sensed before the berry is spoiled», the same as occurs with
worldly pleasures. On the left-hand wing appears the theme of the creation
of Eve by God the Father, as the trusting figure of Adam contemplates it
all. Everything surrounding the scene possesses a maleficent significance;
thus in the central part of the panel an owl appears presiding over a fantastic fountain. This animal was a symbol of wisdom in Classical antiquity,
but of evil in the Middle Ages; for Fraenger it symybolizes knowledge and
wisdom. We think that this fountain which pours its waters into a marshy
area —which is inhabited by simple ducks, proud swans and repulsive ver-

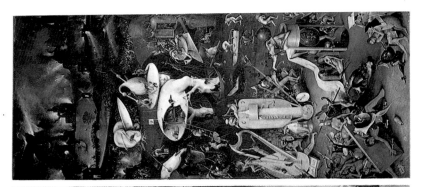

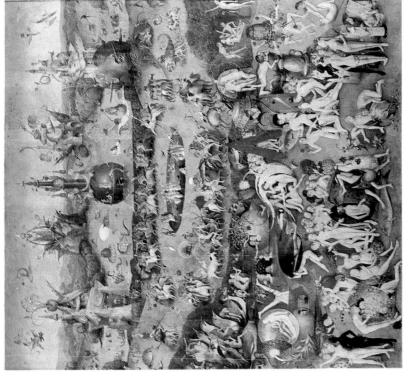

PLATE XV

min—could signify the *tree of life* but a life which although quite new-born already evidences corruption. Fraenger believes that the «Fountain of Life» is represented by the exotic dragon tree (native to the Canary Islands, it had become known through a print by Schongauer); but this tree since it is alongside the first human beings is probably the tree of good and evil; its sinewy, almost diabolical form made it be confused in those times with the mandrake tree. In the lower part, some animals already begin to devour each other. One of them, half-fish, half-duck, must symbolize the stupidity of a certain sector of the clergy, since it is dressed in a frair's hood and reads a book which it may very well not be able to understand. To the proper right of the fountain, a wild bull, the symbol of passion, lies in wait for the white unicorn, which represents chastity. The white elephant, the personification of innocence, has on his back the lustful monkey. Higher up, a great flock of birds leaves the earth, and the rocks take on phallic and anal formations.

In the central panel, the majority of the figures are human beings and all except for one are nude. All of them look very much alike —not because of lack of talent on Bosch's part, but rather due to his desire to portray men in mass. This stereotyped character, which G.-Sévy points out, is «an abolition of space in a place in which time no longer exists». This humanity, which at first glance seems happy, is plunged in melancholy; no pleasures exist which bring enjoyment and a great solitude envelopes them. These pleasures are therefore represented by means of symbols such as fruits, which as Father Sigüenza had already indicated, last a short time; strawberries, cherries, blackberries, raspberries all symbolize the ephimeral character of sexual pleasure. On the far right in the foreground, a man dressed in a camel skin points to a woman behind a glass tube; since she has an apple, she is probably Eve. Isabel Mateo rightly considers this to be a representation of St. John the Baptist, pointing to the originator of sin, and not the Grand Master of the Free Spirit as Fraenger has said. On the other side of the panel, a couple is found inside of a glass ball, which comes out of a flower as if it were a soap bubble. For Combe they signify the *new husband and wife* and he compares it to an alchemist's marriage, but it must really be a personification of the old adage: «pleasure is like a piece of glass, the greater it is, the faster it is shattered». Here the glass bubble will soon explode and burst into tiny bits. This flower in turn blooms out of an ovoid shape from which an envious man (the envy is symbolized by a rat— «envy gnaws at him», says the old saying) through a glass tube watches a couple making love inside of a clam (the representation of the vagina). At the same time, some pearls may be related to the proverb: «happiness is like a pearl, a drop of vinegar is enough to make it disappear». Close to them appears a group of birds; according to Fraenger it might signify the *mating of birds* in which desire is stimulated due to the imitation of nearby couples; a white man and a black woman ride of the back of one of them and another bird offers some symbolic raspberries to some men with his

beak. Three more, trapped by a thistle whose flower is being sucked by a butterfly and one of whose pistils is nibbled by a bird, are hemaphroditic representations, several of which appear in different ways in «The Garden of Delights».

In the center of this panel, there is a great cavalcade which moves around a circular pond, and it possibly represents men who gallop along on the backs of the sins. In the pond, young black and white women have ibis birds on their heads (then related to the Phoenix and to apples). Combe interprets it as the fountain of life, «center of the world around which everything turns». Above this one, another large pond is interpreted by Tolnay as the *fountain of adultery*, but as I. Mateo intelligently advocates (*El Bosco es España*), it is probably the *Fountain of Youth*, since similar medieval representations exist. In the background, the rocks once again acquire erotic shapes and above these, some men are flying through the force of their passion.

The center of Hell is occupied by a monstrous being with a body with the form of a hollow, broken eggshell and legs which recall the skulls of deer or dried up trees, which are braced on boats. His face reminds us of Bosch's self-portrait and this would be very significant, since on one leg a syphillitic sore appears, barely covered by a bandage, which would explain the origin of his misogeny. (This sickness was called the «Gallic» or «Spanish» ill and was ravaging Europe in these times.) Above his head appears a bagpipe, a symbol of homosexuality. Surrounding these figures appear the punishments for the sinners. Thus the clergy appear with bird's beaks, as poor preachers; another one is inside a key: «I knocked at your door and you would not open it». Possibly the most terribly punished group is that of the musicians, imprisoned in their instruments; Fraenger interprets this as a struggle to reach universal harmony. In the lower right section an abbess, who has been changed into a pig, signs a document related to the sale of relics, since a severed foot appears nearby. In the background of the uppert part, a grandiose spectacle, produced by the luminous effects of the buildings in flames, takes place.

Delivered to El Escorial in 1593, in the accompanying document it says that it was acquired at the liquidation of the estate of the prior Don Fernando, of the Order of St. John, who was the illegitimate son of the Duke of Alba (d. 1591). In the Prado Museum's collection since 1940.

PLATE XVII

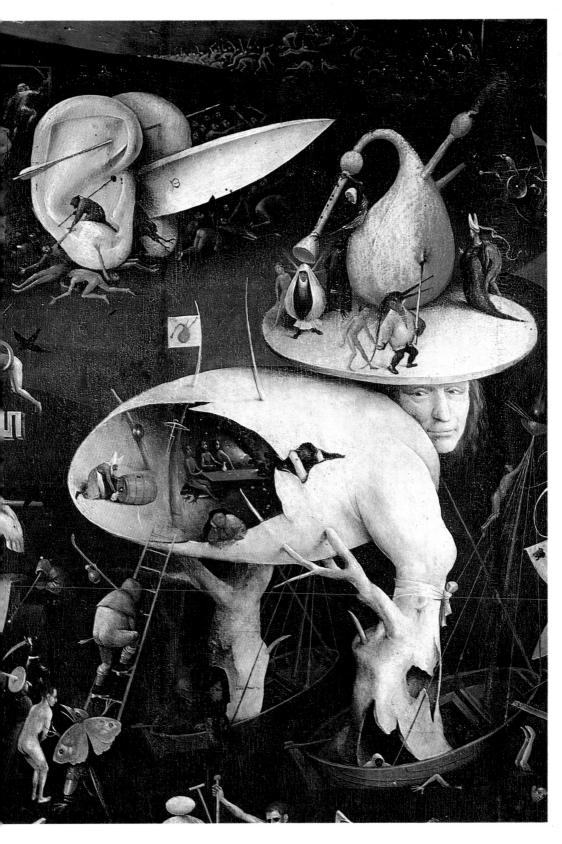

HIERONYMUS BOSCH.
The Hay Wagon (1503-1512). (Center Panel.)
Triptych. Oil on wood, 100 × 135 cm.   C. 2.052

One of Bosch's most usual motifs is the representation of human insanity in its various facets. This is the theme of the central panel of the triptych «The Hay Wagon». Greed is what produces the psychic alteration of the human beings in this work. The general idea is based on the Flemish proverb: «The world is a hay wagon, from which each one takes what he can», which may possibly be derived from Isaiah: «All flesh is grass, and all the goodliness thereof is as the flower of the field. The grass withereth, the flower fadeth» (XL, 6-7).

As may be seen, the hay symbolizes temporal riches, though possibly earthly pleasures as well. Therefore the hay piled up on the wagon is the object of the crowd's greed. There are men attempting to climb onto the wagon with a ladder and others try to grab part of the load with large hooks. Murders, robberies and fights are the results of the struggle for a few wisps of straw. One man will be crushed by the wheels of the cart since he doesn't want to give up his spoils. In the foreground, a fat abbess waits, sipping a glass of wine, for her nuns to bring her abundant stores of hay; one of them watches her devotedly, with the blindness which «the Brothers of the Free Spirit» (see the «Garden of Delights»), claim the petty clergy suffers from; another tries to tempt a young man with a handful of hay, but he's not interested since he carries a bagpipe, a symbol that he is a homosexual. The hay means nothing either for the people with toothaches or for the mothers caring for their children (according to Baldass, they are three gypsies who are telling a young bourgeois woman's fortune). The wagon is pulled by some monsters which symbolized the passions, and traditionally they have been thought of as the deadly sins; behind the cart are the powerful men on Earth who possess all the hay they want.

There are a few people who have managed to climb to the top of the load of hay. These few, who at first seem to be happy since they are singing accompanied by a lute and the trumpet of a gleefully dancing demon, are in spite of their initially placid appearance, corrupted by lust. Behind them, an embracing couple hilden in some bushes is observed by a bystander, possibly the husband of the woman, since over his head is an empty jar, the symbol of marital infidelity. Meanwhile an angel asks for the help of the Lord, who from Heaven looks down on the insane actions of mankind. Bosch shows himself here as a somewhat misanthropic moralist who tinges his sermons more with irony than with anger. On the right side of the central panel appears Hell and on the left, Paradise; when the triptych is closed, Man appears traveling through a world full of perils.

The triptych was bought in Flanders by Felipe de Guevara and sold to Philip II about 1570. It was in El Escorial until 1939, when it was brought to the Prado in exchange for a copy, or replica, of the same.

110

PLATE XVIII

BARTOLOMÉ BERMEJO (B. de Cárdenas).
St. Dominic of Silos (1474-1476).
Tempera and oil on wood, 242 × 131 cm.   C. 1.323

This panel is the one which corresponds to the central part of a retable from the Daroca Church (Zaragoza) which has the name of the saint which is represented here. In it, St. Dominic appears on a throne and with pontifical trappings as corresponded to his title of Abbot of Silos. He lived four hundred years before Bermejo, being born in La Rioja at the beginning of the XIth century, and he was Prior of the Navarran Monastery of San Millán de la Cogolla there. His fame caused Ferdinand I of Castile to call him to oversee the ancient convent of Silos, which he materially and spiritually rebuilt; he was abbot there from 1047 to 1073. From this period date the capitals in the lower cloister, with which a whole period of Spanish Romanesque sculpture is opened: the Silense period.

In this work in the Prado, Bartolomé Bermejo represents St. Dominic, giving him a strongly characterized face, as he really had; its great realism makes one think that it might have been directly inspired, and the portrait of some contemporary of the painter's. This same realistic feeling appears in the hands, while all the rest of the picture is idealized. Bermejo, although he cultivates and is perfectly acquainted with the Flemish style, in the complementary parts of this painting adopts pictorial forms from the Aragonese Gothic tradition; in this region the International style had possessed strong roots. Because of this, he places a golden background on the panel, and has gilded the dalmatica, as well. But he manages to give the metallic element subtle variations. This excessive richness was stipulated as part of the contract for the retable, signed in 1474, in which Bermejo promised to do the relief work on the pontifical ornamentation in gold, and it established besides that St. Dominic would be seated on a throne with the three theological virtues in the upper part and the four cardinal virtues on the sides. These feminine figures add one of the colorful notes to the painting since they were not done in grisaille, imitating sculpture, as was the custom in Flemish paintings, but rather were natural representations and were dressed in brightly colored robes. In contrast, in the representations of the saints on the dalmatica, the two-dimensional figures give a real sensation of being embroidered. The drapery has the tubular pleats characteristic of Hispano-Flemish painting which gives the figure an imposing presence.

The typology of Bermejo's works is close to that of the Portuguese painter Nuño Gonsalves, a fact which would confirm his Cordovan origin, since the Portuguese border is close by; besides, the last name Cárdenas or Rojo, with which he signs, appears in this Andalusian city. Thus Post's opinion that he was so named because he was a redhead (Rojo-red) does not stand up. There is no doubt that, as Elías Tormo has remarked, he is the most energetic of the primitive Spanish painters.

112

FERNANDO GALLEGO.
Blessing Christ (1467-1470).
Oil on wood, 132 × 169 cm.   C. 2.647

Between 1466 and 1467 Fernando Gallego appears working in Zamora; there he does the San Ildefonso retable of the Cathedral. In 1468 he is documented in Plasencia. Later he will move to Salamanca, where he was still residing in 1507. Appearances to the contrary, the «Enthroned Christ» is probably one of his oldest known works; until the XVIIIth century it formed the central part of the San Lorenzo retable in Toro, being painted around 1490 —it displays the coats-of-arms of the founders, Doña Beatriz de Fonseca (d. 1483) and her husband the Infante Don Pedro of Portugal (d. 1492)— which makes one suppose it was done between the death dates of the two. Now then, the panel in the Prado differs from the other ones; its quality is superior and those which remain in place are done with a more expressionist feeling (elongated figures and brittlely pleated draperies) which bring it close to the ancient retable of the Zamora Cathedral, today in Arcenillas, done immediately afterwards (1472-1495). Besides, the «Christ» in the Prado, due to its warm and translucent tones comes close to the best panels of the afore-mentioned Zamoran retable and his oldest known work, a fragment with St. Gregory's Mass (Gudiol Coll., Barcelona). Although the collaboration of the workshop on the Toro retable may be supposed (at this moment Fernando's brother, Francisco, as well as other students are working with him), the stylistic and formal separation is so great that it obliges us to affirm that the panel in the Prado is done in his first years in Zamora, and later placed in the center of the retable in the lovely Morisco chuch.

Formalist Eyckian influences are perceived, but technically it comes close to paintings by Dieric Bouts. In 1907 when this painting was shown in the Golden Fleece Exhibition in Bruges, its Flemish characteristics caused it to be attributed to Van Eyck himself. Its majesty, first-rate execution and attention to the smallest details are such that this error was possible. Today, since we have a profounder knowledge of the works of Spanish Gothic painting such a mistake seems impossible. Nevertheless, this mix-up is a sign of Gallego's great talent, and he was one of the most important painters who worked in Spain in the XVth century.

Christ appears on a throne of Gothic design, similar to the one on which the Virgin sits in the main Zamoran panel; in the paintings at Toro and Arcenillas, the decorative elements are simplified. Christ gives a blessing with His right hand, while in the other He holds a translucent sphere with a Byzantine cross, a symbol of universal power. On His right is the triumphant Church, crowned with laurels and with an upright standard. On the left is the vanquished Synagogue which with great difficulty holds up the Tablets of Law. The symbols of the Evangelists, with billowing filacterias, float in the air.

114

PLATE XX

JUAN DE FLANDES
The Resurrection of Lazarus (c. 1512-1518).
Oil on wood, 84 × 110 cm.   C. 2.935

The most beautiful ensemble done by Juan de Flandes which is preserved intact is the series of panels done for the main retable of the Palencia Cathedral. The commission was given to the Flemish painter by Bishop Diego de Deza on December 19, 1509. It is possible that after he finished this commission the artist began the retable for the San Lázaro Church in the same city, and not beforehand, as some critics have indicated, because he went directly from Salamanca to Palencia to do the main retable for this city's cathedral. Besides the fact that the style is here more advanced than in works proven to be from an earlier period, in the panels for San Lázaro the Flemish painter becomes more Spanish. This is demonstrated in the realism of this «Resurrection of Lazarus», which departs from the idealizing naturalism of earlier works such as in the small panel on the same theme belonging to the «Polyptych of Queen Isabella the Catholic» (Royal Palace, Madrid), with figures —including one portraying the Queen— which are done with a certain conventionalism, which the San Lázaro panels do not follow. In these there is rather an expressionist feeling which brings them closer to Pedro Berruguete or Fernando Gallego.

But still and all, the artist does not therefore abandon a naturalist style. In the background of this «Resurrection of Lazarus» a church appears in a state of abandon, with holes in the roof and broken window panes, and the minor figures have very Castilian features, just as in the scene of the «Pentecost», from the same retable. Unfortunately, this ensemble was dismantled long ago, because before their sale these panels were found set in a retable frame from the XIXth century. The Samuel H. Kress Foundation (in the United States) acquired it several years ago, keeping four panels for itself, which are today in American museums, and giving four panels to the Prado —the two mentioned above, «The Prayer in the Garden» and «The Ascension».

116   PLATE XXI

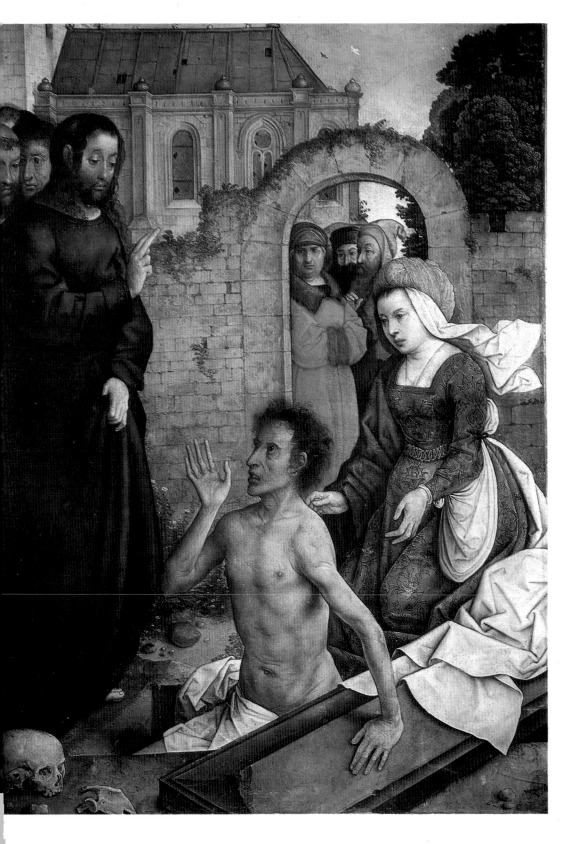

FRA ANGELICO (Guido di Pietro).
The Annunciation (1431-35).
Tempera on wood, 194 × 194 cm.   C. 15

In October of 1435, St. Dominic's Church in Fiesole is consecrated. Fra Angelico did three retables to decorate it; according to chronological order, the first one would be the «Pala de Fiesole» (c. 1430), which was the main retable and its main panel is still preserved .in the convent church; then come the «Pala del Prado» and the «Pala del Louvre» (1434-35).

The «Pala del Prado» is formed by the extremely lovely «Annunciation» and a predella with five small panels. The main panel must have been begun by Fra Angelico inmediately after finishing the main retable. This latter is a masterpiece of a seldom-equaled beauty in any of the artist's works. Therefore the opinions which consider this a work of collaborators or the workshop are inadmissable. There is no doubt that there was some intervention on the part of a collaborator but the entire «Annunciation» scene is unquestionably the work of the painter from Fiesole. The scene takes place inside of a «loggia» (portico) of admirable Brunelleschian architecture in which there is an intense preoccupation with perspective; the columns are of the Composite order, and in the upper part of the center one there is a «tondo» with the face of the Father on it. In the background a small room may be seen in which a violet light models the volumes, in contrast to the golden light which comes in through the window, producing shadow and light effects which are very characteristic of the early Renaissance. The Virgin and the Angel still reflect a sense of Gothic spirituality in their faces; Mary, wrapped in a dazzling blue mantle, with an almost child-like expression, humbly pronounces the «fiat». Meanwhile the hand of God sends down the Holy Ghost among rays of gold. In this entire scene, the only collaboration that may be admitted is in the gilding, a work proper to artisans. On the other hand, the «Paradise» scene is the work of another artist within Fra Angelico's school and at least in the figures of Adam and Eve, it is probable that the hand is that of Zanobi Strozzi.

In the «predella», dedicated to the Virgin, the workshop has also participated. The center panel and the one on each end («Birth and Betrothal», «Adoration of the Kings», and «Death») are probably works which were done at the same time as the «Annunciation». In these scenes the figures are still squeezed in, expressing the Medieval «horror vaqui», while the light comes from Massaccio. In the two remaining panels («Visitation» and «Jesus' Presentation at the Temple»), the structural and spatial system has become more Renaissance, the number of figures has diminished and they are located in a harmonius manner. Therefore these two must have been painted after some commissions («The Linaioli Tabernacle» and the «Pala de Cortona 1433-34) had interrupted the elaboration of this retable.

In the XVIth century it is already mentioned by Vasari. It was in the Royal Convent of the Barefoot Carmelites and from there was transferred to the Prado in 1867. In 1943 it was restored to hide a large vertical crack.

PLATE XXII

SANDRO BOTTICELLI and Collaborators.
The Story of Nastagio degli Honesti (1483). Panels II and III.
Tempera on wood, P. II, 138 × 82 cm.; P. III, 84 × 142 cm.   C. 2.839-40

In 1483, Lorenzo de Mèdici commissioned Botticelli to do four «Cassone» (hope chest) fronts, as wedding gifts for Gianozzo Pucci and Lucrezia Bini. The theme was taken from the Story of Nastagio degli Honesti, as told by Boccaccio in the *Decamerone*. The first panel shows the moment in which the young Nastagio walks alone and deep in thought through the Ravenna pine forest, after his sweetheart, the daughter of Paolo Traversari, has rejected him. Suddenly a knight appears chasing a woman upon whom he sets his dogs. In the second panel, the knight cuts out the heart and entrails of the young girl and gives them to the dogs to devour, but before this he has told his story to Nastagio. In brief it is as follows: Ivo has been condemned by the gods, after his suicide, to chase the woman responsible for his unhappy fate, and to kill her, every Friday of the year. The third panel, which is reproduced here, narrates the moment in which Nastagio invites his disdainful sweetheart and her family to a luncheon at the place where Ivo must appear. Thus, Nastagio astutely makes his sweetheart witness the scene, and convinced more by fear than by love, the young Traversari girl sends a servant to Nastagio with a conciliatory message. In the fourth panel, which is in a foreign collection, the wedding banquet is portrayed.

If in the first panel the feeling of the narration is lyrical, with an extremely calligraphic execution which corresponds to Botticelli's style in 1483: clean outlines, light, mother-of-pearl tones, perfect structural order... on the other hand, the second panel, reproduced here, is of a more epic character. Its personages express more dramatism since in them there exists a psychological, almost psychic preoccupation. Nastagio appears here as a young man filled with spiritual restlessness, the «apparition» bloodily —almost sadistically— cuts the entrails out of the woman's body, which is lying flat on the ground. Besides, the Botticellian calligraphic sense is intensified even more here in the human figures, with the curvilinear lines reaching the point of full forms with a Baroque exaggeration. This is perceived in the white horse, as well, and especially in the two dogs. The white one reminds us of the dragon which Filipino Lippi would paint in the «Story of St. John» in Santa Maria Novella in Florence. The earthen color of the flesh also agrees with his style. Therefore it would not be risky to consider this work, or at least the figures, to have been done by the most important of Botticelli's disciples. We must realize that in this same year they are working together at the Villa del Spadetto in Volterra on a commission from Lorenzo de Mèdici. Besides, in the background there are details which are also characteristic of his style; thus a fox is nibbling at a bush, and a ship is stranded in the port of Ravenna, which at this time of the year is full of mud. The city of Ravenna, which

PLATE XXIII

was on the coast before, had moved six miles inland and a pine forest grew on the land once covered by the waters.

In the third panel, which we have already described in detail, the collaboration of another artist may be noted, almost surely Bartolommeo di Giovanni, working along with Botticelli. Thus the master does the work on the figure of Nastagio and the two «apparitions» whom he introduces to his sweetheart, this latter (who does not appear in the illustration) is also by Botticelli; the old man dressed in black is probably a portrait, and although of miniscule proportions, it is a work with a great psychological perfection. In the illustration, the Mèdici coat-of-arms with its characteristic pearls stands out on the barricade. It is interesting to observe how Botticelli's figures stand out from those of his collaborator's for their vibrant coloring and the talented draftsmanship, besides the astute, penetrating use of his powers of observation. Also very interesting is the «still-life» which appears on the table. Besides the dishes and the cherries —for it is the dessert course— there is a viola da gamba, splendidly drawn; but this is not the only musical instrument to appear, hung on a tree are two small drums, which indicates that instead of witnessing this horrible vision, the guests had planned to dance and sing after the banquet. Now then, this will have to wait for another occasion, which is portrayed in the last panel, which is in foreign hands, in which the wedding festivities are shown.

These four panels belonged to the Pucci family until 1868 when they were sold to Mr. Alexander Barker for a hundred thousand pounds. On his death in 1879, they moved for a short while to the collection of Mr. I. R. Leyland, and in 1892 they were acquired by M. Aynard of Lyon. The three which now belong to the Prado became the property of the famous collector Joseph Spiridon and Cambó, who donated the pieces in 1941, acquired them from him. The fourth one, on the other hand, was bought by Donaldson, who in turn gave it to Watney and it was finally auctioned off at Christie's Gallery in London.

ANDREA MANTEGNA.
Death of the Virgin (1461-1463).
Tempera on wood, 42 × 54 cm. C. 248

A work of miniscule size, though one of the great masterpieces in the museum, the opinion of the subtle thinker E. D'Ors in his *Three Hours in the Prado Museum* that it is the foremost work in the Prado seems excessive to us.

It apparently formed part of a now-dispersed retable, done for the Gonzaga family, who were the Dukes of Mantua. The scene represented is based on the Apocryphal Scriptures, with the narration of the Virgin's death. Called together by the Virgin, after St. Michael advises her of her earthly passing, all of the Apostles have come except for St. Thomas. For this reason only eleven of them appear in the picture. St. John, the youngest, holds the palm which announces her demise, or rather passing, and not death, in anticipation of her ressurrection. The Apostles are portrayed with a sculptural feeling which comes from Donatello, since in Mantegna's formation in Padua the former's influence is decisive. Besides, there is a link between this portrayal and the medieval «mystery plays», since one of them possibly served as the iconographic basis for Mantegna in this masterpiece. This scene is thus narrated in the manner in which it continues to be put on in Elche today. Besides, the action does not take place in Jerusalem, but rather in the Ducal palace at Mantua. In the background, therefore, may be seen the lakes which surrounded this building and whose gray waters have a bluish cast from the reflection of the limpid sky barely marked by a few wispy clouds. Originally the panel was of larger size and in the upper section there was a Christ in glory who received in His arms an infant's figure, representing the Virgin's soul, following iconographic tradition.

When the work was complete the arrangement of the figures in the architectonic setting was perfectly balanced. The spatial effect harmonized by the study of perspective (achieved by the quadrangular pavement and projection of the landscape) has not been lost. The sensation of verticality is not only obtained by the pillastered architecture, in which a simplified Classicism caused Mantegna to abandon medallions—which he had used so much in his previous works—but by the erectness of the figures, the two candlesticks and the height of the horizon. Although the date of execution should probably be fixed between 1461 and 1463, some historians set it even thirty years later.

This work was acquired for Philip IV by Ambassador Cárdenas at the auction of the works of art belonging to Charles I of England, who had bought it from the Gonzaga family. On the back the mark of the King of England still appears.

PLATE XXV

ANTONELLO DA MESSINA.
Pietà (c. 1477).
Oil on wood, 74 × 51 cm.   C. 3.092

Works by Antonello discovered in the last 50 years are extremely rare, and until recently all the pieces known were in a poor state of preservation. Besides, the total number of known works did not reach forty. Because of this, the acquisition of this masterpiece by Antonello's hand by the Prado Museum was a great surprise in the art world.

The «Pietà» in the Prado must have been done after the artist's return to Messina, his home town, in 1476, after he had spent 2 years in Venice and had made a short trip to Milan. His contact with Northern Italian, especially Venetian, painting had tempered his style, and although there still remain Flemish reminiscences in this work, such as the stiff folds of the drapery or the landscape in the background, the angel already possesses the colorist feeling characteristic of a Giovanni Bellini. Especially in his multicolored wings, the idealization of the cherub contrasts with the realism of Christ's face. In the background there are echoes of his two Crucifixions (Antwerp and London) in which there is a multitude of skulls and a cloudy sky in the background. But here there are Mediterranean olive trees and the city of Messina, like an imaginary Jerusalem, as well as two crosses with sorrowing women beside them, which indicates the work's being done in the south of Italy.

The composition, in which there is a prominent *psychological diagonal* which goes from the face of Christ to his right hand, also testifies to the fact that this is a work from Antonello's last period, also reaffirmed by the superb Mantegnesque foreshortening of the left hand, «invented» by Bellini and continued by Antonello, for if it were the reverse, as Salas thinks, the work would necessarily have been done in Venice. This is one of the most perfect and best preserved works by Antonello; only in Christ's hair and in the Cathedral of Messina is there a little carefully done restoration work. There are known to be several versions of a «Christ Tied to the Column», none signed, which repeat the torso and head of this dying Christ. Another *Pietà*, with three angels, exists in the Correr Museum in Venice, but with a different typology.

The one studied here necessarily derives from a Germanic engraving of «Christ, Lord of Sorrows» —used earlier by Mantegna and repeated by his brother-in-law, Giovanni Bellini— which is widely circulated in Venice in the last third of the XVth century, as the present director of the Prado, Don Xavier de Salas, has meticulously studied (*Gazette de Beaux Arts*, 1967, pp. 125 and ff.).

The one in the Prado comes from a collection in Irún which in turn came from Galicia. As Xavier de Salas has wisely stated, it is almost certain that this *Pietà* was at one time in the Monforte de Lemos Monastery.

126   PLATE XXVI

PEDRO DE BERRUGUETE.
Auto-da-fe (c. 1495).
Oil and tempera on wood, 154 × 92 cm.   C. 618

A scene from St. Dominic de Guzman's life (1170-1221) is represented here: the pardon of the Albigense Raymund, while his companions, since they would not repent, are led to the pyre. The scene formed part of a small lateral retable telling stories about the founder of the Order of Preachers, which along with others dedicated to St. Peter, Martyr, occupied the central position of the main altar at St. Thomas' Convent in Avila. Although according to Cruzada Villamil (*Catalog of the Trinidad Museum*) the two were in the upper Cloister of the Kings; in his judgement, they were probably painted between 1480 and 1490, a date which today we would fix a bit later.

In the various scenes of this retable, Berruguete portrays events from the life of St. Dominic in the south of France (in the vicinity of Albi) after 1207, the year in which he receives the Papal order to eliminate the Albigense heresy, which he first attempts to suppress by preaching and miracles. Thus Berruguete narrates in a panel of this same retable the destruction by fire of the Albigense books while the orthodox ones remain unscathed by the flames. On the other hand, here we see the moment of the pardon of a heretic —but the real interest of the scene is rooted in the presence of an «auto-da-fe», in which not books, but rather men are being burned to ashes. A strong sense of realism pervades the scene, attaining truly perfect psychological studies. Thus we see one of the judges put to sleep by the smoke of the holocaust while others chat among themselves, impervious to the human tragedy going on right beside them.

In this work Berruguete demonstrates a great interest in light, due to his acquaintance with the painting of Piero della Francesca and Luca Signorelli, whose works he sees in Urbino, around 1475, while the realistic character of his models is of Flemish origin. The reddish background which reveals a silver preparation below it enriches this composition in which the Renaissance and Gothic styles join hands.

From the Trinidad Museum the pieces were moved to the Prado in 1836 by the San Fernando Academy's Attachment Commission.

PLATE XXVII

RAPHAEL (Rafaello Sanzio).
The Holy Family with the Lamb (1507).
Oil on wood, 29 × 21 cm.   C. 296

When, in 1504, Raphael moves from Perusa to Florence, his painting begins, little by little, to be transformed. Departing from the stereotyped forms of his master Perugino, he will begin the search for his own style, though in spite of this, other painters, especially Fra Bartolomeo della Porta and Leonardo, will influence in the creation of his artistic personality.

This is obvious in «The Holy Family with the Lamb», which due to its delicate handling should be considered one of the masterpieces from the artist's last Florentine moments, in which he reaches his stylistic maturity. It is signed with golden letters on the ribbon of Mary's dress: *Raphael Urbinas MDVII.* (Not in 1505, as it has been read. Besides the clarity with which the date may be seen, the picture's artistic significance fits in with the development of this stage, in which a certain eclecticism still exists.)

Thus, while in the figures of the Virgin and the Baby Jesus may be seen Raphael's unquestionable personal trademark—although a melancholy grimace of Leonardesque origin appears on Mary's face— that of St. Joseph may still be found in the line of Fra Bartolomeo, with the corpulence characteristic of this Florentine painter.

Raphael succeeds in giving this work a seductive coloring, rich in variation of hues, which he will seldom equal. In the background landscape, dewy blues recall those of some of Leonardo's compositions, but this landscape, in general, is inspired by Flemish paintings. Its exotic constructions, such as the strange church, whose tower is topped off in blue, or the house with the sharply-angled roof, are of a clearly Nordic inspiration. The Holy Family, amid dewy leaves, travels along a road toward a «Northern Egypt»; for this reason we believe that this picture represents «The Rest on the Flight to Egypt».

The success of this small and admirable painting is attested to by the multiple copies done during the XVIth and XVIIth centuries. One of them was the property of Lord Lee of Fareham, in Richmond, and is apocryphally dated in 1504. The existence of XVIIIth-century copies confirms the hypothesis that until around 1700 it remained in Rome (Falconieri Coll.), from where it was moved to El Escorial.

It should be pointed out that in this work Raphael still maintains a clear and simple composition: a simple diagonal. Later, in his pictures from the Roman period, he will search for greater compositional complication. Thus, in the «Madonna of the Fish» (C. 297) he will achieve a balanced harmony by means of a series of optic diagonals and he will place, in the foreground, an enormous stone block, which will force the scene backward into an imaginary interior, while the green curtain will push the heads of the Archangel Raphael, the Virgin and the Child out towards the spectator, accentuating this complicated compositional balance.

98.

PLATE XXVIII

RAPHAEL (Rafaello Sanzio).
The Cardinal (c. 1510).
Oil on wood, 79 × 61 cm.   C. 299

This figure which is reproduced is one of the few which was done totally by Raphael's hand during his Roman period (1508-1520). A cardinal appears here who is a prototype for those of the Renaissance whose uncertain identity has converted him into a mysterious personage. A great number of identities have been proposed. Among them we may mention Giulio de Médici, Dovizi de Bibiena, Inocenzio Cibo, Alidosi, Scaramuzza-Trivulzio, Hipolito del Este, Silvio Passerini, Antono Ciocchi, Matias Schinners, Luis de Aragón, etc. Several years ago, Suida affirmed that this same cardinal appears in a work of Piombo's (Kress Coll., USA), since on a small bell on a table the name of Bandinello Sauri, «Cardinal of Julius II's», may be read; he had also been represented by Raphael in «The Disputation Concerning the Blessed Sacrament». This man was a restless person; he was imprisioned in 1517 and this resulted in his death in 1518. Besides, the typology of the face: lean, with a sensual nose, extremely hardened eyes, thin, cruel lips, makes us think of a personage like Sauri, even if Sauri himself is not the one personified.

Venturi considered this picture to have been done between 1510-1511, rejecting the older hypothesis that believed it to be from Raphael's final years. The arm resting on the frame, as if it were a window ledge, not only gives the pose elegance, but also forces the figure backward toward the background of the picture. The sureness of the brush stroke, the refined chromatic contrasts in the cardinal's cape, with a whitish sheen playing upon the carmine surface, and above all the psychological penetration of the subject's face make it one of the most important examples not only of Raphael's portraits, but also of all of those ever done.

The neutral background helps to emphasize this impressive face. Certain evidences of restoration work may be seen in it and a small crack or two are present. In spite of it, the painting is in need of a cleaning to give the volumes and tonalities a greater clarity. Acquired by Charles IV while he was Prince of Asturias, in 1818 it was kept in Aranjuez and was considered the portrait of Cardinal Granvela, painted by Moro, as a placard on the back of the panel indicates.

ANDREA DEL SARTO (A. D'Agnolo).
Virgin and Child with Tobias (?) *and an Angel* (Madonna della Scala).
Oil on wood, 177 × 135 cm.   C. 334

This masterpiece is one of the most important produced by Andrea del Sarto. We could even say that among his compositions, it is the best-achieved, even surpassing the famous «Madonna delle Arpie» in the Uffizi Gallery in Florence. Here the Virgin appears, in the center, with spiritual suffering reflected on her face; on either side is a figure. It has been said one of them could be Tobias and the other is an angel, St. Raphael, since Sánchez Cantón considered that this picture could be of Jesus affirming the authenticity of the *Book of Tobias* because He points to the book. Today it has once again been considered in light of an old iconographical tradition; for Father Santos, historian of El Escorial, said that the masculine figure was a personification of St. John the Evangelist. Viardot therefore called this painting «The Consecration of the Apocalypse».. In this case, the angel would be the representation of a witness prophesying the Passion, which would explain Mary's anguished expression and the figures in the background, St. Elizabeth and St. John the Baptist as a child.

It is painted in Andrea del Sarto's so-called «heroic period», that is, at the mid-point of his life. A «Virgin and Child» exists (kept in the Raleigh, North Carolina, Museum) which is almost a repetition of these two figures, adding in this painting a St. John as a child. Now the painting in the Prado is much more complete, surpassing it stylistically, for its composition is prodigious. The pyramidal sense probably comes from Raphael and the Virgin is based on a Niobe preserved in Florence. There exists a great harmony in the coloring and its tones are already Mannerist. Thus Tobias wears a light pink tunic, with white highlights. The angel has a green tunic with sleeves lined in yellow and the Virgin, whose double «contrapposto» in relation to the Child is Michelangelesque, is wrapped in a blue mantle with a Mannerist form and pleats, as well, while the tunic is red. The landscape which surrounds the figure possessses blue-green tones and the steps, which give the picture its name, are somewhat bluish. A fortified village, very characteristic of Tuscany, also appears. This work was a great succes from this first moment, since many copies were done. Besides, Andrea arranged the composition meticulously, doing quite a few preparatory drawings, some of which are still preserved,

Signed with his characteristic anagram, it was painted for Lorenzo degli Jiacopi. In 1605 it is transferred to the Duke of Mantua, Vicenzo Gonzaga. Bought along with the rest of the Duke's collection by Charles I of England, upon his death, in 1649, the Spanish ambassador, Don Alonso de Cárdenas, acquires it for Philip IV for the amount of 230 pounds. Father Santos describes it when it is in the Sacristy at El Escorial in 1657. It was moved to the Prado in 1819.

ANDREA DEL SARTO (A. D'Agnolo).
Lucrecia di Baccio (c. 1518).
Oil on wood, 56 × 73 cm.

C. 332

Although the identification is not entirely certain, this female figure has the same aspect as other portraits done of Lucrecia by her husband. The type of woman represented is one with a sensual, ambitious and egotistical temperament, but in this bourgeois protagonist there exists an almost animal-like beauty which corresponds to Vasari's description of her as an unfaithful wife. This is the same model who sat for some of Andrea's «madonnas», such as the «Madonna delle Arpie», in the Uffizi Gallery in Florence.

When in 1517 Andrea contracted marriage, Lucretia was a widow, and seemingly she was never in love with the painter. A year later the already famous artist was called by Francis I to paint in his court. After another year had passed, ha secured permission to visit Florence. There, and according to Vasari at his wife's instigation, he squanders the money which he had received from the King of France for the acquisition of art works. For this reason he never returns to Francis I's court.

There exists in this work a certain influence of Raphael, from whom he takes the pose. The composition is quite lovely and the tones are perfectly balanced within a somber chromatic range. But the value of this picture especially stems from its psychological penetration, since the painter unwittingly offers us a complete study on frustrated love.

It is cited several times in the inventories of the Madrilenian Alcazar and from 1794 in the Oriente (then denominated New) Palace.

PLATE XXXI

CORREGGIO (Antonio Allegri).
Noli me tangere (1518-1519).
Oil on wood, transferred to canvas, 130 × 103 cm.   C. 111

This painting is chronologically the first masterpiece by the Parmesan painter. It is characteristic of his first pictorial style with a subtlety in the treatment of the theme and the movement of the figures. In the figure of Christ echoes of Beccafumi are still seen, which demonstrates that this is done before his trip to Rome in 1519. Here Christ appears with his feet crossed in a position of instability which accentuates the see-saw motion of the arms almost as if he were doing a step from a dance; this already anticipates the Correggio of the Baroque and even the Rococo styles. The Leonardesque *sfumatto* appears, especially in the flesh, but Correggio sweetens it, highlighting it with milky flesh tones; instead of «mixing light with shadow», as the painter of La Gioconda indicated, he accentuates the luminous potential and the shadows only delicately define the modeling of the forms.

Mary Magdalen is represented with an expression of burning mysticism, as an anticipation of the «Ecstasy of St. Theresa» by Bernini. Thus, her lips are ambiguously parted and her penetrating look is riveted on Christ's gaze. (This created a very definite facial typology which would be widely accepted in later painting.) The abundant blond hair accentuates the Baroque expression. Meanwhile, hr body trembles and draws back as she hears the commanding: *Do not touch me* from the mouth of the risen Christ, whom she has confused with a gardener (St. John, XX, 2). The pre-Romantic leafiness of the landscape, in which the greens fade into blues in the background, besides producing an effect of compactness, seem to be moistened with an oily substance. This might symbolize the triumph of oil painting over tempera.

Although the majority of the critics dated this work between the years 1523 and 1525 (Venturi, Ricci...) today, after what has been said, we should place it before 1519. Its history may be followed in documents. Vasari already praised it when it was in Ercolani de Bolonia's house. This is confirmed by Lamo in 1560. Afterwards it belonged to Cardinals Aldobrandini and Ludovici. Brought to Spain, it was given to Philip IV by the Duke of Medina de las Torres. In 1657, Father Francisco de los Santos describes it in El Escorial, praising it in an effusive manner. It came to the Prado in 1839.

PLATE XXXII

GIORGIONE (Giorgio da Castelfranco).
Virgin and Child with St. Anthony and St. Roch (1505-1510).
Oil on canvas, 92 × 133 cm.   C. 288

This unfinished picture is the focal point of a debate begun 50 years ago. The problem still stands: Giorgione or Titian? Among the most recent specialists to discuss the problem, Wethey considers it to be the work of the former, while Pallucchini attributes it to the painter from Cadore. Due to its technique, we consider it to be adscribable to the artist from Castelfranco in the last period of his life, and not as a preliminary study of the «Castelfranco Altarpiece», for it is much more skillful than this pictorial technique.

The use of tempera combined with oil is very characteristic of this painter, and here, especially, the carmines of the Virgin and St. Roch, the very posture of this saint recall other personages, such as the one appearing in the «Tempest». The sketchy or synthetic feeling of the landscape possesses a great plastic beauty, but according to some critics it is unfinished. At times, patches of color may be perceived here, as if applied with small palette knives (small reeds in the Oriental manner, such as El Greco would use on occasion?), as as we have observed in other pictures by the painter from Castelfranco. It was already painted on canvas, Giorgione being one of the first artist who would usually do so in Italian painting.

Around 1650 the Duke of Medina de las Torres, Viceroy of Naples, offered this picture to Philip IV. In some of the royal inventories it is listed as done by Zorzo (Giorgione), while in others as done by Pordenone, possibly a mistaken spelling of the name of the painter from Castelfranco. Apparently Velasquez valued it highly, for it was this painter, as chamberlain in the palace, who hung it over one of the doorways in the Escorial monastery.

April 13, 1839, it came to the Prado, where in the first *Catalogs* it appeared as by Pordenone, being rectified in the one for 1920.

TITIAN (T. Veçellio).
Bacchanal (1517-1519).
Oil on canvas, 193 × 175 cm.   C. 418

This masterpiece, along with its companion-piece in the Prado, the «Worship of Venus», and the «Bacchus and Ariadne» in the National Gallery, is one of the «poésies» which Alfonso del Este (1486-1534) commissioned the painter from Cadore to do between the years 1517 and 1519, for his «studiolo» in the fortified palace at Ferrara.

It was Alfonso himself, so it seems, who gave Titian the themes for the paintings, based on Philostratus' «Imagines» which his sister Isabel had translated into Italian. Thus a sleeping Ariadne, based on a Classical sculpture, is portrayed in the foreground, on the spectator's right, and the scene is tranferred from the island of Naxos to Andros, since the Prince delighted in the humanistic complexity of anagram (Alfonso, Andros, Ariadne). Titian's skill is not only artistic but also humanistic; he therefore manages to express and develop the Neoplatonic ideas of the Prince of Este, adapting and recreating the mythological fable, which is converted here into a full-throated song in praise of love and drink. Thus in the center of the composition we find a group, separated from Ariadne by a child relieving himself near a small stream, alongside of which two young women begin to drink after playing on their flutes an ancient French tune: «He who drinks and never drinks again, knows not the meaning of drink». The anagramatic difficulties continue, for on the breast of a lovely blonde, Titian's signature and some violets appear, indicating that it is a portrait of his lover, Violante. Meanwhile in the background, men and women are dancing and drinking, and beyond them in the distance the white sails of a Venetian ship may be seen, which shows us that the scene takes place on an island.

The series was brought to Rome in 1598 by Cardinal Aldobrandini, from Ferrara.

The «Bacchanal» and the «Worship of Venus» were offered to Philip IV by the Count of Monterrey, but it seems that they were really a gift from Niccolò Ludovici, the Viceroy of Aragón. Signed: *Ticians F. N.° 101.*

PLATE XXXIV

TITIAN (T. Vecellio).
The Emperor Charles V at Mühlberg (1548).
Oil on canvas, 279 × 332 cm.   C. 410

The German Protestants are defeated on April 24, 1547 at Mühlberg by the Imperial army led by the Emperor himself. Charles decides that this victory should be commemorated in a painting by the artist whom he considers to be the most important one alive: Titian.

After this famous battle, Charles V spends several months in Augsburg, and that is where he brings his master painter to paint him twice, in his famous equestrian portrait and in a seated portrait which is in the Pinacotheca at Munich. The Prado version was done between April and September of the year following the battle. The Emperor is represented riding out to meet the enemy on a dark chestnut stallion; he wears battle armor and energetically carries a lance in his right hand. Here we have a view of the last king to personally lead his army. Some years later his son will be portrayed by Titian in a bureaucat's office. There is no doubt that this is one of the most impressive psychological portraits in the entire history of painting, for in the same face may be seen Charles' illness and fever, as well as the strong spiritual energy which helps him overcome his physical exhaustion through a superhuman effort which fills his intense gaze. This psychological drama is accentuated by the landscape, in which the light from a reddish sunset of almost bloody tones illuminates a small glade.

Because of imperfections caused by its transport shortly after being painted, it had to be restored in Augsburg by Titian himself, with the collaboration of Amberger; then for a second time after the burning of the Alcázar in Madrid in 1734, and, finally, another recent cleaning has livened up its colors. It came to Spain with the paintings which Maria of Hungary brought in. In 1600 it was in the Casa del Tesoro and in 1619 in El Pardo.

144

PLATE XXXV

TITIAN.
Self-portrait (c. 1568).
Oil on canvas, 86 × 65 cm.   C. 407

Possibly one of the most beautiful self-portraits by the painter from Cadore is this one in which his palette, due to the experience of his maturity and old age, has arrived at a point of admirable chromatic synthesis: blacks, greys, reds and whites manage to make it one of the most synthetic works from the XVIth century. Only Rembrandt and Goya in their last years would reach such a level of abstraction still within a realistic style. This work, along with the «Burial of Christ», is the maximum example of Titian's work from his final period existing in the Prado Museum —and we should remember that this museum possesses the most important collection of the Venetian painter's art in the world.

In this self-portrait Titian appears around the age of 80, expressing all the serenity which he had achieved after a life which was principally dedicated to the observation and representation of beauty. There is no basis to prove that this is the work seen by Vasari in the artist's own home where he «found him, although extremely old, with a brush in his hand». Since it seems that this version must be the one in the Museum of Berlin, the one in Madrid was done at least five years later.

It was possibly acquired for 400 florins in the Rubens auction in Antwerp. In 1666 it was hung in the «Southern Corridor» of the Alcazar Palace in Madrid.

VERONESE (Paolo Caliari).
Venus and Adonis (c. 1580).
Oil on canvas, 191 × 212 cm.   C. 482

This picture, showing Venus with a sleeping Adonis, is a lovely sample from the rich collection of Veronese's work which is preserved in the Prado. This work was possibly done in the painter's prime since Borghini in 1581 described an extremely lovely painting «Di Adone atormentato in gembro a Venere». It would not be necessary for this great connoisseur of the Venetian painting of his times to praise it for us to be able to admire the beauty of this masterpiece. Adonis, tired out after the boar hunt, lies obliviously asleep in the lap of the goddess of love; meanwhile, Cupid plays with some hounds. This is the theme of this lovely composition in which Veronese's decorative sense triumphs. In order to achieve such an effect, he had divided the painting into two triangles with a diagonal which accentuates its rhythmic composition. The opulent coloring, in which the yellows and greens characteristic of Caliari stand out, is mitigated by the blonde Venus' mother-of-pearl flesh tones. Storm clouds framed by the foliage seem to prophesy the tragic death of the protagonist, which Shakespeare would later narrate in verse.

There are two versions painted by Veronese which are related to a picture on the same theme by Titian which is in the Prado Museum, but in these, Venus is shown at the moment in which she attempts to detain Adonis.

This work was possibly acquired by Velasquez for Philip IV in Venice in 1649 or 1650. In an English collection there exists a fragment of a lost painting in which there appears a little cupid with a hare which is related to this painting.

PLATE XXXVII

TINTORETTO (Giacopo Robusti).
The Washing of the Feet (Before 1547).
Oil on canvas, 210 × 533 cm.   C. 2.824

It seems that this masterpiece of Tintoretto's was done for the presbytery of the Venetian church of San Marcuelo, since that is where «The Last Supper» (a canvas somewhat smaller than this one which is considered its companion piece) is kept. The superiority of the painting in the Prado is obvious, however, and, besides, in its background on the right the moment of the Blessing of the Host appears and it would have been redundant to repeat the same theme in the other painting. Due to this, I think that the hypothesis defended by Coletti is not likely. Besides, the pictorial technique of the painting is previous to 1547, as Tietze has already indicated. Later, in the London version (National Gallery), the artist gives the painting a more dramatic feeling and in his later portrayals of the Last Supper the diagonals are more accentuated.

The feeling of depth is the principal stylistic characteristic of this work, in which the spatial element takes on an importance unheard of in those times. The space is projected along an archway toward a pool which ends in another arch and which is bordered by scenic buildings which remind us of those by Palladio, the architect of the Veneto, and a contemporary of Tintoretto's. Gould refers to Serlio as the one who inspires this architecture, but the stage-like feeling and type of capital used here is closer to Tintoretto's friend's work, and besides is closely related to the Teatro Olimpico in Vicenza. The geometric arrangement of the pavement accentuates the spatial feeling and the atmosphere may be sensed below the table. Velasquez will start from this work, which he sees in El Escorial, in his search for a liberated sense of space.

The figures of the Apostles appear like giants here, rhythmically distributed within this spatial atmosphere, forming reference points for a series of diagonals. To the spectator's right is Jesus as He washes one of the Apostle's feet; meanwhile on the left, another one ties his sandal with his foot on the bench, which gives Tintoretto a chance to twist his giant Michelangelesque figure, forcing it outward from the canvas. In spite of the fact that Robusti's principal preoccupation is not that of color, but rather that of space, he cannot get away from the Venetian sense of color. But a livid light gives the colors cold tones accentuating the dramatic feeling and the theatrical expression which the artist seeks, since he is one of the greatest «scenographic artists» from the Renaissance.

This work was acquired by Ambassador Cárdenas in the auction of the collection of Charles I of England. It was in El Escorial until 1940, when it was moved to the Prado.

PLATE XXXVIII

EL GRECO (Domenicos Theotocopulos).
The Trinity (c. 1578).
Oil on canvas, 300 × 179 cm.   C. 824

Here we have one of El Greco's first works to be done in Spain when
the artist comes to the Peninsula from Rome, possibly in 1575. After
spending about a year in Madrid, where the Court was established, he
moves to the old Imperial City of Toledo.   By 1577 he should already be
there, where he possibly came to do the retable for Santo Domingo el Antiguo.   September 11 of this same year, the sculptor Monegro is commis
sioned to carve the retables of this church according to designs by Micer
Domenico Theotocopulos.   The plans of the church were done by Juan de
Herrera.   As may be seen, in his first moments in Toledo El Greco is in
contact with artists who worked for the King, which foretold a success
which he would never achieve in the Court.   The commission was given
to him by Dean Diego de Castilla, the protector and promoter of Toledan
art in his times.   The architecture of the retables opens a stage of the
Spanish Renaissance, since it replaces Plateresque decoration with sculpture of a Classical type.   Corinthian columns carved with a «purist» feeling
support an extremely simple entablure, in the style of the Venetian and
Roman retables.   It has been suggested that the sculptures might be by
El Greco himself.
   Topping off the main retable, in the upper section, the prodigious «Trinity», perhaps the most highly spiritualized Trinity ever painted, appears,
centered between Classical pilasters and under a triangular pediment.   The
group made up by Christ, the Father and an angel in a carmine tunic—
reminds us of Michelangelo's last pietàs, especially the ones in the Duomo
and Academia in Florence.   Camón tells us that the figure of the Son may
have been inspired by «The Dying Slave» by the Florentine painter which
El Greco admired more as a sculptor than as a painter.   Ephebe-angels of
a Mannerist taste surround the central group, while the Holy Ghost in its
traditional form of a dove, flies against a golden sky.   The heads of the
cherubs that appear at Christ's feet are surprising.   In the entire painting
there is a strong Venetian influence, especially in the ineffable coloring.   But
this characteristic is seen even more clearly in «The Assumption» (1577,
Chicago Art Institute) which was directly inspired by one by Titian.   From
this painter he inherits this color which «is the one which fills the eyes
of our mystics in their ecstasy», as Camón has said.
   Sold to the sculptor Salvatierra, it was later acquired from him by
Ferdinand VII for 15,000 reales, pending a favorable report from the painters
Vicente López and Juan de Ribera.

PLATE XXXIX

EL GRECO (Domenicos Theotocopulos).
Nobleman With His Hand on His Chest (1578-1583).
Oil on canvas, 81 × 66 cm.   C. 809

«This unknown man is a Christian / of serious appearance and clothed in black / with no more glitter than the hilt / of his admirable Toledan sword. / A severe face, pale as a lily, / rises above his stiff, ruffled collar / and is illuminated by the inner light / of a devout but waning taper / ... / with a pious and noble and serious gesture / his open hand over his chest / the knight places, as if solemnly swearing his faithfulness.»

We believe that the description of this masterpiece is perfectly given in these inspired verses by Manuel Machado. Much literature has been written about this prodigious portrait, and we shall not try to add to it.

Thus critics have tried to see a symbolic value in the unnatural posture of the fingers, all of them spread apart, except for the ring and middle finger, when this is a pose typical of the Mannerist painters, and of Titian himself. Possibly El Greco took it from this latter since they worked together in Venice. Ricardo Baroja and Willumsen believed that it was a self-portrait, interpreting the gesture as an affirmation of the ego. Camón recognizes that a certain connection exists between it and the self-portrait in the «Pentecost». Others have considered it to be the portrait of a notary, since they interpreted the posture as a sign of testimonial. Cassou relates it to the *Spiritual Exercises* of St. Ignatius, since the saint suggested that a sinner place his hand on his chest each time he sinned.

Angulo Iñiguez has noted that the nobleman's proper left shoulder slumps greatly and that the corresponding forearm «is lost beneath the cloth and may not be seen». This is underlined by the fact that El Greco signed his name in Greek letters on the part of the surface which would normally have portrayed the shoulder. This, and the fact that it is a work done in his first Toledan period, as Cossío and Camón state, make us meditate upon what contact the artist might have had with Cervantes, since he was then living in Toledo as well. The physical and typological characteristics of the face are in accord with a self-description which was given in the *Exemplary Novels:* «This fellow you see with an aquiline face, chestnut hair, a smooth and unclouded brow, a beard... which not twenty years ago was golden, a large moustache, small mouth..., a more pale than swarthy complexion». Besides Cervantes emphasizes the importance of the sword and his right hand, «I know well that in the hard naval tournament/you lost the movement of your left hand/for the glory of the right one». And his «enemy», Lope de Vega, ironically alludes, in poetry, to this kind of portrait: «One of those which touches my conscience / with the hand placed on the chest? / ... / Painters often do this / but at least let it be said / that the canvas is done by a good hand».

Cossío dates it between 1577 and 1584; Mayer before 1580; Camón between 1580 and 1583; and Willumsen, in Madrid, before he settles in Toledo.

PLATE XL

El Greco (Domenicos Theotocopulos).
Portrait of a Gentleman (c. 1600).
Oil on canvas, 51 × 64 cm.

C. 810

«Art has produced few portraits as spiritual and penetrating as this one», astutely comments Camón Aznar referring to this masterpiece; for besides being a prodigious piece of extremely lovely painting, there is a profoundly penetrating psychological study to be found in this bust of a Toledan gentleman.

El Greco always gives fundamental importance to the eyes of his subjects, and here he has achieved perhaps one of the most mysterious looks in all of his painting. These eyes are very clear, but he darkens the sclera with gray tones which make the eyes seem like bottomless wells in which life-long sorrows seem to have been calmed by serene meditation. The prominent cheek bones, with small hollows, speak of times of scarcity and misfortune or they could also be the product of a psychological exaltation, of a devotion reaching the ascetic mysticism characteristic of the times of Philip II. El Greco, with a slight facial dissymmetry and the oblique sense of the beard has accentuated the pathos of this face. The forehead, usually smooth in most of the Cretan painter's works, is marked here by horizontal wrinkles which accentuate the still hopeful pessimism of the subject. Azorín fancifully associated him with the gentleman who gave Lazarillo de Tormes shelter in the Imperial city of Toledo in the «sorrowfull and ill-starred house where they neither eat nor drink»; unfortunately this is only a lovely literary speculation.

Theotocopulos achieves here one of his portraits of most delicate and inspired technique. Carmine touches lend a succulence to the surfaces and transparent grayish shadows define the flesh of the face. This technique shows that this work is not among the early ones done in Toledo, but rather may be dated around 1600. According to Cossío, between 1684-1694 it figured along with other portraits by El Greco in the inventories of the Madrilenian Alcázar of 1686. Velasquez had them hanging in his workshop.

PLATE XLI

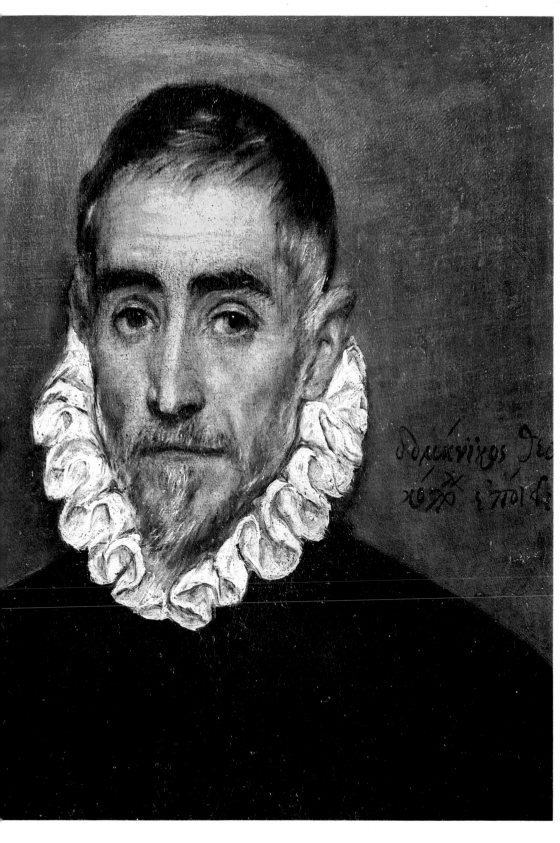

El Greco (Domenicos Theotocopulos).
The Adoration of the Shepherds (1612-14).
Oil on canvas, 180 × 319 cm.   C. 2.988

On August 26, 1612, the son of El Greco, Jorge Manuel, rents a crypt in the Convent Church of the Dominican Sisters in Toledo, Santo Domingo el Antiguo, to serve as the burial place for him and his father. He promises that his father will build and decorate a retable for it. It is possible that El Greco began the work on the main canvas for this altar after the contract was ratified on November 20.

The result was a masterful work: «The Adoration of the Shepherds», in which as Wethey has expressed, «each brush stroke is brimming over with form and meaning». But in spite of an illusionistic technique the description of the beings and objects is minute. The coloring reaches surprising levels here, standing out starkly and dazzlingly against a lugubriously profound background. Reds, oranges, jade greens, golden yellows and dark blues are livened up or attenuated by the light which radiates from the new-born Babe, Who like a living beacon dominates the center of the composition. The illumination defines the surfaces, filtering between the figures which it surrounds with atmosphere and space. In the background, on the left, are depths defined by arches which extend backwards until a curtain, reminding us of a retable, cuts them off. It is possible that the artist had the structure of the Toledo Cathedral in mind. In the upper part angels fly about holding a filacteria with the inscription «Gloria in Excelsis. In terram pacis». *Peace on Earth* is what El Greco must have desired at this moment; peace for him, peace for mankind. At that time of world-wide conflicts, he was personally suffering from sickness and his creditors were pestering him as well. When he dies in 1614, the canvas remains in the Church of Santo Domingo, but his mortal remains do not, since his son, Jorge Manuel, could not pay the maintenance costs of the crypt. His remains are moved to another convent and then later to the common grave. As a result his ashes are today mixed with the earth of Toledo, just as it should be. His tomb is all of Toledo, the entire city shelters him. For, as Góngora said, here «lies El Greco. Heir of Nature and Art, Art he studied. (He was) Iris to color, Phoebus to light, if not Morpheus to shadows.»

In 1618 Luis Tristán, his disciple, says that he saw El Greco working on the piece, saying that «he was there». This makes us think that the shepherd in the foreground is the last self-portrait that El Greco does, and this is confirmed by the facial features which are similar to other self-portraits of his.

The picture was sold to the federal government by the nuns in 1954 for 1,600,000 pesetas, thus saving it from the danger, which was imminent, of its being exported. It came to the Prado Museum on December 31, 1954.

PLATE XLII

LUIS DE MORALES.
Virgin and Child (c. 1568).
Oil on wood, 64 × 84 cm.   C. 2.656

Without a doubt the most important Spanish painter among El Greco's contemporaries is Luis de Morales, whom the people gave the name of «The Divine One». Of an almost autodidactic background, he attains a very delicate technique and becomes well-acquainted with the painting of his time. For this reason, although painted with an archaistic technique reminiscent of the XVth-century Flemish masters, there is not lacking in this «Virgin and Child» a certain Mannerist feeling which is close to the Italian painting of the times. According to E. Du Gué Trapier, it may thus be related to the «Virgin of the Holy Family» by Luini, which since early times had been in Spain and still remains in the Prado. Besides, a Leonardesque feeling lends a halo of mystery to Mary's oval face, blurring her features somewhat and partially covering her fair hair with a transparent veil obtained by retouching the already finished painting. There are very few painters who have succeeded as well as Morales in penetrating maternal psychology. Thus, the Mother appears here as the prototype for all them in the world, painted with an infinite tenderness; while her offspring searches for her breast, the Virgin looks at him affectionately. These pious pictures made Morales the painter most esteemed by the bourgeosie, clergy and popular class in Extremadura and the southeast of Portugal in the second half of the XVIth century.

Other versions of these works exist, but none suceeds in raising the maternity theme to the sublime heights of this one. Here the bony frames characteristic of the Estremenian painter almost disappear to give us a more idealized type which brings it closer to certain creations by the painter from Crete. Unfortunately for Spanish art, Philip II did not give Morales' art its proper due and he denied him artistic entry into the royal palaces and churches, much as he had done to El Greco. This work, therefore, as well as many others by Morales in the Prado, proceed from recent purchases and donations. This lovely painting is owed to the legacy of Pedro Bosch, one of the few patrons who have helped to enrich the foremost collection of Spanish painting, as we see.

JOACHIM PATINIR.
Charon Crossing the Styx (c. 1510).
Oil on wood, 103 × 64 cm.   C. 1.616

Although Patinir himself was not the inventor of landscape painting, this genre was developed by him, giving it a new character. Also a creation of his is the type of landscape which will be used by the Flemish and Dutch painters in the XVIth and XVIIth centuries. In general, in his landscapes there is a predominance especially of greens, whether it be in the waters of the rivers, or in the trees and the bushes on their banks; at times, even the cloudly skies overhead take on a greenish cast. These greens run the gamut from an almost black tone to a light emerald color.

The landscape here contains some qualities which are rather surprising for the times: although the horizon is still very high, following Medieval typology, a new sense of curvature in the distance is perceived, owed to the new theories of the spherical shape of the Earth, confirmed by the discovery of America. Thus the horizon is not undefined as in earlier painting, but rather a radical cutting-off point is perceived. The old landscape —a «road without end»— which according to Spengler was the fundamental characteristic of Nordic painting, no longer exists.

But a terrible loneliness emanates from the broad river, illuminated by a frozen light, in spite of the living beings which appear on both shores. In the middle of the water, at the prow of the boat, a nude young man's hair stands on end in fright, while Charon, the oarsman, takes him to the Tartarus' shore. It is easy to imagine the howls of the damned which reach the passenger's ears, since terror reigns on the right-hand bank. Alongside a stone tower where a lugubrious stream empties, Cerebus guards the Gates of Averno (Hades); a decapitation scene is in progress in the tower. In the background, fires remind us of H. Bosch's «Hells». In the Elysian Fields, on the other hand, there exists a placid boredom; angels, accompanying seraphic spirits, stroll through gentle fields where glassy structures similar to ones by the painter of the «Garden of Delights» rise.

Very few panels by Patinir are conserved, although in many of the paintings by contemporary Flemish painters, the landscapes are by his hand. The Prado Museum possesses, along with El Escorial Monastery, the most important collections of his work. And «Charon Crossing the Styx» is, with «St. Christopher», in El Escorial, one of Patinir's key works. It belonged to Philip II's collection and was saved from the fire of 1734 in the Alcazar and in 1799 it was found attributed to Bosch in the Buen Retiro inventories.

162

PLATE XLIV

Jan Gossaert (Mabuse).
Virgin Child (c. 1527).
Oil on wood, 63 × 50 cm.   C. 1.930

The Virgin is represented here in a niche very characteristic of the Flemish Renaissance, already within the Mannerist style. The structural organization of the painting develops inside of a harmonious sense of compositon. Mary is the center of the scene and in her we find a feeling for rounded forms which, like in many of Mabuse's paintings, tend toward an exhuberance which reminds us of forms which will later be employed by Rubens. Thus her face is round, her lips full and her body exhuberant. But nevertheless her bared breast is not, as has been said, a worldly symbol, but is rather related to Medieval iconography, in which the Virgin Mary appears as «The Virgin of the Holy Milk». The Child, although His aspect here is Mannerist, holds an apple in His hand, like in representations from the previous century. But this work, in the formal aspect, is within the artistic domain of Rapahel's painting. This is logical since Gossaert arrives in Rome the same year as the painter from Urbino (1508). The triangular composition and the profiles of the Virgin and Child make this origin clear.

Certain Leonardesque influences may be observed in this work, as well, especially in the manner of modeling the figures with the light, in which Leonardo's *sfumato* is present. Mabuse has used the Flemish «velatura» technique (with layered brushstrokes) in order to bring out the textures, as in the veil which covers part of the Virgin's shoulder. This technique later comes to Spain where it is used by Morales among others. Due to all this, Gossaert may be considered one of the first Mannerists, along with Alonso Berruguete and Pedro Machuca, outside of Italy.

Although this work is neither dated nor signed, its excellent state of preservation makes its exhaustive study possible in the technical and stylistic aspects. Thus the subtle, minute technique which is preoccupied with the least detail, like the ruffled pages of the book, the above-mentioned «velaturas» which achieve subtle transparencies or the interest in emphasizing the qualities of the smallest things, such as the pearls in the diadem make this picture the unquestionable masterpiece of this important Flemish painter. It may be dated around 1527, as Weiss has said, since stylistically and formally it is related to the «Danae» (Pinacoteca in Munich), dated the same year. Besides, in 1530 Hans Baldung Grien does a copy of this painting (Germanic Art Museum, Nuremberg). Von der Osten believes that this Virgin, along with the «Man with the Rosary» (National Gallery, London) formed part of a diptych. This is not possible since the man portrayed does not return the Virgin's look and there exists no architectural identity between the pictures. From 1572 on it was in El Escorial, and after 1814 it moved from there to the Prado Museum.

                                                        PLATE XLV

QUENTIN MATSYS.
Ecce Homo (1527-30).
Oil on wood, 160 × 120 cm.   C. 2.801

At first glance, what seems to be represented here is a scene from the Passion of Christ, but if we look carefully we will see that there exist, decorating the architectural background, scenes simulating sculpture whose symbolic content will explain to us the secret meaning of this painting.

The composition seems initially to be a bit helter-skelter, following Medieval tradition, and thus there are certain reminiscences of Bosch's *Ecce Homos*. Nevertheless, the technique is already Renaissance, for there is a certain Leonardesque feeling in the manner of modeling the faces with light and some of the caricaturized types not only recall the sarcastic expressions of the painter from Bois-le-Duc, but also the caricature drawings by Leonardo and Dürer. Now Matsys goes much further; a fervent reader of Erasmus and acquainted with Luther's doctrines, the old painter from Antwerp has expressed in this picture a social satire against the bourgeoisie and against the abuse of power, using an entire system of symbolism, in which he sharply criticized certain social problems of the XVIth century, by-products of the transformation that was taking place in Europe during the Renaissance. The new capitalist economy in these moments gradually susbstitutes the Medieval corporative order; financial manipulation, commerce in gold and silver, and market speculations favored the amassing of great fortunes. This controls the industries and transforms the old artisans into proletarians, bringing many families to misery. Antwerp, under the reign of Charles V, is the great monetary market for Europe. The Emperor protects those financiers who support his European and American policy.

All this is what Matsys is strongly criticizing here. Thus in the first «grisaille» (on the spectator's left), the figure of Pilate, with a certain caricaturized similarity to Charles V, appears as a symbol of power, having his feet washed by the people. In the center, this representation of power restricts a famished figure of Charity, who only gives the bare necessitites to the people (represented by starving children) to keep them from dying. And on the other side, Truth or Liberty looks with avarice at a solid gold star which is held up instead of a torch, since only with money is liberty or truth attained. On the front of the balcony Caesar appears, portrayed as Alexander the Great, since he carries on his helmet Minerva's owl and on the golden shield the «imperial eagle», which also flutters on a pennant. Meanwhile on a frieze there may be partially observed a flaying scene. It should be noted that those who ask for the death of the Divine Lamb are also wealthy men, since they wear rich clothing and jewels.

This is a work from Matsys' final years. It belonged in the XIXth century to the Marquis of La Remisa. It was left in 1936 in Mariano Lanuza's legacy and entered the Prado in 1940.

Marinus (Marinus Claeszon van Reymerswaele).
The Money-Changer and His Wife (1539).
Oil on wood, 83 × 97 cm.   C. 2.567

Marinus takes from Quentin Matsys the theme of «The Money-Changer and His Wife», but he does not limit himself to merely presenting us with a pair of money-changers or bankers with certain sarcastic overtones, but rather develops the theme accentuating its dramatism in a series of paintings such as «The Tax Collectors» and his bankers, in which he mercilessly vents his fury against a class newly enriched by underhanded means. The greed is almost caricaturesquely reflected in the faces of these personages; this occurs in «The Money-Changer and His Wife» in the Prado, in which a burgeois couple anxiously recounts the coins with trembling hands, accentuating the feeling of avarice which Matsys had shown in his painting in the Louvre.

In the background of these pictures there exists a reflection of the social transformation which was going on at the beginning of the XVIth century in Europe, which we have already mentioned in the commentary for the previous plate. The new capitalist economy was precipitatedly taking the place of the aristocracy, which it was ruining. In turn, the old artisans were converted into a proletariat as the villages were abandoned for the cities. Taking advantage of the social and industrial flowering, a new class of men and women made its living from usury. «Although the Church severely prohibited lending money for interest, the progress of the capitalist economy obliged it to soften its rigid position» (Marlier).

Therefore, what is represented in this panel is a pair of usurers who are checking the exact weight of the coins with a small scale, since the majority of the gold and silver pieces were filed down or shaved thin. This might also be considered a representation, as Winkler has said, of tax collectors, who were also criticized in Renaissance literature. Thus Erasmus was very firmly against them.

It is signed «Marinus me feci a (nno) d (omini) 1539». Other versions exist, one of them in El Escorial, on loan from the Prado. The work which we speak of here was left by the Duke of Tarifa and entered the Prado in 1934.

168

PLATE XLVII

PETER BRUEGEL, The Elder.
The Triumph of Death (c. 1565).
Tempera and oil on wood, 162 × 117 cm.

C. 1.393

A terrifying vision of the triumph of death over life is presented here, expressing in Renaissance terms a favorite theme from Medieval times, which had been represented in frescoes like those in the cemetery at Pisa or in books such as the illustrated manuscripts in the Libraires of Paris or El Escorial. During the XVIth century they were still profusely represented in Germany by artists such as Holbein and Baldung Grien. The theme recalls another work of Bruegel's the «Dulle Griet» (1564, Antwerp Museum), but here the technique as well as the composition are superior, which may indicate that this one was done several months later, although Friedländer and Genalle considerer it to have been painted four years earlier.

In this «Triumph of Death» all living beings are killed; nothing, no one is saved from death's destructive power. Almost in the center of the composition (which is based on the *Apocalypse*, VI, 8), a skeleton appears on a bony old mount cutting short with his scythe the lives of the rich and the poor, of the powerful and the plebeyans. A plentiful army of skeletons dispatches death on all sides and not even the kings or high officials of the Church are excepted. Only some brash soldiers uselessly try to fight against their fate; on the extreme right of the painting, two lovers strum instruments and sing. They'll die without suffering, accompanied vocally and instrumentally by one of these macabre figures. In the ocean in the background, ships founder and sink, and on the coast buildings are set in flames.

Here Bruegel diverges from the popular themes so characteristic of him and of which there is a prodigious collection in the Vienna Museum. It is possible that an echo of Hieronymus Bosch may still be heard in this piece, for Bosch had greatly influenced Bruegel in his early works. The composition here is still somewhat motley, bringing it close to his first productions; around 1566 he uses fewer figures and places them in a more systematic order.

This painting was in Antwerp until after 1614, since in this year it was listed in Philips van Valkenisse's collection. Therefore its mention in 1604, by Van Mander, «the Dutch Vasari», is not at all clear; it appears in an inventory at La Granja in 1774. It is included in the Prado's collection in 1827. It has recently been restored and the cleaning has confirmed its quality.

HANS BALDUNG GRIEN.
The Stages of Human Life (1530-1545).
Oil on wood, 61 × 151 cm.

C. 2.220

This *allegory*, along with its companion piece: «Beauty, Poetry and Music», is a metaphorical diptych in which the perishable reality of life is contrasted with a harmonious idealization of beauty in constant renovation, symbolized by the birth of little children.

The majority of the Germanic artists from the Renaissance, so scarcely represented in the Prado, liked to cultivate these allegorical themes and Hans Baldung Grien would come to be truly obsessed by symbolism, since paintings by his hand in which themes of this type do not appear are very scarce. In spite of all this, in the planning out and representation of the pale nudes such as we see in the allegories in the Prado, there exists a Gothic-like echo which separates it from the Renaissance structures. Thus if we compare Dürer's «Adam and Eve» with these figures we notice at a glance an obvious difference. Perhaps the artist's training as an engraver influences him; this may be seen in the outline of the human figures, in the graphic sense of trees and in the lineal feeling in the landscape. Baldung works especially in two university cities, Freiburg and Strasbourg, where he is in contact with the German humanists. Thus the possibility exists that the theme of these two panels is based on a suggestion from them or on other sources of the humanistic literature of the times. The panel which is reproduced represents, as we have said, the ephimeral element of life. A sleeping child holds in his hand a lance, a symbol of vitality, but which has been broken by death; meanwhile a young maiden is undressed by an old woman, whose arm is held, at the same time, by death, which is personified by a rotting cadaver. In the face of this woman who is already past maturity, we may see a certain influence of Dürer, but there is a closer affinity to Cranach, especially in the younger faces. In the background of this panel an alpine landscape appears; in the foreground there is a tower in flames, like in Bosch's paintings. It is probably done at the end of his life.

The companion piece had an inscription on the back, which does not exist today, which said that it had been given to Juan de Ligne, Baron of Barbazón, by Federico de Solms, January 23, 1547, in Frankfurt-am-Main. It belonged to Philip II and was listed in the Madrid Alcazar's inventory of 1600. In 1814 it was in the Oriente Palace; when the Prado Museum was created by order of the prudish Ferdinand VII, these panels were kept in the special «nude rooms», since he did not want «the public to see the indecent pictures in any event».

172

PLATE XLIX

ALBRECHT DÜRER.
Adam and *Eve* (1507).
Oil on wood, 209 × 81 and 209 × 83 cm.   C. 2.117-18

The great intellectual and professional capacity of Albrecht Dürer, along with his Humanist feeling, brings him to practice all the pictorial techniques and genres known in his time. For this reason, he will base the principles of this art on a knowledge of the sciences. Thus he searches for a perfection of the proportions, basing himself on the theory of the «golden section» which he studies in the treatises of Euclid and Luca Pacioli; he is initiated in these by Jacopo de Barbari —whom he will later recall, affectionately referring to him as an «amiable and good painter»; possibly through him he became acquainted with the theories of Leonardo. In this way, Dürer as well preoccupies himself in his writings with diverse questions, such as the manner of fortification and partition of space with the circle and square, or human proportions. Although he translates to the German realistic style the idealizations of the Italian, he searches for beauty in nature just like Leonardo; due to this he draws with exactitude animals and monsters, plants and mountains, and, above all, man, the axis of humanity and king of Creation —for being a «Humanist», he does not set aside the Medieval spirit; therefore he will engrave and then will paint with special attention the progenitors of mankind: «Adam» and «Eve».

These two panels, done separately, form a homogeneous ensemble which was composed upon Albrecht Dürer's return to Nuremberg after his second trip to Italy. Certain Renaissance touches may be noted. This is especially so in the «Eve», in which there are echoes of the nudes being done at that time by Giovanni Bellini, Giorgione and Titian, but above all of the «Eve» sculpted by Antonio Rizzo which is in the Doge's Palace. As we can tell, the Venetian influence in Dürer is obvious in these two works, since even the «Adam», in spite of its Germanic style, shows signs of Northern Italian art.

If we compare these two works with an engraving on the same theme —«Original Sin»— done by Dürer three years before, we will see that the forms are softened and the monumental, stony feeling which existed in this engraving has been set aside. Although it has been said that the engraving is more Renaissance in style than the paintings, we do not share this opinion, because here the Germanic flavor disappears in favor of a greater flexibility which gives it a strong *cinquecento* flavor almost previewing the Mannerist style. Besides, these nudes are the first in German painting to be done life-size, although with a canon of nine heads, which elongates the figures, accentuating their slenderness. This brings them closer to a typical Mannerist feeling, which in turn recalls the stylized forms of the Gothic style, and we must realize that in Mannerism there are certain resurgences of the Gothic spirit. Here the lines of the anatomy, although exact, are softened, obtaining what Bialostocki calls Dionysian characteristics. Its lyricism makes it one of the most beautiful nudes from this period.

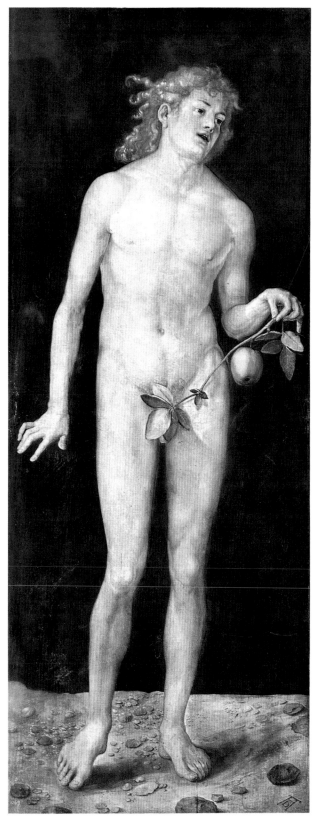

PLATE L

Proud of these masterpieces, Dürer has signed them with his anagram, on the ground in the «Adam», and in the «Eve» on a cartellino, on which he also puts the date. Ancient copies of them exist in the Ufizzi in Florence and in the Museum of Maguncia in which there appear symbolic animals, just as in the engraving, which are lacking in the pair of panels in the Prado Museum. As the copies and the double signatures testify, these paintings were done independently, although they complement each other and form a greater whole which is symptomologically unified.

Both panels were presented to Philip V by Christina of Sweden. They were in the San Fernando Academy of Fine Arts from 1777 until 1824, and since they were considered «indecent» they were kept in the «restricted entrance» salon of the Prado until after Ferdinand VII's death.

PLATE LI

ALBRECHT DÜRER
Self-portrait (1498).
Oil on wood, 41 × 52 cm.   C. 2.179

This self-portrait is perhaps the first of its kind to be independently done, thus breaking with the traditions of the guilds, at least in Germany, according to the great Dürer scholar Panofsky. It was painted before the end of the XVth century, a time when —except for in Italy— artists were considered little more than artisans and therefore not allowed to do a self-portrait which was not to be included in a larger composition. «1498. I painted it as I was at the age of 26. Albrecht Dürer», is how he has signed this painting, showing that at this time Dürer was proud of the artistic triumphs he had achieved which allowed him to associate with princes and aristocrats. This same year he did engravings for and published his *Book of the Apocalypse*, which enjoyed a success unprecedented in the Europe of his time.

He portrays himself elegantly dressed, like a «dandy» of his times, in the latest style; the light colored suit with a broad, open neck gives him a Renaissance air which a refined pose accentuates. The frizzy hair which appears in his self-portrait of 1493 (Louvre) here has been carefully curled and his long, delicate artist's hands are wearing gloves. According to Panofsky, Dürer completely bases this work on a portrait by Dieric Bouts from 1462, for the composition, but we consider the work to be closer to Giovanni Bellini's portraits. Besides, in the background through the window an alpine landscape may be seen, which must have been done from the sketches he made during his trip to Italy from 1494-1495, which tends to clear up this question.

Other self-portraits by Dürer exist, but none as daring, life-like and direct as this one in the Prado. Given in 1636 by the city of Nuremberg to the Count of Arundel, it came into the power of Charles I of England and after his execution it was bought at public auction (1686) for the Spainsh Royal Collection. It enters the Prado in the year 1827.

PLATE LII

HANS HOLBEIN, The Younger (Attributed to).
Portrait of an Old Man (2nd Quarter of the XVIth century).
Oil on wood, 62 × 47 cm.   C. 2.182

This prodigious portrait of an old man, with ruddy skin full of personality and life, inspires in us not only aesthetic feeling but also a deep respect, in spite of his bulbous, deformed nose. It is one of the masterpieces of Nordic Renaissance painting in the Prado Museum, although critics have debated its attribution. Since 1873 it has been cataloged, with doubts, as by Holbein; in the 1920 catalog, this attribution was categorically rejected, according to the opinion common among critics at that point, since they attributed it almost unanimously to Joos van Cleve («The Master of the Death of the Virgin»), considering it the masterpiece of his final period. Now, although Cleve had done stupendous portraits, none was equal to the quality of this one, not only due to the psychological forcefulness of the expression but also due to the formal qualities themselves. Thus the hands are comparable to the loveliest ones painted by Holbein; their texture recalls the ones done during his last stay in Basle (1528-1532), between his two trips to England. The black material of the clothing and the tactile quality of the parchment which is held in the left hand, are characteristic of the painter from Augsburg. This opinion was communicated to the Director of the Museum at the time, Sr. Alvarez de Sotomayor, by various Swiss scholars, on the occasion of the *Geneva Exposition* (1939). Today the most accepted opinion tends toward this position since the old attribution to Joos van Cleve has been abandoned.

Around 1900 the identity of the personage in this portrait was proposed to be Sebastian Münster (1489-1519), the famous cosmographer, but this has been rejected by Winkler and other specialists. According to information sent to the Prado Administration by Dr. Eggerphed of Berlín, the deformation of the nose is due to *rhinoscleroma*.

In the times of Charles II it was inventoried in the Madrilenian Alcázar as an original by Albrecht (Dürer?). It was saved from the fire of 1734.

ANTONIO MORO (Anton van Dashorst Mor).
Mary Tudor, Queen of England (1554).
Oil on wood, 84 × 109 cm.   C. 2.108

Antonio Moro, upon coming to work in the Spanish Court, lays the foundation on which will be raised the great school of Spanish courtly portrait artists, which begun by his own student Sánchez Coello and continued by Pantoja de la Cruz, will culminate in Velasquez.

This is one of the most important portraits by Moro, the richest collection of whose works is in the Prado Museum. It represents the second wife of Philip II —to whom she was married the last four years of her life— seated, in a full portrait. Mary wears a dress of velvet which is vented and has a ramiform design, and its pineapple motif may indicate that it was woven in Italy. She wears a purple greatcoat which contrasts with the embroidered velvet chair. A rich collection of jewels, as well, tries to enhance her poor figure. The red rose of the House of Tudor is held like a scepter in her scrawny right hand, while the left one holds some gloves.

In this painting, as in all of Moro's work in general, the colors are muted and the technique is rigid, but this is not noticed because the splendid lines and modeling make us overlook it. Moro's success is principally owed to the true-to-life manner in which he does the faces of those portrayed. Thus in this feminine face we perceive a life which was sterile in all respects, and on her thin, cold lips is an almost imperceptible grimace of ambition which accentuates her penetrating, steely eyes.

Charles V was the one who commissioned this portrait of his daughter-in-law, since he was the one who arranged this marriage of which he was very proud. It seems that thanks to this marriage the longed-for alliance between England and Spain was achieved, but it was only an apparent and ephimeral one. When in 1556 the Emperor retires to the Monastery at Yuste, in Extremadura, he demonstrates his fondness for the picture (and the subject) by taking it with him. The painting is signed on the left under the ruffle on the sleeve: «Antonius Mor pingebat 1554». It was back in Madrid from Yuste by 1600 at the latest.

PETER PAUL RUBENS.
Maria de Medici (1622-1625).
Oil on canvas, 108 × 130 cm.   C. 1.685

Rubens practices all the pictorial genres in an admirable manner and the Prado Museum preserves splendid examples of his various types of production to an extent which is unequaled in any other museum. Among the portraits, that of the Duke of Lerma, which was acquired recently stands out in the Madrilenian Museum as possibly the most important of his youthful portraits, along with that of the Queen of France, Maria de Medici. At the time this portrait was done, the daughter of the Duke of Toscana, Francesco Medici, was around fifty years old and was then ruler of France, since it had been more than twelve years since Henry IV had died (1610). If we compare the clothing of the Widow Queen of France with that of her Spanish equal there is an immense difference. For example, Doña Maria of Austria, who was the wife of Philip IV, wears a nun's habit, while the French Queen is elegantly and very richly dressed, although also in black and white. Big pearls, jewels which may be worn while in mourning, adorn her neck and earlobes, like an echo of past beauty, since in spite of her double chin and puffy cheeks, Rubens shows us traces of her blonde loveliness.

The Flemish painter in this period is doing, with collaborators, a cycle on the life of the Queen of France, today in the Louvre, and which was planned for the Luxembourg Palace. Between 1628 and 1631 the artist from Antwerp worked on another pictorial ensemble in which the story of her husband's life was narrated; but the disagreements with their son, Louis XIII and his adviser Richelieu's intrigues caused the project to be abandoned since the Queen Mother ended up financially ruined, with Rubens even loaning her money at one time.

This work was acquired at the sale of Rubens' estate in Antwerp, and according to Mayse it was brought to Madrid in 1636. It is known that by 1686 it was in the Alcázar.

PLATE LV

PETER PAUL RUBENS.
The Three Graces (1639?).
Oil on canvas, 221 × 181 cm.

C. 1.670

In June of 1626, when Isabel Brandt, Ruben's first wife dies, the painter, to get his mind off his loneliness, begins diplomatic activity for the Spanish Crown. His mission was an old dream for the Flemish painter —to reestablish peace in Europe, unobtainable since the beginning of the Thirty Years' War. Trips to Madrid and London, besides distracting Rubens and serving political ends, also enabled him to look for more clients. But painting and diplomacy do not occupy him entirely, and his strong personality required a woman's hand. Four years after the death of his first wife, he will marry her niece, Elena Fourment, a youngster of only 16, while Rubens was around 53 at the time. From this perilous match Rubens will receive immediately new vitality. This will be the last decade of his lifetime, as he dies in 1640, at the zenith of his creativity. Extremely lovely paintings by his hand come from this period, such as a portrait of Elena with only a fur coat thrown over her shoulders, and a stupendous imaginary celebration in the garden of his home in Antwerp: «The Garden of Love», in the Prado (C. 1.690). But probably the earliest of Rubens' works in the Prado Museum is «The Three Graces», in which the painter from Antwerp shows off his artistic talent, obtaining a masterpiece of formal beauty. The physical attributes of the three young women portrayed are truly oppulent and the pink-toned flesh, obtained by layers of glazing, achieves prodigious chromatic effects. The Graces are portrayed here joined in a ring, in a manner identical to that of Raphael's work on the same theme. He, in turn, was inspired by a Classical sculpture of serene beauty, known in several versions, one of them in the Piccolomini Library in the Siena Cathedral. Rubens, on the other hand, made the figures of Jupiter's daughters and the nymph Erynome more Baroque. Above the heads of the goddesses of joy and merry-making appears a garland of roses symbolizing the condition of the servants of Venus, which is underlined by the deer in the background. The exuberance of composition and freedom of execution remind us of poet Rafael Alberti's line: «He was a man of passion and life».

In the XVIIIth century this feeling was not appreciated and the work was placed in the secret gallery of the San Fernando Academy of Fine Arts. Today a recent cleaning has revived the admirable coloring of this work which was acquired by Philip IV at the auction of Rubens' estate.

PLATE LVI

ANTHONY VAN DYCK.
Self-portrait with Sir Endymion Porter (1630?).
Oil on canvas, 144 × 119 cm.

C. 1.489

The final years (1632-41) of Van Dyck's short life —he died at the age of 42— were spent in England. There he manages to become the painter for an oppulent, aristocratic society and fulfill his desire of living elegantly among distinguished and cultured people.

The Belgian painter who is totally integrated into English society accepts its customs and gains the friendship of the noblemen and is spoiled by the gentlewomen, many of whom often fall in love with him. But these enjoyable pleasures also bring him a premature death.

Among his friends, the Viscount of Arundel, Sir Endymion Porter (d. 1649), famous collector and connoisseur of paintings, as well as poet, politician and diplomat, stands out; he gave his services to the Duke of Buckingham, as a specialist in Spanish affairs, and thus visits Madrid in 1622 to take part in the later frustrated plans for the marriage of Doña María, the King's sister, and Charles I of England. In 1628 he returns once again to Madrid, the city where he was born and where he had learned courtly etiquette as a page of the Duke of Olivares. It was possibly Porter who convinced Van Dyck to go to England in 1632.

This double portrait was possibly done between 1629 and 1630, before his move to Britain, when in Antwerp Sir Endymion acquires «Renaud and Armida» from the painter for Charles I's collection. The style and face of the painter make this affirmation possible, although authors such as Schäffer date it around 1640 and Van Puyvelde thinks it was done a bit earlier than this. Above all, the particular pictorial technique with a fine, close brush stroke, makes one think it is a work previous to his final period. Perhaps the English diplomat requested that Van Dyck portray himself alongside such an illustrious subject. In this way the painter could satisfy his personal taste and eternalize Sir Endymion by having him forever accompany the famous artist throughout posterity. The elegant stances of the subjects, the elegance of the silk suits, the expressions and psychological depth of the faces caused a profound impact not only on contemporary English artists, but also on later ones. One may therefore say that Van Dyck is the creator of the English school of painting (Plate LXXXIV). Besides, the use of a column and curtains in the background will be repeated not only in England, but also in European painting during the XVIIth and XVIIIth centuries.

Isabel de Farnesio, Philip V's second wife, and a collector of exquisite sensitivity, acquires the picture. In 1746 it is already listed at La Granja Palace (Segovia).

PLATE LVII

JAN BRUEGEL DE VELOURS.
Allegory on Sight (1617).
Oil on wood, 65 × 109 cm.

C. 1.394

In Flanders during the XVIIth century, a pictorial genre develops in which large rooms are represented completely decorated with paintings, sculptures, drawings and curios; these pictures are called *Cabinets d'Amateurs*. It will be around the beginning of the century when the first painting is done in which a real «collector's room» appears. It is painted in 1617 by Bruegel de Velours, since this is when he signs his «Allegory on Sight», the most significant from the pictorial point of view in the series on «The Five Senses» in the Prado. This ensemble is painted by Bruegel between 1617 and 1618. In each painting many more or less artistic objects appear filling the room; the panel in which the most number of paintings appears is logically the one on «Sight». Even so, in another painting in the Prado by the same artist, «Sight and Smell», once again a veritable gallery of art works is represented.

This «Allegory on Sight» is one of the most beautiful paintings from Bruegel's production. According to S. Peth-Holteroff («Les peintres fls. de cabinets d'am»), the half-nude young woman which personifies this sense in represented by Venus, but since identical figures appear in all of the pictures, it may be presumed that it is a nymph. Also this same author tells us that she is contemplating her reflection in a mirror, when she actually looks at a picture of herself, which possesses allegorical meanning since it represents «The Cure of the Blind Man». The same as in «Sight and Smell», it is inspired by the Gallery of the Archduke Albert and Archduchess Elizabeth who were Bruegel's patrons, for in a prominent spot on a table on the spectator's left their double portrait appears and almost in the center of the painting is a smaller versión of the large «Equestrian Portrait of Archduke Albert». At the same time, homage is paid to Rubens, since on the spectator's right and in the foreground «The Bacchanal» (Ermitage M., Leningrad), painted three years before, is reproduced along with «The Virgin of the Garland» (Louvre) on which Bruegel collaborated, doing the garland of flowers, of which he was very proud and which he copies here with all exactness, in miniature. Some of the other pictures may be documented but they are less important, such as a copy of the St. Cecilia by Raphael. In the background are shelves with sculptures, among them busts of Laocoön, Seneca, Galba, Lucius Verus, etc. Besides on the floor there appears a great number of scientific instruments.

The painting was acquired inmediately after the completion of the series on «The Five Senses» by Duke Pfalz-Neuburg who «gave it to the Cardinal Infante (Don Fernando) and his Highness to the Duke of Medina de las Torres, and the Duke to his Majesty», as it would be inventoried in the Palace in Madrid in 1636. In this inventory it was indicated that the figures were by Rubens (?).

190

PLATE LVIII

DAVID TENIERS, The Younger.
The Old Man and the Maid.
Oil on canvas, 64 × 49 cm.   C. 1.800

Flemish painting in the Baroque period cultivates mainly religious themes and portraits, but, even so, it does not for this reason neglect genre painting, and painters exist who specialize in the representation of popular scenes. The most famous is David Teniers, the Younger. His paintings are almost always small in size and are quite different from the ones being cultivated at the time by the Dutch painters, since in spite of the proximity between Flanders (Belgium) and Holland, religious, political, sociological and cultural differences between the two neighboring countries were very marked. This explains why Teniers' painting was not intrinsically popular, in contrast to Dutch painting in which everday life acquires a genuinely intimate character. At the beginning of the century the difference was not so pronounced; in both countries drinkers, barmaids, courtesans, soldiers... and especially «kermesses» were painted; but little by little this typology began to disappear in Protestant, Puritan Holland in which painting will become linked to everday homelife. Meanwhile, in Belgium the traditional typology continues, although separating it from a truly popular character as it loses its intimacy. Thus in Teniers' painting the festivities in the country are seen from the point of view of a spectator, in contrast to Brouwer or Van Ostade who narrates the diversions and hijinks of the people almost with a reporters's viewpoint, so that the rich and powerful may contemplate them. A good example is this maid surprised by her master while she is cleaning. Like in the theater of the times, she just puts on an ingenous look. The roguishness is accentuated by the fact that the old wife appears in the background. On the other hand, the chiaroscuro atmosphere, in which the objects are meticulously studied, reminds us of Van Ostade's pictures.

Philip IV had already acquired paintings by Teniers in the artist's lifetime through his Viceroy; possibly because of Holland's isolation from Spain, a fundamental cause of the lack of Dutch works, he had to be content with genre paintings by this painter. But it was Isabel de Farnesio who showed a special predilection for Teniers, collecting numerous works such as the one which is reproduced here. This one was in La Granja by 1746 and later it was moved to Aranjuez.

REMBRANDT.
Artemisa (1634).
Oil on canvas, 142 × 153 cm.   C. 2.132

Chronologically this is one of the first masterpieces by the artist from Leyden. According to some critics, it represents Sofonisba receiving a cup of poisoned wine, sent by her husband, the Numidian King Siphax, a prisoner of his enemy Masinissa, since he was afraid she would be forced to succumb to Scipio: she would submissively drink it. It is now necessary to accept the ancient attribution in which Rembrandt is understood to have represented the Pergamene queen ready to drink the ashes of her husband which have been dissolved in a drink —since after a recent restoration an old servant appears in the background carrying the ashes wrapped in a cloth.

The scene which we see is a symbol of conjugal love in the Platonic sense. We believe we can recognize the companion piece to this picture in the «Scholar», in the National Gallery in Prague, which in this case would represent Plato, since their dates and dimensions are identical, besides the themes being similar (see *Goya* Mag., No. 95, March-April, 1970). This series of a philosophical type already has an antecedent in «Aristotle Contemplating the Bust of Homer», «The Blind Homer», and «Alexander», which belonged to the Rufo Collection in Messina. The scene is related to Rembrandt's own life, since it is dated 1634, the year of his marriage to his first wife, Saskia, the most profound love of his lifetime. Although some critics have denied that it is a portrait, its relationship with other such ones from the same period is doubtless. For here she appears just the same as in «Sampson's Banquet», awaiting a child, which somewhat changes her appearance.

The scene is probably based on a picture by Rubens, a copy of which according to Konsnetzov, although Gerson has rejected this hypotesis, exists in Sansousi (Berlin) with the same theme. But here the textures, as well as the sense of color, are superior, which makes this work one of the most expressive mythological scenes from the XVIIth century. Signed on the arm of the chair: *Rembrandt f. 1634.*

It was acquired in 1769 for 2,500 reales at the Marquis of La Ensenada's auction; Mengs took part in the transaction. Rembrandt's «Plato» was also in Spain until the XIXth century.

PLATE LX

GUIDO RENI.
Cleopatra (c. 1635-1641).
Oil on canvas, 110 × 94 cm.   C. 209

Among the best examples of Guido Reni's work which the Prado possesses are «Hippomenes and Atalanta», «A Young Girl with a Rose», «St. James
the Apostle» and this lovely «Cleopatra» represented at the moment of her
death due to the poison of the asp which has bitten her. In this work Guido
Reni created a composition characteristic of the Baroque style, for Cleopatra is shown with her eyes fixed on the skies, with an attitude which
though taken from the Mannerist style takes its proper form, especially
in Italy, in the XVIIth century. Many of Reni's feminine figures appear
with the same posture no matter whether they are religious or secular
subjects. In this grandiloquent manner this painter expresses the painful
end of life, almost as if it were the end of an opera.

Pérez Sánchez, in his important book *XVIIth-Century Italian Painting
in Spain,* catalogs it as a work characteristic of the artist's final years. The
softness and simplicity of the coloring, which tends toward a grisaille-like
monochrome in olive-gray tones, is typical of the last part of his life. In
these final works the illumination is softened, toning down the Caravaggiesque dramatism, which is diminished here. Malvasia, the first one to
study Bolognese painting, in 1678 says that «for the Lucretias, Cleopatras
and others, he used the Countesses Branchi and Barbacci as models», which
indicates first, that Reni did several versions of these themes (and while
it is true that various Cleopatras are preserved, the one in the Prado is
one of the most important), and second, that the studies were done from
live models, since there were two different ones for this type of figure. This
Museum possesses, although they are workshop pieces, a «Lucretia» (C. 208)
and a «Judith» (C. 226), as well.

Another «Cleopatra» exists in Spain which was done in a very different
manner from this one. It is in the Marchioness De la Zenia's collection in
Majorca. The version in the Prado appears inventoried for the first time
in the Oriente Palace in 1814. Zoeller did a lithograph of it (Litographical
Coll., Vol. II). It is not included in the latest catalogs (1963 and 1972).

196

PLATE LXI

FRANCISCO RIBALTA.
Christ Embracing St. Bernard (1624-1626).
Oil on canvas, 158 × 113 cm.   C. 2.804

Among the most admirable pictorial representations of the Spanish as-
cetic-mystic vein is this «Christ Embracing St. Bernard» by Francisco Ribalta. Its iconography is taken from *The Life of St. Bernard* by Father
Rivadeneyra which narrates the moment when the founder of the Order
of Cistercians is in ecstasy in front of a crucifix and Christ comes down
from the cross to embrace him. As we admire this work we may remember
the line from a famous Spanish mystic poem: «Forgetful rapt, I lay, My
face reclining on my lov'd one fair».

Ribalta has done here a pictorial work in which the realism of the
earliest Spanish Baroque style is already present; if in Christ's muscular
body there still exist echoes of Mannerism —perhaps reminiscent of the
artist's formation in El Escorial— on the other hand the saint's figure is a
splendid example of realism, since it appears as a clear study in observation
of reality, expressed in the lassitude of the body and face of the saint
who experiences mystic union with Jesus. Translucent shadows take shape
among the pleats of the Cistercian habit, in a way similar to the paintings
of monks by Zurbarán; due to this, at the turn of the century this work
was attributed to the painter from Extremadura.. Although this seems
strange if we remember that Ponz in his *Travels in Spain* (Letter VII, 7)
describes this painting in the Prior's cell in the Carthusian Monastery in
Portaceli (Valencia), saying: «It is the most beautiful, best painted and
most expressive work which Ribalta has produced; nothing else compares
with this painting». As may be seen, the praise could be no more effusive,
especially coming from a critic full of a frigid melancholy whose feroce
reaction to the Baroque style was obvious.

Now this picture continues today to impress the spectator, not only for
the psychological profundity with which the artist studies the subjects, but
also because of the formal beauty of the painting. The stongly illuminated
lighting of the main figures leaves barely visible among the shadows in the
background a pair of angels; possibly this is the result of Ribalta's contact
with the Italian painter who created Tenebrism: Michelangelo Merisi, «Il
Caravaggio». It is in Italy that Ribalta copies and studies the works of
the creator of a new style, realism, as Ainaud de Lasarte has shown.

The work disappeared from the Portaceli Monastery at the time of the
Disentailment Acts; it was acquired in 1940 with funds from the Count of
Cartagena's legacy.

PLATE LXII

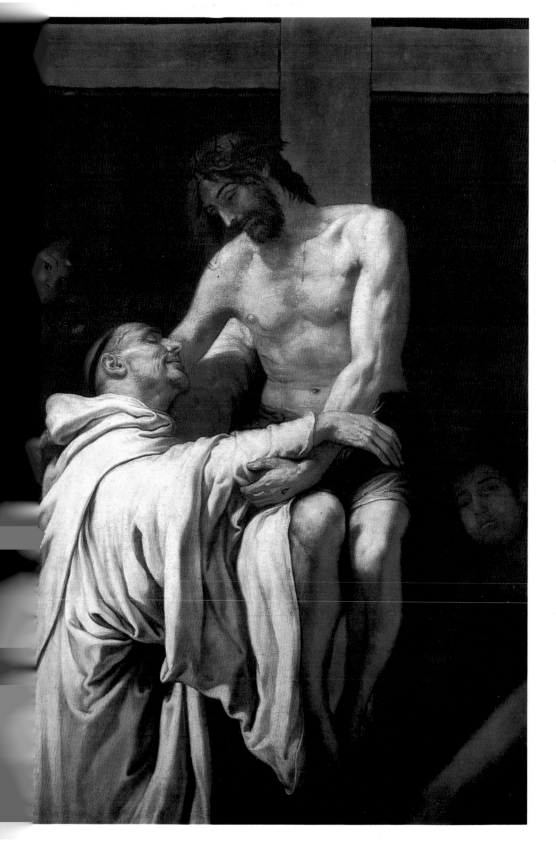

JOSÉ DE RIBERA.
St. Bartholomew (1632-1635).
Oil on canvas, 77 × 64 cm.   C. 1.099

   This fragment of a head which is reproduced here is a good example
of the technical capacity of Ribera's painting. And it is possible that this
Spanish painter is one of the most talented in his generation. In him the
profession of painter attains an admirable virtuosity, the fruit of many
hours of work and an acute observation of reality, since along with his
talent for execution there exists a preoccupation with penetrating the surrounding atmosphere and the spirits of the personages portrayed. In his
extremely agile technique and in his realism he even goes beyond Caravaggio himself, the initiator of the Tenebrist style. Already some of Ribera's
Italian contemporaries, among them Mancini, compared his painting with
that of Caravaggio himself, praising the execution; for his brushwork is
denser, more dazzling and produces a sensation of relief with which he
attains textures, or what is referred to in painters' studios today as «substance». This formal preoccupation makes «Il Spagnoleto's» works be as
important for their pictorial technique as for what is pictured in them.
   This figure is possibly a portrait taken from direct observation. It is
known that Ribera used the beggars and stevedores of Naples as models.
Therefore the wrinkles, beard and the eyes and nose reddened by alcohol
make the type represented here a very characteristic model within the artist's
production. Points of light strengthen the coloring and its realistic, popular forcefulness is such that, thanks to similar portrayals, the Russian
scholar Malinskaya has remarked that Ribera is the most important popular painter of his century. The entire painting represents «St. Bartholomew» in a less than half-figure portrait, with a red tunic and white mantle.
In his right hand he holds the knife which is a symbol of his flaying.
   The work forms part of a series on the Apostles painted in the full maturity of the artist (according to Don Elías Tormo between 1632 and 1635);
it was in the Casino del Príncipe at El Escorial; from there it came to the
Prado.

José de Ribera.
St. Philip or St. Bartholomew (1639 or 1630).
Oil on canvas, 234 × 234 cm.   C. 1.101

The date of this masterpiece by Ribera has been debated, since although at first glance it seems to be signed 1630, the faded signature can be read differently, and besides, the free style of the brushwork and greater colorist feeling depart from the Tenebrist style of the artist's early works. The composition also possesses a greater freedom here which gives the painting a sense of spatial ambience which was unknown in El Spagnoletto's work up to that moment; the forms are perfectly structured and defined by an inverted triangle formed by two clear diagonals and the vertical lines produced by the mast where the martyr is being strung up and the Classical striated shafts of the columns, witnesses to Ribera's love of Ancient art.

Delphine Fitz Darby tells us that this canvas does not represent the martyrdom of St. Bartholomew, as was traditionally accepted, but rather the crucifixion of another younger Apostle who had been tied to the instrument of martyrdom: St. Philip. (Normally St. Bartholomew is portrayed with a graying beard.) In the XIXth century Ribera is considered «the painter of bloody martyrdoms», which is far from the whole truth. Thus, he departs from the bloody aspects in this work in contrast to his contemporary Poussin, who in his «Martyrdom of St. Erasmus» (Vatican), presents us with the moment of torment just as the executioner rolls up the saint's intestines with great care. Ribera, on the other hand, takes as his theme the preparatory moments which makes possible the portrayal of a herculean nude, perhaps modeled for by a Neapolitan stevedore, with all his muscles tensed, which recalls the titans of the Mannerist style. Meanwhile a group of spectators are classically represented on the right as not overly interested in the action; nevertheless on the far left there are some figures of an extremely popular feeling which, due to their realism, remind us of ones to be painted by Goya almost two centuries later.

In 1666 this work was already to be found in the Alcázar in Madrid and it moved to the Prado at the times of its foundation, for it is inventoried in the *Catalog* of 1828. It is signed on a stone in the lower right-hand corner: «Jusepe de Ribera Spaniard 1639 (?)».

PLATE LXIV

FRANCISCO DE ZURBARÁN.
Still-life. Bodegón (1632-42).
Oil on canvas, 84 × 46 cm.　　　　　　　　　　　　　　　　　C. 2.803

Zurbarán is one of the Spanish painters who has done the most beautiful and serene still-lifes. It would have been enough for this painter from the tiny town of Fuentedecantos to have painted the «Still-life» with oranges, lemons and a cup, which has recently left the Contini-Bonacosi Coll. in Florence to go to the Metropolitan Museum in N. Y., to achieve the reputation he enjoys today, because this is one of the most beautiful works within the genre.

The Prado Museum preserves another still-life (illustrated here) which is smaller and less pretentious than the one in New York, but is filled with a special enchantment. Three clay objects and a bronze chalice on a paten are serenely lined up to form this diaphanous «bodegón». Each object here possesses its own independent individuality due to the fact that their properties are delicatey studied and individualized in concept in such a way that if any of them were hypothetically broken, it could not be replaced by any other piece. Each one of these objects has such a highly spiritualized personality that it reminds us of the very Spanish expression of St. Theresa's: «God may be found even among the cooking pots».

These still-lifes are extremely Baroque. As Orozco Díaz has said, this style «broadens the range of objects which may be represented, searching for pictorial and expressive elements beyond the human figure». Because of this, the «bodegón» and still-lifes appear as a consequence of the realistic tendencies proper to the Baroque style. Earlier, in the Renaissance and Middle Ages, the «bodegón» did not exist as an independent genre, but rather as an integral part of another picture. In the case that one might be painted it was only done as a preliminary study, bacause this kind of painting is developed only beginning in the XVIIth century.

The one in the illustration was donated to the Prado Museum by the illustrious politician and patron of the arts Don Francisco A. Cambó, in 1940. Another version is preserved in the collection which the same patron donated to the Barcelona Museum. In this latter the objects are less defined and do not possess as much vivacity, but nevertheless the plasticity is more intense, which makes us think that it might have been done by the artist's son, Juan de Zurbarán, a splendid still-life painter, as well, who followed in his father's footsteps. The two versions, especially the one in Barcelona, are very close to the ones in the Moscow and Kiev Museums which are signed by Juan de Zurbarán.

PLATE LXV

FRANCISCO DE ZURBARÁN.
The Defense of Cádiz Against the English (1634).
Oil on canvas, 302 × 323 cm.   C. 656

Until 1945 when María Luisa Caturla found, after a difficult search, the document which certified that «The Defense of Cádiz» was done by Zurbarán, the majority of critics had been attributing it to the painter Eugenio Cajés. Today this seems impossible to us, especially after Robert Longhi, in 1927, attributed it to the painter from Fuente de Cantos. Nevertheless, Meyer and other scholars of Spanish painting continued to insist on its «false paternity», which had been assigned since the XVIIth century by Ponz in his *Journey* and picked up by Ceán Bermúdez in his famous *Dictionary*. Nevertheless, the German historian pointed out that in it there appeared «very interesting portraits of soldiers who in their bearing and modeling recall somewhat the art of Zurbarán; but Zurbarán is simpler and better in all aspects». Today we cannot leave this painting outside of the orbit of the Extremaduran painter's work, nor consider it an unimportant piece either.

The scene represents the moment in which the English, who besieged Cádiz on November 1, 1625, are repelled. Don Fernando Girón, Governor of the Plaza, gives orders to the military chiefs, seated in his «sedan chair»; he wears a black suit and only his red sash livens the figure up a bit. A starched collar frames a splendid face, full of majesty; in it as well as in the hands, may be seen reminiscences of the paintings of the artist's friend, Velasquez, who introduced Zurbarán, at the Court. This may be observed as well in the knight of the Order of St. James in civilian clothing, with a document in his hand, who stands behind the Commander-in-Chief. The other personages who appear in the scene wear bright clothes, only permited in Spain in combat. Thus, in the center, may be found the Duke of Medina Sidonia (?) with embossed half-armour, a red sash and purplish trousers; a little more to the spectator's right, another quite old general, perhaps Don Lorenzo de Cabrera, is elegantly dressed and the three young soldiers, who receive orders from him, are even more richly dressed. In the background, on shore, the English trooops begin to be repulsed by the Spanish. Meanwhile, at sea, the fleets of the two sides combat harshly, covering almost the entire surface of the water, giving the picture a somewhat archaic feeling. The landscape somewhat recalls that of Cádiz, which Zurbarán might have known.

In April of 1634, Zurbarán moved from Seville to Madrid. On November 13 he was paid a hundred thousand ducats for this painting and «The Labors of Hercules» (also in the Prado), which formed part of the decor of the *Monarchs' Salon* in the Buen Retiro Palace, along with «The Surrender of Breda», by Velasquez, «The Reconquest of Bahia», by Mayno and other paintings commemorating Spanish victories done by Cajés, Carducho and J. Leonardo, besides the royal equestrian portraits done by Velasquez.

PLATE LXVI

Francisco de Zurbarán.
St. Casilda (c. 1640).
Oil on canvas, cut down to 90 × 184 cm.   C. 1.239

This adorable feminine figure is a representation of a saint, but at the same time it is an equally enchanting portrait of a young girl from Seville's «high society» from the beginning of the XVIIth century. We know that it was the custom in certain of Seville's processions for the young maidens to parade with the symbols of the saints, that is why this St. Casilda is portrayed walking along. Her «pose» reminds of those of the models in a present-day fashion show. She is wearing a brocade and richly jeweled dress. Meanwhile her timid yet at the same time bold glance catches the spectator's eye.

This picture is possibly the representation of the saint whose name is Casilda, since in her skirt appear the roses which the pieces of bread which the saint took to the Christian slaves of her father, the King of Toledo, were changed to. Now although her dress is the product of imagination, it has nothing to do with Moorish costumes. Very characteristic of Zurbarán is an anachronistic outlook. Besides, as was customary, the drapery seems to be placed on a mannequin. With this, he achieves very characteristic effects: thus transparent shadows, obtained by layers of glazing, appear in the crisp pleats. With the apparent brittleness of the draperies and the warm tones of the surfaces, he achieves almost pre-Cubist effects. And besides, here, as in almost all of his important works, the feeling of repose, since there doesn't exist the slightest hint of a gesture or movement, is such that he creates a characteriscally static feeling, divorcing himself from the grandiloquence of the contemporary Italian painters. This and the ascetic feeling of his works make a strong spirituality emanate from his paintings, but here in turn there is also mixed in a slight shade of frivolity and coquetry.

These figures of saints formed part of a series to be placed for effect around the walls of a room, generally in a sacristy, although sometimes they were done as single pieces; this has been demonstrated by the literary allusions discovered by Orozco Díaz. In these series, the artist's students intervened and some of the series were repeated by his followers. On other occasions Zurbarán does true saints, whose virtuous expressions differ from this one of Casilda's —who though modest, is nevertheless a gentlewoman.

This «St. Casilda» has lost at least 10 centimeters from the left-hand margin. An engraving exists of «St. Emerenciana», a work by David Teniers, the Elder, which possibly served as the basis for the composition of this painting. Until 1814 it would not be placed on the Palace inventory list (as «a fireplace piece»), which makes us suppose it must have been the fruits of the Napoleonic pillaging of Seville. It is included in the Prado Catalog from 1828 on.

PLATE LXVII

ALONSO CANO.
Dead Christ, Held by an Angel (1648-52).
Oil on canvas, 178 × 121 cm.

C. 629

Alonso Cano, in his first period (Seville, 1624-1638), cultivates, the same as his one-time companion in the workshop, Velasquez, a marked Tenebrist style, which he had taken from his teachers Martínez Montañés and Pacheco and to which he adds elegantly decorative forms of a Sevillian Classicism in his final years in this city. But when he comes to Madrid he begins little by little to abandon this chiaroscuro Naturalism, to a great extent due to the influence of Ribera, for a greater expressivity in color, especially after the restoration of Venetian Renaissance paintings after the fire in the Buen Retiro Palace in 1640. In the retables of the Magdalena Church in Getafe (1645) this change is already noted because although the backgrounds are a bit dark, there is a soft pictorial illusionism in the drapery and flesh which evidences a direct contact with the work of Titian and Veronese. This may be seen as well in «The Kings of Spain», in the Prado.

Possibly the most characteristic of these works in which the new light battles with the old shadows is the «Christ Held by an Angel» (Prado, C. 2.637) in which the importance of color is still only relative, since the grey and white tones are the ones which predominate. We believe this version, although dated by Wethey between 1646-52, due to its Tenebrist feeling must be from the beginning of the artist's Madrilenian period, but previous to the Getafe retables. The work reproduced here is by this time from the last years of the Madrilenian period, in which the shadows are practically dispersed from Cano's paintings, here he only uses those required for the theme and he bases the composition on a picture of Veronese's (today in the Boston Museum) in which two angels appear, while the former picture was taken from an engraving by Golzio. A deathly pale pervades Christ's limp body and the white of the shroud is distinguished from that of the flesh only by subtle gradations, similar to those used by Malevich, the great abstract artist. The color becomes intensified in the lavander tones of the angel's tunic, his face appears in semi-darkness and the hair is copied from the Venetian painting. In the foreground is a washbasin as well as the crown of thorns and the nails which have just been removed from Christ's body; these are the last vestiges of the Passion. Thus the painter, with a mystical feeling, wanted to remove all signs of violence and pain from the Lord; His face is serene and His body relaxed. The carmineblues of the sketchy landscape, in which a small, mysterious city may be intuited, accentuate the dramatic tension. In spite of Wethey's negative position, we think this version is an original replica with a student's intervention.

The work was acquired by the Marquis of La Ensenada in 1769. In 1772 it was in the «passageway to the King's bedroom», in the Oriente Palace; later it was moved to the private oratory. A third workshop replica exists in the Prado.

DIEGO VELASQUEZ.
The Adoration of the Magi (1619).
Oil on canvas, 125 × 203 cm.

C. 1.166

This is the only work by Velasquez in the Prado which is without doubt from his initial Sevillian period. In it, as was usual in his first period, it is possible that members of his family served as models, considering the intimate feeling of the picture. Thus, it is very probable that his wife Juana Pacheco served as the model for the figure of the Virgin. There only exists one portrait of his wife which is completely documented, the one which was done by her son-in-law Juan Bautista del Mazo, in «The Painter's Family» in the Museum of Vienna, in which she appears as a grandmother taking care of her grandchildren. This makes it difficult to identify other portraits by comparing it to the Vienna one, since the facial features are old and wrinkled by this time. Another portrait, on the other hand, the «Sibyl», in the Prado Museum must be rejected, since there is no proof that it is in fact a portrait; nonetheless, the face of the «Frere Immaculate Conception» (1618, National Gallery in London) is very similar to the one of the Virgin in this «Adoration of the Magi». Besides, it is very close to some Immaculate Conceptions by Pacheco, and may suggest that she modeled for both her father and her husband. Velasquez marries his teacher's daughter on April 23, 1618. (Buendía, *Goya*, No. 23, 1950, pgs. 281 and ff.)

Besides this possible portrait, the figure of the kneeling King has been identified as a self-portrait of Velasquez himself, and that of the other King who accompanies him, as his father-in-law Pacheco. Recently there has also been an attempt to identify the Baby Jesus as the painter's eldest daughter. As we see, the iconography coincides with the date which appears on the painting: 1619. Although some have read it as 1617, this must be rejected, not only because newer technical methods, such as the quartz lamp, clearly show that it is a nine, but also because the pictorial method employed by Velasquez is different from the one he uses two years earlier, since here he has almost abandoned the use of earthen tones and utilizes asphalt more moderately than in previous paintings. Although certain Caravaggiesque touches remain, the stylistic influence of Luis Tristán may be perceived, and is confirmed by literary texts. The color is also intensified here in comparison to his previous painting, especially in the greens and blues. The drapery still forms broad, thick pleats, reminding us of Montañés' sculptures. In the background is an abbreviated landscape with cloudy skies which remind us of Toledo. Velasquez uses a diagonal composition, which had already been utilized in the Mannerist style and was still cultivated by some Baroque artists.

Although in the Prado Catalog it is considered to have come from El Escorial, where it had been attributed to Zurbarán, it is more probable that this was the work Velasquez did for the San Luis Novitiate House of the Jesuits in Seville. According to R. Twiss (1775), a painting with the same theme existed in the collection of Don Francisco de Bruna, in Seville.

PLATE LXIX

DIEGO VELASQUEZ.
View of the Villa Medici Gardens (1630).
Oil on canvas, 38 × 44 cm.   C. 1.211

The two views of the Roman villa which belonged to the Medici Family are without a doubt the two most beautiful landscapes done by Velasquez and only the dazzling background of «Las Lanzas» may be compared to them. They are done, so it seems, during his first trip to Italy in 1630 while he was living in the above-mentioned country home; in an attempt to escape from the torrid Roman summer, he sought refuge among the lovely trees and cool relaxation of this ancient villa. But he becomes ill, possibly with malaria, and he is obliged to leave the villa and move to a branch of the Spanish Embassy. This hypothesis, rooted in tradition, has been documented, since in 1634 Juan de Villanueva acquires four landscapes from Velasquez to be given to Philip IV; two of them are the ones preserved in the Prado. Today this is upheld by José Camón Aznar and López Rey, refuting another wide-spread theory with a formalistic basis, which —due to the spontaneity of the technique, which is almost Impressionist— considered them to be from Velasquez' second stay in Italy.

There is no doubt that the execution is so advanced that it reminds us of his later periods; their rapid, sketch-like qualities —and they could well be sketches— bring them close to the first pictures of the early French Impressionists or of the realist Corot. But these paintings have been taken directly from nature. Velasquez must have set up his easel in the garden, painting two «pleinair» which must have been among the first ones to be done in the entire history of painting. Up to that time, landscapes had been almost always the background for some scene, with some exceptions —such as the landscape which appears in the «Death of the Virgin» (Plate XXV) by Mantegna— they were all painted in the studio without worrying too much about reality.

In this sketch of the landscape the light falls almost vertically with the dazzling solar illumination filtering straight down through the branches, producing intense shadows which fall with a leaden weight. (In the Prado the light is filtered through like this only in Veronese's painting of «Venus and Adonis» (Plate XXXVII) and possibly the Venetian painter did this only by fortuitous accident because he never repeats the effect in any of his other paintings.) Because of this lighting effect, Lafuente Ferrari rightly calls Velasquez' painting «Noontime»; while he calls its companion piece, which has a more waning light, «Afternoon». This second landscape is a of a freer technique than the first, the two figures which appear in the foreground are also «Impressionistic» and in the background, in the Palladian archway appears the famous statue of Ariadne.

In 1666 the two paintings were in the Alcazar in Madrid, and after the fire of 1734, they were moved to the Buen Retiro Palace.

PLATE LXX

DIEGO VELASQUEZ.
The Surrender of Breda, «Las Lanzas» (1634-1635).
Oil on canvas, 367 × 307 cm.   C. 1.172

Here we can see the moment in which Ambrosio Espinola, commander-in-chief of the Spanish infantry in Flanders, receives the key to the reconquered city of Breda from the hands of the Dutch governor, Justino de Nassau; the storming of the city took place on June 2, 1625, nevertheless the symbolic surrender of the city was enacted 3 days later. Eight years passed before Velasquez was commissioned to immortalize the scene as one of a series of Spanish victories for the Monarchs' Salon in the Buen Retiro Palace.

As usual, Velasquez does background work for the painting, but this time with special care, as Angulo and other critics have shown. Thus, he uses different sources for the compositon, among which, for the central group, stands out an illustration of Essau and Jacob which appears in various versions of the *Bible* from the time of a Lyon edition in 1553 on, and which still is in use in the beginning of the XVIIth century. Now then, this composition in turn—or possibly the one of Velasquez himself—is based on the representation of «Concordia» in the famous «Emblemata» by Alciato, since the theme of the picture is a settlement. Amiability is expressed in Espínola's face and his placing of the hand on the shoulder of the conquered enemy, who tries humbly to kneel is an eternal symbol of pardon and peace. For this group he also took into account the «Christ and the Centurion» by Veronese, the composition of which he also keeps in mind, as well as El Greco's «San Mauricio», for the group of Spanish soldiers. The portrait of Espinola is based on real life, for Velasquez met him on his first trip to Italy (1629-30) and for the one of Nassau, he referred to an engraving. The faithful interpretation of the Dutch countryside is admirable, especially since, basing his work on inferior paintings, he achieves one of the most beautiful «plein-air» pictures in painting, applying a perspective system very close to that of the Dutch landscape artists. The overall composition, as in other scenes by Velasquez («The Drunkards», «Vulcan's Forge», «The Spinners») is opened out with a vertical line on the extreme left and closed by an oval curve on the right, similar to the «Pietà» by Van der Weyden. Recent X-ray studies have revealed numerous changes made by the artist; the horse, for example, was originally almost in the center of the painting.

Saved from the fires which destroyed the Buen Retiro Palace in 1640 and the Alcázar in 1734, it was moved to the Royal Palace and then to the Prado when it was opened.

PLATE LXXI

DIEGO VELASQUEZ.
Prince Baltasar Carlos (1635-1636).
Oil on canvas, 173 × 209 cm.   C. 1.180

This equestrian portrait of Prince Baltasar Carlos is done at the same time as the other equestrian portraits of his parents and grandmother which are in the Prado and were painted for the Monarchs' Salon of the Buen Retiro Palace in Madrid, and in which the paintings were already hung by 1637.

Here Baltasar Carlos, though he seems to be happily riding in the hills of the Pardo —the Guadarrama mountain range, with the snowy peak of La Maliciosa standing out, may be seen in the background— his expression is full of melancholy sadness, although Velasquez has kindly painted it somewhat out of focus, as he will later do with the Palace buffoons. The Prince's poor health will bring him to an early death.

This picture was placed quite high up over a doorway, which would explain a certain disproportion in the horse's belly, but also one must realize that this animal was painted by Velazquez after it had died and then been stuffed at the request of the Prince. But in spite of this, the horse's head is a splendid example of realism and the animal's snorting energy makes us think of the poet Góngora's line: «In vain the foam of the Andaluz horse, strains at the bridle of silvery gold». Confirming the King's painter's capacity for observation of reality is the fact that he represents the Prince's boots filled out so that his small feet rest more firmly in the stirrups. The figure of the Prince is delicately painted in harmonious colors: a black hat, with a feather; a gold tissue jacket and pants of green velvet embroidered with gold; a lace vandyck collar, a pink sash and a general's staff.

Copies of an original lost today of a more naturalist type exist showing the Prince at the Royal Riding Academy with the Duke of Olivares in the background.

218

PLATE LXXII

DIEGO VELASQUEZ.
Don Sebastián de Morra (c. 1644).
Oil on canvas, 81 × 106 cm.   C. 1.202

Lafuente Ferrari, with great precision, has called the four portraits of the buffoons which cover the wall of one of the Prado's rooms the «polyptych of the monsters», since these figures were animated by lives which were physically and mentally mutilated. We know their names: Juan Calabazas («Calabacillas»), Diego de Acedo («The Cousin»), Francisco Lezcano («The Boy from Vallecas»), and the one which is reproduced here, Don Sebastián de Morra. Now not all the buffoons or jesters at the Court were deformed; rather some of the «comedians» who had the talent to distract the King and his Court with jokes, card and magic tricks, etc., were perfectly normal. Moreno Villa, who has done an exhaustive study of them, affirmed that they were a sort of escape valve for the rigid customs of the Palace.

The jester «Don Sebastián de Morra» is without a doubt the most beautiful picture in the series, at least as far as coloring goes, since his red overcoat with gold braid stands out vividly in contrast to the green breeches and doublet. Don Sebastián (the title «Don» didn't really mean much) was in the Court from 1643 on, when he left the service of the Cardinal Infante Don Fernando, who was at that time in Flanders, for that of Prince Baltasar Carlos, who grew fond of him and left him a set of steel arms when he died. Don Sebastián dies in 1649. Velasquez, as he does in other paintings, such as in his equestrian portrait of the powerful Duke of Olivares (whose hunchback he disguises), attenuates with the posture of his subject his defects, but without hiding them. In this manner, placing his small figure seated and facing the spectator, the shortness of his legs is disguised, but his short, deformed arms make his dwarfishness obvious. Although Velasquez usually gives the buffoons a humanitarian touch, possibly Morra's strong character —which may be seen in his harsh features— makes the artist ridicule him with this absurd posture, in which the soles of his shoes confront the spectator and which makes him seem like a rag doll, or rather as Justi writes, «like a dog chained to his doghouse».

The portrait was painted around 1644. It was damaged in the fire at the Alcázar, and then had to be cut down and reframed. At least for a while it had an oval frame, and its silhouette may still be seen. In 1746 it was already in the Buen Retiro Palace.

PLATE LXXIII

DIEGO VELASQUEZ.
The Family of Philip IV, «Las Meninas» (1656).
Oil on canvas, 318 × 276 cm.   C. 1174

The zenith of Velasquez's painting is the work which is called in the Palace inventories from 1666 on, the «Picture of the Family». No one dared to change this title until Don Pedro de Madrazo in his *Catalog* of 1843 gives it the name of «Las Meninas». The success of this new nomenclature was complete, to such an extent that this is how it is generally referred to today. We should note that the Portuguese term «meninas», little girls, was applied in the Palace to the «maids of honor».

Since this painting was done in the XVIIth century, its fame has constantly grown. Thus Luca Giordano, when he stood for the first time in front of this work, called it «the theology of painting», an opinion which even today no one considers exaggerated. Theophile Gautier, surprised by the spatial effect, asked «where is the picture»?», broaching the problem of its volumetric character. Camón Aznar, one of the scholars who has best penetrated its secrets, considers that it is not a «passive space», such as in Gothic or Renaissance painting, but rather that its depth is determined by the «interdistances», by the light, by the «reciprocal relationships between the objects» and the postures of the personages, which create «a dense and palpable spatial complexity». The lack of tile which neutralizes the floor obliges us to substitute a new spatial perspective for the old optical one. Therefore although the ambience is totally real there exists a certain atmospheric idealization, balanced by a systematization of the perspective, which has been attained by using a colorist system which had already been initiated by the Venetian painters. Here, though, it is simplified since the chromatic atmosphere tends toward an almost monotonous sobriety. In order to help achieve it, the space is syncopated by graduated splotches of light which are mixed in with the gray tones of the shadows on the floor and walls; thus the lack of tiles, which neutralizes the floor, is compensated for by the black frames of Mazo's paintings and the perspective distribution of the figures, since as Alpatov has demonstrated, the canvas is composed according to the rules of the «Golden Section». As we see, Velasquez has substituted the traditional optical perspective with a new one based on space and lighting. This last element, in an especially complicated sense, achieves the perfect distribution of the various sources of light in the pictorial space which have been adroitly interlaced. From a door, invisible for the spectator, which is opposite the one in the background, a first flood of light focuses on the figures in the foreground and on the painter himself, and projected in a syncopated manner from the balconies, luminous spotches subtly put the various personages into or out of focus. From the door in the background a great torrent of light, extending along the stairway, penetrates the room accentuating the perspective relief. With all this the most perfect example of aerial perspective in the entire history of painting is achieved.

                                                                          PLATE LXXIV

But this is not the only pictorial problem studied here, rather as Birkmeyer has said, there is also a search for a «fourth dimension». This is based on the attainment of the forward movement, which this author calls «contrast», since it alternates, moving back and forth from the outside to the inside of the painting and rebounds from the interior to the exterior. Thus the easel and the open door in the background are used by Velasquez as «foils» to reflect and disperse the light. Besides this, Velasquez, the Infanta, Maribárbola and the chamberlain, by fixing their stares on the spectator, accentuate the tensión; and even more, with the ghostly appearance of the King and Queen reflected in the mirror confronting the spectator, the projection of the painting toward the exterior is intensified. This complex feeling created by Velasquez is accentuated even more if we think that Velasquez has represented himself inside the picture while painting the King and Queen, of whom we only see, so it seems, their effigies because they themselves must be situated outside of the picture, almost at its very edge, more or less the place from where Velasquez painted the work. Now, the faces which are reflected are not the real flesh and blood ones, but rather the painted images which Velasquez was doing on the canvas which is stretched on the easel in the foreground and only a fragment of which is captured, because if the sovereigns were being reflected in reality, their size in the mirror would be smaller, as the architect Moya has demonstrated («Arquitectura» Mag., 1961).

In spite of the extremely complicated setting, «Las Meninas» gives such a sensation of simplicity that it caused Ortega y Gasset to remark: «Its total candor makes it fabulously sublime». For Sánchez Cantón the theme is almost that of a Dutch collective portrait: the Infanta bursts into the artist's studio, is thirsty and a «menina» offers her water in a vessel from Estremoz whose clay cools and sweetens the water; meanwhile, another maid curtsies to her in this moment when the maids of honor bow down, Velasquez makes the King and Queen appear in the mirror. All of this reminds us of some of the theatrical scenes of the times; Valbuena Prat, before anyone, related Velasquez to Calderón.

To make a brief description of the personages, we start on the spectator's left: forming an undulating line appear the painter himself, Isabel de Velasco, the Infanta Margarita, María Agustina Sarmiento, the dwarves Maribárbola and Pertusato. In the middleground we see as well the duenna Doña Marcela de Ulloa and a ladies' escort, who according to some is Diego de Azcona, though it is hard to be sure, since as we have said he is sort of blurred in semi-shadows. On the stairway in the background, the Palace Chamberlain, José Nieto Velasquez appears opening the curtains. And in the mirror we have the King and Queen, But there exists an extremely important yet invisible personage —the spectator— for as Orozco astutely indicated: «We are like another personage which has started to open another door and with an instinctive curiosity we stand watching what is going on in the room where Velasquez is painting».

PLATE LXXV

DIEGO VELASQUEZ.
Dispute Between Pallas and Arachne, «The Spinners» (c. 1657).
Oil on canvas, 289 × 220 cm.   C. 1.173

In 1948, the illustrious historian of Spanish art, Angulo Iñiguez dug up the old name for «The Spinners» as it appeared in the Inventory of 1664: «The Fable of Arachne». Here is the myth which served as the basis for the painting according to Ovid's *Metamorphoses*: Minerva, inventor of the loom, is considered to be the most important weaver in the universe, but in Lydia the young Arachne weaves material which is the wonder of the entire region and Minerva therefore challenges her to a contest. In the foreground of this painting we see the dispute, with the two principal figures based on two *Ignudi* by Michelangelo in the Sistine Chapel, which makes Professor Angulo think Velasquez painted this in homage to the Florentine artist. Meanwhile, in the background, we see the moment of vengeance, in which the goddess changes the young Lydian girl into a spider, before a tapestry which represents the Rape of Europa, as portrayed by Titian. And in the foreground, next to one of the ladies who contemplate the scene, is a cello which may allude to the use of music to treat spider bites, but Professor Azcárate has suggested, referring to Ripa's *Iconology* (a copy of which Velasquez had in his library), that it is a symbolic envisionment of obedience to the Monarchy and punishment of rebels —a political allusion to the Spain of the painter's own times, which would confirm Tolnay's theory of the Neoplatonic nature of this painting. But the artist, who always bases his work on the tangible world, will take as a source of inspiration the Santa Isabela Tapestry Restoration Workshop in Madrid. When Justi proclaimed that this was the first time that a workshop had been pictorially represented (he was ignorant of the Dutch and Flemish precedents), «the *socialist holier-than-thou* attitude of the turn of the century», says Ortega y Gasset, «fervently picked up this formula». Now then, the illustrious thinker recognizes that «none of the figures is individualized» and later adds that «without doubt it was to keep the attention from being fixed on any particular component of the picture and to make it be the work as a whole which acts upon the spectator». He is correct, for in this picture—which he previously called «The Fates»—there is only one essential protagonist: the symbol of service to the State. Now then, by balancing the compositional harmony and lighting, as he would do in «Las Meninas», the artist converts it into one of the summits of art.

In 1664, as «The Fable of Arachne», it was owned by the royal huntsman, Don Pedro de Arce. In the XVIIIth century, with the motive of a restoration carried out to remedy the damage caused by the fire in the Alcázar (1734) an upper section of 48.5 cm. was added with a very Goyesque arch which altered the calm equilibrium of the original composition. In spite of its defective state of preservation, this painting, along with «Las Meninas», ranks as *the* masterpiece by the «King of Painters».

226   PLATE LXXVI

CLAUDIO COELLO.
St. Dominic of Guzman (c. 1683).
Oil on canvas, 160 × 240 cm.

C. 662

This superb painting formed part of a series done by Claudio Coello around 1683 for the Madrilenian Rosarito Convent (Dominican Order). From among these works, the Prado possesses a «St. Rose of Lima», which is a companion piece to the picture which we are discussing and, besides, in the San Fernando Academy is «The Virgin Appearing to St. Dominic». Perhaps also belonging to this group is the impressive «St. Catalina», which has been in the Wellington Collection in London since it was appropriated from King Joseph Bonaparte in the Battle of Vitoria.

A method which is very typical of Claudio, the «trompe l'oeil», that is, the art of deceiving the spectator's eye, is used here. In this way the saint's majestic form in black and white is emphasized by placing it against a simulated pedestal of gilded wood, which makes it recall a figure from a retable. Two arches supported by low, thick columns with Doric capitals, as well as draped red curtains, frame the saint, with the scenographic feeling characteristic of the last third of the XVIIth century. In his right hand, St. Dominic carries a black and white processional cross, the emblem of the Order of Preachers, and in his left, he holds the white lilies which are his symbol. Meanwhile, a dog at his feet has a lighted torch in his mouth and next to it appears a globe of the earth. In the background we see a hint of the blue-green cloudy sky which is very characteristic of Claudio's painting. All of this, as we have said, lends this work the aspect of an ecclesiastical set, whose symbolic meaning is derived from the exaltation of Faith and of the Order of Preachers.

It proceeds from the Trinidad Museum, along with the «St. Rose of Lima», where the two had been provisionally attributed to Claudio Coello.

BARTOLOMÉ ESTEBAN MURILLO.
The Good Shepherd (c. 1660).
Oil on canvas, 123 × 101 cm.   C. 962

Murillo's final period begins with the paintings done for the Church of Santa María la Blanca in Seville, although we could also consider them, as Mayer does, as the culmination of his second style. They must have been painted in 1665, when work had just been finished on this famous Sevillian church, which was founded to commemorate the brief in which Pope Alexander VII had proclaimed the Dogma of the Mystery of the Immaculate Conception. Seville, which had been a fervent supporter of it since the XVIth century, showed its happiness in this way. Torre Farfán, in his description of the festivities celebrated for the inauguration of this church, describes for us an altar painted by Murillo in which a «Good Shepherd» appeared; the *Catalog* identifies it with this one, but as Angulo points out, it must not be so, for the Sevillian figure wears sandals, while the one in the Prado is barefoot. But the masterpieces done by the Sevillian painter for this church are the poorly-nicknamed «semicircular arches», today in the Museum in Madrid as well, in which there is a reference to the founding of the Church of Santa Maria Maggiore in Rome. Of these two paintings, the most lovely is «The Patriarch's Dream». Possibly it is Canon Justino de Neve, a learned man, who commissions them and gives the themes to Murillo.

The Child Jesus Who is portrayed here has been painted sitting down by Murillo, in contrast to other versions, in which he shows Him standing. His pose, as Mayer has indicated, is derived from an engraving done by Stefano della Bella for his *Metamorphoses* by Ovid, to represent Cupid. The Child rests His left hand on a lamb, which is painted with a realism worthy of Zurbarán; in the hazy background the flock may be seen. In His right hand He holds the crook. And behind Him appears part of a Classical entablature, and a little further back the base and lower part of a striated Roman shaft; it is possible that Murillo was directly inspired by ruins in Italica, sung by the Sevillian poets of his times. Although the expression and posture of the little personage are a bit preciosiste —since this painting, like the majority of Murillo's work, is done to please a heterogeneous public— the pink carmine of the clothing possesses a great beauty and the landscape is done with a lyrical feeling characteristic of Murillo's last period, in which the atmospheric ambience gives almost Rembrandtesque qualities to the backgrounds —in them the greens and blues are modified with thin reddish glazes. There are also certain reminiscences in these landscape backgrounds of the Neopolitan painting of the times, especially that of Salvator Rosa. Thus we see that Murillo does not lock himself up in a Sevillian ivory tower, but rather through paintings and engravings is in contact with his epoch, creating a personal style, in which though there is room for affectation he also achieves creations of a subtle beauty and elegance in the formal aspect.

PLATE LXXVIII

Nicolas Poussin.
Parnassus (1625-1629).
Oil on canvas, 197 × 145 cm.   C. 2.313

Around 1620, Poussin makes his first trip to Italy; motivated by the admiration he felt for the Classical world and by his passion for Raphael's painting, he abandons Paris for Rome. After twenty years he returned to France but only for a short stay of two years; his adopted homeland for his entire life will be the Italian Peninsula. Altthough he spends his first four Italian years in Florence, he will settle in the Eternal City, studying Classical sculpture and architecture without neglecting literary studies of Antiquity which will be very useful for thematic iconography and composition of his works, in which a formal order reigns. A good example of this is the «Parnassus», a work done in his early Roman years and in which his devotion for the painter from Urbino makes him stick close to the composition of the same theme which the latter did in the Stanza della Segnatura, in the Vatican.

Now just like his Italian comrades, the Bolognese Eclectics, headed by the Carracci Brothers, and possibly due to their influence, Poussin's work falls under the sway of Titian's coloring. Thus the landscape setting and the amorinos fluttering about in the trees of Parnassus can be seen to have been freely copied from the «Worship of Venus» (C. 419), which at that time was still in Italy. The nude girl in the foreground, representing Castalia (the personification of the fountain of the Oracle at Delfos) is somewhat reminiscent of the nude which appears in the «Bacchanal» (Pl. XXXIV), although executed in a colder manner due to the influence of Classical sculpture. Behind her, with an academic air, appears Calliope, crowning Homer with laurels. The artist's love for Classicism makes one see in some of the Parnassian figures a direct inspiration in Roman sculptures, especially in the delicate group on the right. In this masterpiece, Poussin combines the expression of «ideal beauty», which will be the main aesthetic factor in his painting, with a realism which is still within the early Baroque style, which caused it to be beloved by Eugenio D'Ors who highly praises it in his well-known little book *Three Hours in the Prado Museum*.

Already in 1746 the «Parnassus» figured in the inventory of Philip V's collection. A preparatory sketch for it is conserved, and before 1667 an engraving of it had been done by Jean Dughet.

STYLE OF NICOLAS POUSSIN.
Landscape with Ruins (after 1648).
Oil on canvas, 98 × 72 cm.   C. 2.308

If we had to pick the painter most opposed to Velasquez' style, it would be Poussin, a strict contemporary of his. A French painter of a critical, almost glacial temperament, he scarcely takes anything from reality, since his figures are inspired by Classical sculptures, which lends his compositions an abstract feeling. In the landscapes something similar occurs; starting from the Carraccis' ideal conception, the evasion of reality reaches even greater proportions than it had in the Bolognese school. Poussin visits Rome and its surroundings, and with passion, but also with a great delicacy, he does sketches of everything that interests him. He later transforms and composes these sketches to paint his landscape pictures and sometimes he adds forms which are inspired by Classical literature, which he so loved.

There is nothing more removed from the two landscapes of the Medici Villa by Velasquez than the work which is reproduced here. Although it seems it is not the work of Poussin, since Blunt definitely attributed it to Jean Lemaire (1598-1659), it is within Poussin's style. Here not the least feeling of reality exists; rather this work is the result of an intellectual re-creation. The first thing the spectator who contemplates this picture notices is its formal beauty, achieved in part by the harmonious balance produced by a series of diagonals quite within Baroque Italian taste, which had already been used in the Mannerist Period. These lines divide the space in an even manner. The figures are also placed throughout the picture in a harmonious way, which by means of the touches of color accentuates the serenity. However, human beings do not appear, but rather statues, for Poussin —and Lemaire, his faithful follower— men and statues are the same. The buildings, geometrically stylized, are pure cubic forms; even the monumental ruins have been reelaborated as well. The grey-gold light accentuates the greenish blues, achieving an effect of frozen beauty.

Blunt supposes that it is from Lemaire's final period, after 1648, the date of a painting by Poussin which served as a model for this one. In 1746 it is found among Philip V's paintings in La Granja, which had been bought from the painter Carlo Maratta.

Claude Gellée, «Le Lorrain».
Port Scene: The Embarkation of St. Paula Romana at Ostia (c. 1648).
Oil on canvas, 145 × 211 cm.   C.2.254

Along with Poussin Claude Lorrain was one of the few French painters from the XVIIth century to be included in the Spanish Royal Collection. Philip IV, in spite of being a great connoisseur of the painting of his times, did not come to appreciate the French painters of such a popular and realistic taste as Le Nain or La Tour, but he did, on the other hand, know the works of the principal courtly painters of Spain's neighboring country. For this reason there are important examples of Claude's works in the Prado. But perhaps his masterpiece from among the pieces in this collection is this «Port Scene». It forms part of a series of four vertical pictures more or less of the same size and of similar themes which the painter was commissioned to do directly by Philip IV.

The work which is reproduced was done when Claude Lorrain was at the height of his powers. He can therefore achieve effects of wispy light in the clouds which stand out above the blue-green waters of the port; but more surprising are the mother-of-pearl effects which he attains in the intermediate zones and which, except for Turner, no painter has so perfectly executed. All this is framed by buildings with a Classical feeling which give the composition a majestic equilibrium and help to establish a sensation of depth, not discontinuous, as in other works of his, but which is rather perspectivistic and luminous.

As in the majority of works from the artist's prime, the figures are minuscule in comparison to the scenic background which surrounds them and perhaps Claude was influenced by the predominant philosophical idea of the times: man's pitiful stature in dramatic comparison to the harmonious beauty of Nature or even in comparison to the majesty of his own artistic creations.

The following inscription may be read on a tablet in the painting: «imbarco Sta. Paula Romana per terra Sta.»; and on a large stone block: «Portus Ostiensis a A(ugusti) et Tra(ini)».

Along with the companion pieces—the «Burial of St. Serapion» (C. 2.252), also of paleo-Christian hagiography, like the one described, and two others with Old Testament themes: «Moses Rescued fron the Nile» (C. 2.253) and «Tobias and the Archangel Raphael» (C. 2.255)—it was already in the Buen Retiro Palace at the beginning of the XVIIIth century.

JEAN-ANTOINE WATTEAU.
The Marriage Contract (1714 ?).
Oil on canvas, 55 × 47 cm.   C. 2.353

This little picture is a good example of the *fête galante*, a favorite theme of Watteau's, in which the high society and bourgeoisie of the XVIIIth century appears elegantly enjoying themselves in leafy parks. Nevertheless the eternal happiness and idyll of love are enveloped in just a shade of melancholy, reminding us that the farce will soon be over with the curtain coming down.

«The Marriage Contract» forms a set along with the canvas, «Festivity in a Park», and these are the only works by the «libertin d'esprit» which the Prado possesses. They may be dated near the end of the artist's short life (d. 1721) while tuberculosis was already undermining his health; this is documented by 1714.

Underneath the shade of some trees the bride and groom-to-be are seated and they are accompanied by relatives and a notary. The marriage vows, according to ancient custom, are accompanied by festivities of music and dancing in which the oppulent countrymen —or aristocrats— since the fine clothing and willows in the foreground set a courtly scene, enjoy themselves. Some of the guests take advantage of the occasion for flirtation. All of this at first glance produces a sensation of sickly sweetness which disappears when we study the work carefully, because a tenuous melancholy flows around the little figures and takes over the atmosphere of the small painting as well as the spirit of the spectator. This is normal in the *fêtes galantes* by Watteau, in which no one laughs. But here some extraordinary things come up. We may observe that one of the heads is deformed —to the point of having two faces. Thus we see that on the right side of the reproduction a lady kisses her gallant, but she has another surfeited face which avoids the kiss that the twin mouth accepts. Similar episodes are repeated with more or less clarity, and are the results of Watteau's sarcastic character. His friends said of him that «il était né caustique» («he was born caustic») and in him the sarcasm is an expression of the bitterness of an intelligent but shy person, incapable of overcoming the society that surrounds him. In «The Marriage Contract», Watteau poses the problem of «erotic contradictions», before Goya does in his «Dream of Lies and Inconstancy» in which there also appears a double face, on the figure of the Duchess of Alba. But if the Aragonese painter uses satire because of his robustly healthy jealousy, Watteau does so due to a misogynist's impotence, as an embittered person who has never loved.

The memory of Rubens' «Garden of Love» is present here. It was possibly acquired while Watteau was alive, by Isabel de Farnesio; in 1746 it was listed among the paintings belonging to this queen in La Granja Palace.

PLATE LXXXII

GIOVANNI BATTISTA TIEPOLO.
The Immaculate Conception (1767-1769).
Oil on canvas, 152 × 279 cm.   C. 363

This «Immaculate Conception» is one of the most delightful representations of its kind in the Prado Museum; according to Sánchez Cantón, no
more beautiful version of this mystery than this one existed in Italian
painting. Mary is represented with a proud beauty and almost sculptural
majesty, and the sensation is reinforced by her spindle-like shape. While
in the majority of Spanish paintings on this theme she appears as a child,
such as in Murillo's works, here Mary is a fully mature woman who stands
with a triumphal air over the serpent which writhes on the earth. This
New Eve appears surrounded by cherubim and the Marian symbols in a
misty blue sky.

Tiepolo is invited to Madrid by Charles III, arriving June 4, 1762, accompanied by his sons Domenico and Lorenzo. He immediately begins the
frescoes in the Royal Palace in Madrid and finishes them in 1766. In September of 1767 he accepts a commission to do the altar paintings for the
Franciscan Convent of San Pascual in the Royal Seat at Aranjuez, and
among them is this «Immaculate Conception». In August of 1769 they
were already finished and in place on the altar; but the winds of artistic
fashion shifted to a Neoclassical taste, which cooled the convulsions of the
Late Baroque style. As a result, these works were hidden away in dark
rooms and were even fragmented. But in spite of Father Eleta's harsh
persecutions this «Conception» scarcely suffered harm and now presents
us with a prodigious expression of Rococo technique, so characteristic of
Giovanni Battista's final work. It is possible that a minimal participation
of his sons exists, but the work is characteristic of Giovanni Battista.
Besides, it is signed: *Dn Juan Ba(tis)tta Tiepolo inv. et pinx.*; that is, it
was thought up and painted by him .

Today, besides the other paintings which made up the retables at Aranjuez conserved in the Prado («St. Francis Receiving the Stigmata», C. 3.652;
«St. Anthony of Padua with the Baby Jesús», C. 3.007; «St. Pascual Bailón»,
C. 364 a, damaged), others are preserved in various collections, such as the
picture of «St. Pedro de Alcántara», of an oval shape, which matched the
«St. Anthony», kept in the Royal Palace in Madrid, and the «St. Charles Bo-
rromeo», never installed, possibly because he was protector of the Jesuits
during his administration of the Milanese see; this work is today conserved
in the Cincinnati Museum in damaged condition, but thanks to its preparatory sketch, it can ideally be reconstructued.

In the collection of Lord Kinnaird (London)—before, it was owned by
Bayeu—a preparatory sketch existed and an engraving of this «Immaculate
Conception» is known. Since 1828 it figures in the catalogs of the Prado
Museum.

PLATE LXXXIII

JOSHUA REYNOLDS.
Portrait of a Clergyman.
Oil on canvas, 77 × 64 cm.   C. 2.858

   Sir Joshua Reynolds (born in Plympton-Earlys [Devonshire] on July 16, 1727; died in London on February 23, 1792) is, along with Hogarth, the true creator of English painting. His originality is strengthened by a basis of perseverance in his studies. He begins his artistic career imitating the gentle Ramsay and Van Dyck, along with Hogarth and Rembrandt. In Rome (1750-1752) he discovers Raphael and Michelangelo and with them, the secret of the «grand style», even doing portraits inspired by Classical statuary; thus he represents «Commodore Keppel»—who had treated the artist to the trip around the Mediterranean and took him to Italy—with the pose of the Belvedere Apollo and «Lady Blake» as a Juno. The influence of Reni also makes itself felt, for Reynolds adopts his chiaroscurist modeling (Pl. LXI), achieving his loveliest portraits between 1760 and 1770. Success in society accompanies him and he creates the Royal Academy. At the end of his life, due to Rubens' influence, he moves closer to reality, doing groups in which the personages comport themselves in a relaxed manner.
   Although this is not one of the British painter's masterpieces, it is representative of his style. This is one of the characteristic, officially-done portraits which were hung in the picture galleries of institutions very typical of the social structure of Great Britain, such as asylums, hospitals, poor houses, etc. Possibly this personage was an important member of one of these centers since he reminds us of the type of administrator described by Dickens. He is dressed simply, in accordance with his dignity as a clergyman or magistrate, in a black suit with a white collar and he wears a wig. This feeling of sobriety is very characteristic of the painting from Reynold's middle period. In the face we may note a careful observation of the personage. Therefore, although it is not an exceptional picture, it is a work of sociological and psychological interest.
   It was bought from the Marquis of San Miguel by the Ministry of National Education in 1943, and is among the paintings which the Prado has acquired in the last thirty years in an attempt to remedy its lack of English paintings. Neither do there exist important samples of this country's painting in other public Spanish collections; only the Lázaro Galdiano Museum in Madrid possesses an important group of paintings from this school.

PLATE LXXXIV

Thomas Gainsborough.
Doctor Isaac Henrique Sequeira (1770-1774).
Oil on canvas, 102 × 127 cm.   C. 2.979

This portrait is an important work within Gainsborough's production. It was possibly done in the final years of his stay in the wonderful English spa of Bath, where from 1770 to 1774 the artist painted the English aristocracy which went there to cure its afflictions or boredom.   It might also be considered (as Waterhouse thought, but was not sure) to be from his last London period (1774-1788).   Now its stylistic relationship with the portrait of William Lowndes, dated 1771, and with other portraits from this same epoch makes us fix its date earlier, and we believe it must have been executed between 1770 and 1774.   In this moment his portraits have a hazy quality which make the faces appear somewhat blurred, as if they were out of focus, and it would not be unusual that this was an influence from Velasquez, whom he so admired.   In his final London period the technique is denser and more realistic, possibly because he restudied Van Dyck's work more directly.   These last years at Bath are the greatest ones of his artistic career, since he does a series of paintings, such as the one reproduced here, in which he makes no concessions to the people who commission the works. From this moment are the lovely draperies of the famous «Blue Boy». Goya, on occassion, allows himself to be influenced by the English painting of Gainsborough and Reynolds; thus his portrait of Ceán Bermudez recalls the one of Sequeira —the poses are almost identical.

The figure of the doctor, Isaac Henrique Sequeira, appears in this picture dressed in blue, like in the above-mentioned «Blue Boy», the colbalt shades have a touch of green, giving them an especially elegant tone.   The Doctor is seated on a Chippendale chair and rests his hands on a book with elegant abandon.   The powdered wig distracts our first glance from the uneasy look on his face, reflected in his penetrating eyes, strained from years of study, and accentuated by the bitter smile on his thin lips.   Sequeira was born to a Jewish family in Portugal; he emigrated to Bordeaux, then moved to Leyden, where he studied medicine.   He practiced his profession in London, where he was the painter's doctor.   He dies at an advanced age in 1816.

This painting belonged to the Sequeira Family until it was auctioned in London in 1901.   In 1953 Mr. Bertram Newhouse, a famous antique dealer in New York, donated it to the Prado in exchange for an exportation permit for another work of art.

There is another painting by Gainsborough in the Prado which is earlier than the Sequeira portrait; it is of Robert Butcher (c. 1765) and is a replica of another one at Williams College (Mass., USA).

PLATE LXXXV

Anton Raffael Mengs.
Maria Luisa of Parma (1765).
Oil on canvas, 48 × 38 cm.   C. 2.568

Mengs' fame has been diminishing since the beginning of this century. Impressionism and artistic currents which diverge from reality made possible this disdain for the most famous of the Neoclassical painters. But today his past prestige is again being recovered. His paintings in which he moves away from an Academic style, such as in his own self-portraits, are once more interesting modern spectators. His most personal works are those in which minutely reflected reality is poetized by his sensitive spirit. Some of these paintings remind us of the early Goya.

One of the most delicate works in the important collection of Mengs' art in the Prado Museum is this study of a woman's head, which represents the Princess of Asturias, Maria Luisa of Parma. In this young girl's enchanting face, adorned only with a pink ribbon at the neck, the bohemian artist achieves a creation which, though within the Neoclassical style, is full of life. The Princess possesses a beauty here which is quite different from what we will later see in Goya's pictures. It is really difficult to believe that the toothless, ridiculous sovereign at the end of the century is one in .the same with this delicate personage.

This study was the direct sketch done for the portrait which, once in the Count Del Asalto's Collection in Madrid, is now in the Metropolitan Museum in New York. This latter, large in size, shows her standing with part of her dress draped across a chair, as if she had just stood up; the silk dress has yellow and white stripes with red flowers. In her right hand she holds a miniature box with the likeness of the future Charles IV, her husband-to-be, since this portrait was probably done a short time before their wedding, in 1765. It has been suggested that it might have been done in Parma, although no documentary evidence exists. According to Ceán, around this time Mengs goes to Italy, visiting Naples, Rome, and Florence, which means that the portrait could have been done in one of these cities before he came to Spain. This is confirmed by the Princess' likeness because in this portrait it looks as if she had not yet reached the age of fourteen, which is when she married.

Manish, Mengs' most recent biographer, dates the painting 1763 (?). Other portraits of Maria Luisa of Parma exist. In the Prado there is a version in which she appears quite a bit heavier, possibly awaiting a child, which means it was done after her marriage, and thus is later than this one. There are replicas of that portrait in the Louvre and in Aranjuez. There is a copy of the one illustrated here in Holland; and a preparatory sketch for it existed in the Carderera Coll., now in a private collection in Madrid. It was donated to the Museum by the Duke of Tarifa in 1934.

43

LUIS EUGENIO MELÉNDEZ.
Still-life: *a Slice of Salmon, a Lemon and Three Vessels* (1772).
Oil on canvas, 62 × 42 cm.   C. 902

In Meléndez' paintings all the elements of composition are subordinated to the «whole» of the painting. The things —inanimate beings— represented here are the protagonists of the work. This causes them to have a markedly unified character, with no element of distraction. His «still-lifes» —it would be better to call them inanimate— are the results of a conscious and reflexive study, based on a great dedication to his work, which made possible his careful technique, almost like that of one of the primitives. Thus in spite of the too-polished surface, so in vogue in his times and which repels us today, the artist's paintings are attractive to the contemporary spectator.

Meléndez has been called the «Spanish Chardin», but we think that he is closer in spirit to Zurbarán. If his affinity to the French painter is purely technical, his affinity to the artist from Extremadura is based on a Spanish tradition which has never been lost. Thus in these objects there is the feeling of a portrait, especially due to the carefully and faithfully studied quality. The main protagonist of this little painting is the prodigious slice of salmon, anticipating the one which Goya would later paint (Oscar Reinhart Collection, Winterthur); the secondary, but still important, personages are the lemon and some vessels. All of this is placed on a rough kitchen table on whose edge we may read the signature and date: *L. M˟ D° IS° P'. AÑO 1772.*

This was possibly painted along with other still-lifes in the series in the Prado for the Aranjuez Palace, for they proceed from there and were done between 1760 and 1772. In the earliest ones is perceived a certain Baroque ostentation which becomes more simplified in the last ones, reaching a synthesis and schematic treatment (such as in the one reproduced here), the fruit of the reigning Neoclassicism which brings it close to the *bodegones* which at this time were appearing on the walls of the mansions at Herculaneum and Pompeii.

It is a shame that the Prado, at this time, is totally lacking in any representation of the superb portraits which Meléndez did, among which stands out his «Self-portrait» (Louvre) in which Goya's popular bravado will be anticipated and a «Young Girl» (Castejón Coll., Madrid). The Museums of Barcelona just acquired one, and we hope that the Madrilenian pinacotheca follows their example, for in these works as well there exists the simplicity and domination of line which appear in the still-lifes, not counting the special personal attraction of his personages. An example of this domination of drafting is his «Young Girl» in the Uffizi; he also used pastels, such as in his portrait of Moratín (Navarra Museum, Pamplona).

LUIS PARET Y ALCÁZAR.
Charles III, Lunching with His Court (1768-73).
Oil on wood, 50 × 64 cm.   C. 2.422

One of the most lovely works from XVIIIth century Spanish painting is this «Charles III, Lunching with His Court», done by Paret in his youth. This small picture is at once a historical painting and a genre scene since the historical narration is done in a festive, almost joking manner. Very characteristic of Luis Paret's first period are paintings, almost always small ones (*tableautin*), which are exponents of this sense of humor and satirical character, which unfortunately forced him into exile. In this work, the King appears engaged in an everyday but at the same time ceremonial activity: his luncheon. Due to the influence of the French Bourbons, the sovereign was usually the only one to dine, though the entire Court was present at the meal, as well as occasional guests who «came to observe». While the courtiers serve the King course after course, Charles III directs his attention exclusively at a dog, maintaining a silent dialogue. Another animal seems about to attack the food. The Count of Fernán Nuñez describes a similar moment for us: «In the middle of the meal, the hunting dogs broke in somewhat excitedly and you had to be careful to keep them from running between your legs and dragging you around the room, as happened to the Marquis of La Torrecilla... who ended up mounted bareback on one of the large dogs, named Melampo...» In this painting even the signature has an ironic touch; it is signed in Greek and reads: «Luis Paret, son of his father and mother, did this.»

Although Charles III lunched in the Gasparini Salon of the Royal Palace and dined in the antechamber of the same salon, the setting for the action of this painting seems to be the fruit of the artist's imagination, though based on elements from reality. Thus the walls are adorned with French tapestries from the XVIIIth century in the style of Boucher or Fragonard. On the ceiling are figures which remind us of the ones which appear on Tiepolo's ceilings in the Palace. All of this is permeated by a spatial atmosphere whose blue-green tones give it an unreal character. A distant and wide perspective, like the view through a «wide-angle» lens, accentuates this feeling. At the same time, rhythmical diagonal movements create a sensation of instability in the painting. Paret's personality has achieved here, as in all of his great works, a masterpiece of Rococo painting.

Osiris Delgado, Paret's biographer, dates the painting between 1768 and 1774. According to its style it must have been done after «The Costume Ball» (C. 2.875) and «The Shop» (1772, Lázaro Galdiano Museum, Madrid). Acquired in 1933 with funds from the Count of Cartagena's legacy, it came from the Gatchina Palace in Russia.

PLATE LXXXVIII

FRANCISCO DE GOYA Y LUCIENTES.
Self-portrait (c. 1815).
Oil on canvas, 35 × 46 cm.   C. 723

Here we have one of the most penetrating portraits which Goya would do of himself. The painter from Fuendetodos (the Spanish town with the most democratic denomination, «fountain for all», and whose name seems to foretell Goya's influence on almost all the later pictorial styles —Romanticism, Realism, Impressionism, Expressionism and Non-figurativism) appears portrayed here around the age of 70, with an immensely forceful look, with his eyes expressing his energetic and creative spirit.

Comparing it with a similar portrait which is signed in 1815 (San Fernando Academy of Fine Art), it may be considered to be from the same period, that is to say from a convulsive period in Spanish history, since the last Napoleonic troops had just left and the «versatile» Ferdinand VII, of whom the artist does several portraits at the time, had just been reinstated on his throne. So it seems Goya had once more become the painter for great personages: the «Duke of San Carlos», founder and first president of what is today the Bank of Spain; «Don Ignacio Omulryan», member of the Privy Council and Colonies Board, etc. Also in this same year, he portrays friends such as «José Luis de Munarriz» (S. F. Academy), in which we may see remote influences of El Greco. Here, on the other hand, we may note the influence of Rembrandt —since the dark background contrasts very little with the figure, painted with clothing of an intensely dark chestnut, almost black color. And in the same manner as the Dutch painter had done on occasion, he paints himself in a work smock; only the white shirt collar offers a certain feeling of light here. Psychologically as well as technically, especially in the way the face is illuminated, we see reminiscences of Rembrandt. We must remember that Goya had said: «And my only masters are Velasquez, Rembrandt and Nature».

In this penetrating psychological study of his face we may sense the introverted man —to a great extent the result of his deafness which each day separated him more and more from the superficial exterior world and caused him to turn more within himself, thus learning to more profoundly capture the essence of things. He therefore represents himself with his hair mussed and his collar open, like a simple man who doesn't think about his appearance. This face has a certain expression which reminds us of the portraits of his contemporary and kindred spirit, Beethoven. Around this time the artist would begin to prepare his series on the *Tauromaquia*, since in 1816 he proudly advertises his engravings in the newspaper, «Diario de Madrid».

In the upper part of the background he has signed the painting: *Fr. Goya. From Aragon. By himself.*

Acquired in 1866, by the Trinidad Museum for 400 escudos from Don Ramón de la Huerta.

PLATE LXXXIX

FRANCISCO DE GOYA Y LUCIENTES.
Blindman's Buff (c. 1790)
Oil on canvas, 41 × 44 cm.   C. 2.781

When Spain changed dynasties and lost many of her possessions at the end of the War of Succession, domestic and foreign policies changed their orientation, initiating not only a politcial, but also an economic centralization, in contrast to the course of dispersion followed by the Austrias. Until then, the manufacture of tapestries was prohibited in Spain, giving Flanders a monopoly. The factories in Madrid, Pastrana, Salamanca, etc., could only reweave those in poor condition or do coats of arms. In 1720, when the first Bourbon, Philip V, founds the Royal Tapestry Factory in Madrid, a new stage of the Spanish industrial arts commences. In the early moments, the themes employed were mythological and biblical; but at the beginning of Charles III's reign, the popular themes are developed. Under the direction of Francisco Bayeu, a series of artists, including José del Castillo and Goya, does a great number of cartoons with these themes. The difference between Goya's canvases and the others is not specific but only qualitative.

The appearance of popular scenes in the tapestries is based on the change in literary tastes. At the end of the XVIIIth century Rousseau makes an apologia of rustic life, and very soon his ideas spread to other writers; in Spain Meléndez Valdés, in 1779, wrote his «Eulogy of Rustic Life», which won a prize from the Royal Academy of Letters in 1783. Goya cultivated this writer's friendship and did his portrait. When he began his first cartoons (1774/75) he does somewhat common hunting and fishing scenes which may only be attributed to him thanks to documentation published by Sambricio. On the other hand, in the following period (1775/80), the influence of Meléndez may now be seen in his popular scenes. Thus the «Pottery Vender», «The Dance on the Banks of the Manzanares», «The Washerwomen», etc., are done with an ease and mastery which is unequalled by anything else from the Royal Tapestry Factory. In the last two periods (1786/88 and 1791/92), he reaches even greater technical and artistic heights, which were difficult for the tapestry weavers to carry out, being unable to match the prodigious chromatic effects which Goya created. Two works from the third period: «The Flower Venders» and «Blindman's Buff» are perhaps the two best works by the painter from Fuendetodos in this genre. Thus in «Blindman's Buff» he achieves a sense of force and popular elegance which he will only surpass, in a different aspect, in the paintings from the Black Period.

Goya did reduced versions of the cartoons. The «Blindman's Buff» reproduced here is the reduction of the famous cartoon. Variants exist: the addition of one figure in the circle and various in the background, among others. It was painted for the Alameda de Osuna after 1790; the cartoon had been turned in to the Tapestry Factory in 1787. It comes from the Fernández Durán legacy.

Francisco de Goya y Lucientes.
The Nude Maja (1796-1797).
Oil on canvas, 190 × 97 cm.   C. 742

The «Majas» have occasioned the creation of a legend with multiple variations which have the Duchess of Alba appearing as the model and romantic protagonist. Goya painted and drew the Duchess several times between 1795-98 using symbolic elements which clear up for us the reality of the affair between her and the painter from Fuendetodos. Thus he signs *just Goya* on the sandy soil of the Rocío (Huelva) marsh on which is seated her figure dressed in mourning (Hispanic Society, New York); her husband had died several months before and Goya accompanies her to her secluded Andalusian ranch (1797). But previously, in her enchanting portrait done in white tulle (1795, Duchess of Alba's Coll.), on two plaques, placed on the left arm, very close to the heart, appear in an inverted fashion only legible for her, an A and a G (Alba and Goya). Later, in the portrait in New York the names will then appear complete on two rings (see my article published in *Goya*, 1971, N.º 100, pp. 240-245).

Although the figure in these works corresponds to the Duchess' proportions, with a broad chest and ample thighs, her face—with a glacial stare accented by thick, dark brows—is made to resemble a mask. The discovery of a double frame with the dimensions of these pictures—in which the *dressed* one would logically be placed over the *nude* one— at the Rocío (Ayamonte) estate, property of the Albas, caused the problem to be raised once more; besides, these paintings correspond stylistically to the period of the lovers' stay at this estate. The spontaneous style and succulent coloring of the «Dressed Maja» are close to the angel-majas in San Antonio de la Florida (1798). Godoy bought these works, so it seems, at the auction which took place after the Duchess of Alba's death. In the catalog of the former Prime Minister's works of art (1808) they were listed under the title of «Gypsies». With the attachment of Godoy's property, they become the property of the Crown.

Although the «Dressed Maja», from the stylistic point of view, is supe rior to its companion, this latter, due to its intimate character and its being one of the few female nudes in Spanish painting, must be considered one of the Aragonese painter's masterpieces, and one of the principal attractions in the Prado.

PLATE XCI

Francisco de Goya y Lucientes.
The Family of Charles IV (1800).
Oil on canvas, 336 × 280 cm.   C. 726

In 1799 Goya reaches his zenith at the Court, obtaining the highest position an artist could hold in Spain, that of «Painter of the King's Chamber» (first among the Royal Painters), a position held a century and a half before by Velasquez. Probably motivated by this promotion, he has the idea of doing a painting similar to the one Velasquez did of the Family of Philip IV, since by portraying the figures in a standing position and contemplating a mysterious figure who is posing for the painter, it brings the work closer to «Las Meninas» than to the portrait of the «Family of Philip V» by M. van Loo done in 1743 (C. 2.283) in which the figures are seated, as is conventional, and listening to music.

Possibly the isocephalic feeling which Goya gives to the painting, placing the figures in a straight line and in the order required by royal etiquette, is an obligation placed on him by the King. It is in strong contrast with the freedom of the execution. The figures wear courtly dress and honorary decorations; thus the gentlemen sport the Order of Charles III and the ladies, the Order of María Luisa. In the center, Queen María Luisa of Parma appears and on her left is the Sovereign—thus contrasting the haughty expression of the Queen with the insignificant and insipid figure of her husband, who although he is 51 around that time, seems to be older. On the left is the future Ferdinand VII, accompanied by a lady whose face is mysteriously turned away; the figure represents his bride-to-be and her identity at that time was not yet known. Between the two is the hideous countenance of María Micaela. At the other end of the group, the lady with the child in her arms is Princess María Luisa, who is accompanied by her husband the Prince of Parma.

But whom is the Royal Family looking at? Sánchez Cantón has offered an intriguing hypotesis: the «Prince of Peace», Manuel Godoy, who had progressed from a simple Guard of the Corps, by way of the royal marriage bed, to become the person who held the destiny of Spain in his hands. Goya looks out with a scrutinizing stare, but he has not been able to achieve the sense of artistic freedom which Velasquez gave us in his masterpiece.

A recent and careful cleaning has revived the tones and in one of the paintings in the background two monstrous figures have appeared which may symbolize the protests of the people, and in one of them, so it seems, Goya, did another self-portrait, although with physiognomical deformations appropriate to his style and period, in which masks and masquerading are highly developed.

PLATE XCII

FRANCISCO DE GOYA Y LUCIENTES.
The Executions of the Third of May (1814).
Oil on canvas, 266 × 345 cm.

C. 749

Goya does not remain inactive during the War of Independence since his indomitable spirit, his preoccupations and anxious curiosity bring him to reflect the tragic happenings or capture the aspect of the people who took an important part in the strife. When on May 2, 1808, the almost unarmed people of Madrid rebel, ferociously attacking Murat's troops, Goya was in the city. And the first bullet to kill a «mameluco» was shot from the house of an in-law of Goya's son. It is not unusual that the Aragonese painter might be on the scene, which he would record in a sketch which is known today (Duchess of Villahermosa's Coll.). Later he would change the setting, in the definitive version, to a famous event: «The Charge of the Mamelucos».

According to tradition, Goya, accompanied by a servant, was also present at the executions at Moncloa. The sketch for this must be the one preserved in the Hispanic Society in New York. Its definitive version will be the psychological reverse of «The Charge» —for if in this latter momentarily victorious people are represented, in «The Executions», on the contrary, in a lugubrious dawn, the heroes of the previous day have their lives cut short. Before an execution squad a group of patriots confront death, meanwhile the soldiers of the Napoleonic army are represented with their backs to the spectator. Goya hides their faces not out of pity, but to show them as mere instruments of repression. In contrast, the Spanish group is heterogeneous; each person faces death in a different way. A large lantern illuminates their faces with a ghostly, yellowish light. In the foreground, a man stands out, with his white shirt and yellow pants, from his companions, who wear dark clothing. He throws back his arms and his head, with staring eyes, while the others pray or yell insults or cover their eyes so as not to see their own death. One of the heroes from the previous day now gnaws his knuckles in terror. The cadavers of those already executed lie on the ground, like mere inert carcases, almost as if they were animals. In the background is the Príncipe Pío hillside, done with colors appropriate for an Expressionist painting.

The two pictures which commemorate the uprising of the people of Madrid against the Napoleonic troops were done, from sketches, in 1814. They were commisioned by Cardinal Luis de Borbón, President of the Regent's Council, before Ferdinand VII returned, to «perpetuate by means of brushes the most notable and heroic events of the glorious insurrection against the «Tyrant of Europe». So it seems, they were placed on a triumphal arch built to celebrate the arrival of «Ferdinand, the Desired One». Now Goya has left us here, more than a portrayal of heroic events, a pathetic anti-war testimonial.

260

PLATE XCIII

Francisco de Goya y Lucientes.
The Witches' Sabbath (1820-1823).
Mural painting in oil, transferred to canvas, 140 × 438 cm.   C. 761

Persecuted, sick, in anguish, Goya spends his final years in Madrid, before moving to France (from which he will make only one short trip back to Spain), in a modest two-floor country home which was on the bank of the Manzanares River, past the Segovia Bridge; coincidentally it was already quite appropriately named «The Deaf Man's Villa». Tormented by memories and hallucinations, his physiological pains augmented by his psychological suffering which an old liberal would feel in an Absolutist Spain —where the cry «Long live our chains!» could be heard— Goya, hidden away from the outside world, searched for an escape valve in his extremely personal creations. With only a range of smokey blacks, whites, earthen tones and a little red, he will do the most fantastically independent cycle within all his work. This is due to the fact that the fourteen compositions from the villa are perhaps the only works which he did exclusively for personal motivations.

In «The Witches' Sabbath», possibly held in the Cabrón Meadow, the He-Goat (Cabrón) appears as a demoniacal representation, wearing ecclesiastical garb and zealously preaching to a hair-raisingly frightening group of women. There is only one young woman who appears somewhat divorced from the action; seated to one side she wears mourning dress and buries her hands in a fur muff. As in the other pictures of this series, there have been atempts to discover hidden meanings in this one; thus Ramón Gómez de la Serna sees here an «allegory of the Confession»; Sánchez Cantón says, on the other hand, that he is resigned to see no more in the decoration than a flight of fancy and, at the most, a reference to «the sleep of Reason» (which produces monsters).

Earlier Goya had already painted cruelly biting episodes and witches' scenes—in «Los Caprichos», small paintings for the Duke of Osuna (Lázaro Galdiano Museum), etc—but in the «black paintings»—so-called not due to their color, but rather because they represent the black period Spain was going through in the artist's times—he does not limit himself to merely portraying these terrible scenes, but also adapts his pictorial technique to the episodes represented, expressing with palette-knives and brushes an artistic freedom unknown before that time.

PLATE XCIV

FRANCISCO DE GOYA Y LUCIENTES.
Saturn Devouring His Son (1820-1823).
Mural painting in oil, transferred to canvas, 83 × 146 cm.   C. 763

On either side of the entrance to the dining room in the «Deaf Man's Villa» were a «Judith and Holofernes» and a «Saturn Devouring His Son», a theme which at first glance might seem to be ill-suited for dining-room decor and inexplicable for those who have not delved into Goya's subconscious. He may possibly be expressing with the decapitation of Holofernes the justification of the assassination of a tyrant, as Donatello, Botticelli and other artists before him had done. In this picture, on the other hand, the voracity of the tyrant may be the subject of the allegory. But it is more likey that he refers to Quevedo's assertion: «Spain devours her most gifted sons».

Few times in the history of art has the expression been represented with such cruelty. Here realism oversteps all reasonable bounds to approach a genial anticipation of Expressionism. Not even Rubens' painting on the same theme (also in the Prado), nor the portrayals of Cronus devouring Time diminish the revolutionary originality of this «Saturn». Here the chiaroscuro, bitter medicine of the «black paintings» has reached its maximum expression. The pigmentation for the flesh is applied with a burning ferocity worthy of the picture's theme. The reddish tones of the blood offer the only colorful note. Once again the staring eyes of lunacy appear riveted on the spectator.

Probably the artist's fear of being swallowed by the «Absolutist Reign of Terror» for having supported the Constitution of 1820 is what motivated Goya to paint this hair-raising work. Shortly after it was finished, Goya would abandon Spain in 1824 when he was 78 years old. His pretext was to visit the baths at Plombières; but more than corporal hygiene, he needed spiritual purification. When he left, he gave the villa to his nephew Mariano. Slowly it falls into disrepair; the oil, directly applied to the plaster walls, begins to crack. Such an inappropriate technique, has caused its actual state of preservation to be very deficient because periodic restorations were required which altered the original pigmentation. In 1873, Baron Emile d'Erlanger acquires the «Deaf Man's Villa», and hires the famous restorer Salvador Martínez Cubells to carefully lift the paintings from the walls and transfer them to canvas. They were shown at the Universal Exhibition in Paris in 1878 where they were not appreciated. This made possible their presentation to the Prado Museum in 1881.

T 536

PLATE XCV

FRANCISCO DE GOYA Y LUCIENTES.
Bullfight Scene: The Picadors.
Oil on canvas, 38 × 46 cm.   C. 3.047

As Xavier de Salas has masterfully shown («Burlington M.», 1964), the five known paintings of bullfight scenes, including this delightful work, although for a long time attributed to Eugenio Lucas, are unquestionably works by Goya. Of a high quality and carefully done, split reeds were used as spatula knives to achieve effects of great pictorial relief, following a Goyesque technique which has already appeared before 1812. But although they serve as a basis for the lithographic series of the Bordeaux bullfight scenes (1825), these tiny paintings must have been done previously and then taken by the artist into exile with him. In my opinion, they are works from between 1813-1818, a period in which Goya lives isolated from the world in his *Deaf Man's Villa* in Madrid, where he executes, along with his famous Black Paintings, scenes of a strongly popular flavor («The Dirigible», «The Procession», «The Carnival» and «The Fair») which possess a close stylistic relationship with these bullfight pictures. Just as in the former these latter have a densely smoldering technique, and the superposition of chromatic pigments lends them qualities similar to those of Rembrandt's final moments. The effects of light reach a new feeling of perspective which is applied in this picture to the sand in the bullring, directing our attention across it to meet the dark wooden barrier and the phosphorescent, flashing forms of the spectators. In the center of the bullring, picadors and bulls which dramatically slash open the horses' bellies shock the spectator.

This work was acquired by the Prado thanks to a private donation, in 1962 by Thomas Harris, a British painter. It is necessary to accept the wise opinion of Salas who considers it done at the same time he did the «Bullfight» (Marchioness of Baroja's Coll., Rome) and two pictures with similar themes acquired at Christie's (London), as done by Eugenio Lucas, to whom they had been attributed; when the one in the Baroja Coll. was given by Goya himself to his friend Joaquín María Ferrer, this latter noted on the back: *Painted in Paris in July of 1824, by Dn Fran(cis)co Goya J.M.F.;* a fourth version was also auctioned at Christie's.

COPY OF POLYCLITUS.
Diadumeno (Original c. 420 B.C.; Copy c. 100 B.C.).
Copy in marble, 212 cm. high.   C. 88 - E

This sculpture is the best copy which remains of the original of the «Diadumeno» by Polyclitus, which has been lost. The original was cast in bronze and was the masterpiece of the artist's final style. The ease with which the anatomical structure of the body is executed and especially the mobility and flexibility of the musculature makes one think of the influence of Phidias. The band around the head, an emblem of the winners in sporting events, is so tight that it presses hard on the hair, making us note the plastic relief, like in some of Phidias' works, such as the «Athena Lemnia».

Restoration work from the XVIIth century has somewhat lessened the formal beauty of this extremely lovely version. The only original parts of the legs are from the knees up; the statue's proper right arm, which is extended here instead of curved, as in the original, is also partially the product of restoration, and the same is true to a great degree for the support and for the entire plinth. Unfortunately, almost all of the old patina has been removed, with only a little remaining on the hair. The beauty and tone of the marble make us think it may be from Pentelicus.

This is not, at all, a mere copy of Polyclitus' original but a Hellenistic interpretation of it since, some details, especially the posture of the arms, differ from the original, since as Blanco has said, «in accordance with the taste of the times, the arms and head try to create an impression of spatial volume which is foreign to Polyclitus». In another version, preserved in Delos, a quiver appears on the support for the statue, which has made some suppose that it is not simply the representation of a mere athlete, but rather of the god Apollo. As with the majority of sculptures which come from the Spanish Royal Collections, its origins are unknown, but since the original was in Athens in ancient times, it may be supposed that this one, like almost all the direct copies, was done in that city. It was in the sculpture collection of La Granja de San Ildefonso Palace; Ponz limited himself to saying that these works had come from Italy.

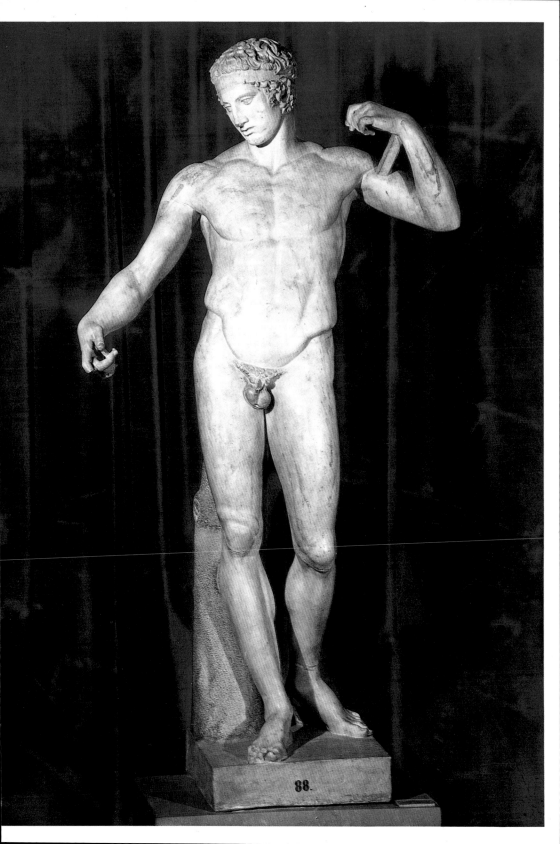

88.

STYLE OF LYSIPPUS.
Masculine Head (Beginning of IIIrd Century B.C.).
Original in Bronze, 45 cm. high.   C. 99 - E

This impressive head, a Hellenistic original in bronze, represents a young man of perfect Classical features, and its iconography has for many years been the subject of controversy. Whom does it represent? Is it a real or a fictional character? As early as 1899, Kieseritzky interpreted it as being Alexander. Buschor considers it the portrait of a young man with facial features like those of the Macedonian ruler, since the profile reminds us somewhat of the figure which appears in the mosaic of the «Battle of Ipsus» (National Sculpture Museum, Naples). There is no doubt that the physical features are very similar, not only to those of the figure in the Neopolitan mosaic, but also to those of other busts which are believed to be portraits of Alexander done by Lysippus. For this reason we believe that this may be a Hellenistic god-like idealization of his face, in the form of Meleager or Hercules, possibly this latter, since we should note that Alexander was called «the Macedonian Ares». This idealization of a person is another detail which might indicate that the sculpture in the Prado was done after his death. Its style and plastic beauty, already within the Hellenistic eclectic style, make one think that it must have been cast in the workshop of one of Lysippus' direct disciples, in the first years of the IIIrd century B.C. As Blanco Frejeiro has astutely pointed out, the only thing that makes us think it might be a portrait is the manner in which the curly hair is treated, scarcely falling over the forehead the individualized character, which at first glance the face seems to possess, is owed to the fact that the head suffers from imperfections, particularly on the left side of the face, resulting from a blow which has flattened it a bit. All this makes Blanco consider it the idealization of a deified athlete.

Arndt hesitatingly observed that it might have been the portrait of the Athenean intellectual, politician and governor, Demetrius of Faleros. In old sculpture catalogs of the Prado Museum it was considered to be the head of one of the Dioscuri, only because of its colossal size. Its origin is unknown, but Winckelmann, in 1812, affirmed that Philip V had bought it for 50,000 pistolas (coins similar to escudos), money used in the south of Italy, which means it may possibly have come from Magna Graecia. It was in La Granja de San Ildefonso, where it was even absurdly referred to as a portrait of Christina of Sweden. Recently is has been cleaned, removing the pitch which filled the inside; the old marble pedestal has been replaced by a metallic support which sets off even more its brooding beauty.

GRECO-ROMAN ART.
San Ildefonso Group (1st Century B. C.).
Original in marble, 161 cm. high.   C. 28 - E

The «San Ildefonso Group» is one of the most beautiful productions of
Rome at the time Augustus (or at the end of the Republic), since it may be
dated in the 1st century due to its markedly Hellenistic character. This
work has the same eclectic feeling, for example, as the «Orestes and Elec-
tra» from the Ludovisi Collection in the National Museum in Rome and as
the «Mercury and Vulcan» from the Louvre. These are related to the art
of the followers of Pasiteles (a sculptor from Magna Greacia who settled
in Rome at the beginning of the century). The group in the Ludovisi Collection is the work of Menelaos, a student of Estafanos, who in turn was
a disciple of Pasiteles. Now the group preserved in the Prado is the loveliest of the series. In it, the figure on the spectactor's left reminds us of
Praxiteles' «Sauroktonos Apollo», and, in contrast, the one on the right is
related to works by Polyclitus. This group is formed by two adolescent
nudes, the younger one resting his arm on the shoulder of his companion,
who holds two torches, one of them close to a sacrificial altar, the other,
a modern one of wood, slants over his own shoulder and his friend's arm.
To support this figure there is an archaic statue of a goddess dressed in a
«chiton» (tunic) with long sleeves and a «peplos» (shawl). The small altar,
which appears in the foreground and at which the figures direct their gaze,
is surrounded by garlands which hang from stylized bucranes and are
centered by rosettes. This altar's typology confirms the date of this group
as the 1st century B.C.

The traditional interpretation was that it represented the Dioscuri: Cas-
tor and Pollux, at the moment they offer a sacrifice to Persephone. But more
imaginative is the hypothesis suggested by Winckelmann, that it might
represent Orestes and Pilades, offering a sacrifice in front of the tomb of Aga-
menon in which event the goddess would be Artemusa. It should be observed that in Pasiteles' workshop groups of this type, based on Greek
tragedy, were done and also in Hellenistic paintings these heroes are represented with torches. Later, an ancient head of Antinoo, Hadrian's «favorite», was added to the figure on the spectator's left which made Elias
Tormo believe and advocate that this group was a funeral monument raised
by Hadrian to the Bithynian slave, with the Emperor's figure accompanying
him. But the severage was not the result of a break, the cut between the
head and body was purposefully done, and besides the typology of the head
is totally different from the rest.

This group has, besides this alteration, suffered quite a few restorations.
Its origin is unknown. It was in the Ludovisi Villa in Rome, and was
acquired by Queen Christina of Sweden, being transferred later to the
Odescalchi Collection and from there to that of Philip V, who moved it
to La Granja de San Ildefonso.

FRANCO-ITALIAN GOLD WORK.
The Dauphin's Treasure: Saltcellar.
Middle of the XVIth century.
Onyx with a gold mermaid 17,5 cm high.

The gems which Philip V inherited from his father, the Grand Dauphin of France (son of Louis XIV), when he died in 1712 are called «The Dauphin's Treasure». This was an important part of the inheritance since the rest was reduced to an income of 40,000 pounds coming from his lands. This was assigned to the first-born son, the Duke of Burgundy; the jewels were divided between the Duke of Berry and the King of Spain. A portion of them had previously been sold at public auction to pay some debts contracted by the father.

Since its arrival in Spain this collection of gems and precious stones remained in the Royal Seat at San Ildefonso until Charles III decided in 1767 to give them to the Natural History Foundation created by him in the present building of the Prado as samples of minerals and metals (!), paying no attention to their artistic worth. In 1813, in deplorable condition, they were taken to Paris by Napoleon's troops; the collection was returned two years later, but the majority of the pieces came back broken and with important losses and twelve were missing altogether. Transferred to the Natural History Museum, they were recovered for the Painting Museum by the Director of the Prado, Don Pedro de Madrazo, in spite of strong resistance. In 1818 eleven pieces were stolen and thirty-five were mutilated. Since 1944 they have been kept in a salon built especially for them. In spite of robberies, mutilation and losses, this treasure still offers a splendid collection of Italian, French, Central European and Oriental gold work; the majority of it comes from the Renaissance and Baroque periods. It forms a companion ensemble to one which belonged to the French crown exhibited today in the Louvre.

Although it is difficult to select one sample from this rich collection, we have chosed this lovely «saltcellar» in onyx, with a mermaid in gold, covered with enamel on the lower extremities. According to Madrazo, the piece was not cast, but rather sculpted in gold leaf worked with small mallets. A blue-green tone predominates in the enamel, with flecks of red, white, blue and green appearing also. This gem is adorned with one hundred and seventy-seven rubies and two diamonds. On the lower part of the mermaid there was a small dolphin which was lost during the trip to France. This mermaid is possibly meant to evoke the sea, as a triton would do in another saltcellar which belonged to Francis I of France. It seems that this work was done in France in the middle of the XVIth century since its marked Mannerist character places it in the sculptural schools of Fontainebleau, and although certain influences of Cellini may be noted (he resides in France until 1545), its style makes us think more of the work of the famous French sculptor Jean Goujon.

274

PLATE C

BRIEF VOCABULARY OF PAINTING

bodegón. Painting in which diverse objects are represented (dead animals, fruit, ceramic pieces...); in general with a certain ostentation, which distinguishes it from the simple **still-lifes.**

brushwork, brush stroke. Manner of application or personal touch in the use of the brush.

cartoon. A drawing which is employed as a model for a tapestry, fresco, stained glass window, etc. Generally it is the same size as the projected work; it may be done in **grisaille** (fresco) or in full color (tapestry). Its name comes from the material on which it is done (It. **cartone,** pasteboard), although other similar ones may be used.

color. Essential element of a painting along with the drawing. From a prism the seven basic ones are obtained: three primary ones (red, yellow and blue), three secondary (green, from mixing blue and yellow; violet, from red and blue; and orange, from red and yellow) and white. Those which refract light are called **hot** colors (red and yellow) and those which absorb it **cold** (green, blue and violet). Complementary colors are the ones which when they are mixed produce white (red and green, yellow and violet, orange and blue).

coloring. Totality of colors.

color print. Copy of an engraving. Widely circulated in **workshops** and used by painters for their compositions.

composition. Harmonization of the forms and colors in a picture.

easel. Support used to hold the canvas. **Easel painting** designates that which is done using this support.

execution. Personal manner of doing a work.

figure. Representation of a human body.

foreshortening. Search for an effect of depth in a figure by means of perspective or by twisting the forms.

fresco. Technique proper to wall-painting; while a uniform layer of plaster (a mixture of lime and sand) is still moist, colors dissolved in water are applied, resulting in a reduced **range** of matte tones.

genre. **Genre painting** is that which narrates scenes from everyday life.

glaze. Tenuous layer of transparent color, superimposed on another one which has already dried. At times it is dissolved in a **varnish.**

grisaille. Painting in which grays and blacks are used; generally they almost always imitate sculptures.

halo. Luminous outline which emphasizes the superhuman or saintly value of the figure which it envelopes.

impasto. Thick brushwork, at times in relief.

imprimatura. Monochromatic preparation which previously covers the canvas before the picture is executed. In the **workshops** it is also referred to as **staining** or **priming.**

material. The totality of chromatic impasto. This is the same as **texture.**

miniature. Pictorial ornamentation of a manuscript. A picture of reduced size.

nimbus. Luminous outline which surrounds only the head of sacred personages.

obrador. See **workshop.**

oil. Chromatic pigments dissolved in oil, generally vegetable oil (linseed, nut oils...).

palette. Instrument used for holding colors and mixing them; until present times it was usually made of walnut or pear wood. In the figurative sense: the **scale** or **range of colors** used by a painter.

palette knife. Instrument which is used to clean the palette or to impaste the surface of a picture. At times, reeds cut lengthwise are used as palette knives.

perspective. The art of representing the third dimension, that is, depth and distance. By means of drafting, lineal **perspective** is achieved, using oblique lines which converge at a **vanishing point** placed on the horizon. By means of physics and optics, or through personal intuition, **aerial perspective** has been achieved (see Pl. LXXIV) in which the air is placed between the object and our sight.

range. Chromatic shading according to the predominance of hot or cold tones. Its graduation gives the **scale of colors.**

retouching. Corrections which a painter makes in his work.

seascape. Picture with marine or coastal scenes.

sketch. Colored study done to discover the projected chromatic effect of a painting. It should not be confused with the partial studies or outlines which are preparatory drawings. **Sketchy,** or open, may be used to describe freely-executed work.

still-life. Bodegón. But, in general, it is the more reposed bodegones which are referred to by this name.

structure. Manner in which the parts of a whole (a picture, sculpture...) are arranged in relation to each other. In painting: the primacy of the relation of the totality of the picture with respect to its components. The problems which it poses has given rise to a new science: **artistic structuralism.**

style. Particular manner of composing or executing typical of a period, school or artist.

tempera. Paint dissolved in water, tempered with a binding (egg, animal or vegetable paste).

texture. Expression achieved through the use of the materials employed in the execution of the painting.

tone, tonality. Chromatic variations or shades in which a certain color predominates.

trompe l'œil. French expression meaning illusionism in spatial effects.

values. They are obtained by the comparison or relationship of the tones in a painting. The one with the greatest value is that which stands out over all the others. It is irrespective of the color itself, for a quieter color may be predominant over a brighter one (such as green over yellow). While in the Renaissance there was a search for a balance in the values, in the Mannerist and Baroque periods the artists prefer to contrast them.

varnish. Transparent liquid generally derived from resins, though today there exist plastic varnishes, which preserve paintings done in oil. With time it becomes rancid and turns yellow changing the tonalities; thus, blues become greens; therefore a careful cleaning is necessary, but taking into account that on occasion the painter may use **glazes** in a second coat of varnish.

workshop. Place where the artist executes his works. In Spain it was called the **obrador.** Also designated by this name is the group of artists which collaborate with a teacher, or master, on the works which come from the shop.

INDEX OF ARTISTS MENTIONED IN THE TEXT

NOTE: The numbers in boldface indicate the most important references to each artist.

INDEX OF COLOR PLATES

285

INDEX OF BLACK AND WHITE ILLUSTRATIONS

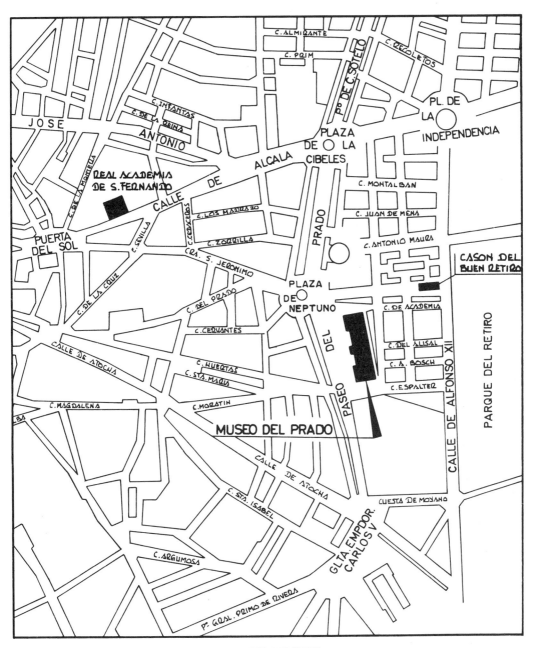

MUSEUM'S LOCATION

291

TOPOGRAPHIC INDEX

ROMANESQUE STYLE: Rooms 51 A, 51 B

GOTHIC STYLE: Rooms 49, 55 B, 56 B, 56 C, 57 C

FLEMISH, DUTCH AND GERMAN PAINTING, XV-XVIth CENTURIES:
Rooms 40 to 44, 63, 63 A, 64, 65, 68

ITALIAN PAINTING, XVIth CENTURY: Rooms 2, 5, 6, 7, 10, 10 A

    Raphael: Room 2
    Titian: Rooms 5 to 10
    Veronese: Rooms 7 A, 8 A
    Tintoretto: Rooms 8 A, 9 A, 10 A

SPANISH RENAISSANCE PAINTING: Rooms 49, 50, 55 B, 56 B, 56 C

    El Greco: Rooms 9 B, 10 B

SPANISH BAROQUE PAINTING: Rooms 1, 8 B, 25 to 29, 59, 60, 60 A, 62,
62 A, 83, 86, 87

    Ribera: Rooms 26, 61 A, 62 A
    Zurbarán: Rooms 11, 11 A, 30
    Velasquez: Rooms 12 to 14, 14 A, 15, 27
    Murillo: Rooms 28, 29, 60, 61, 62

ITALIAN BAROQUE PAINTING: Rooms 89, 89 A, 90, 91, 96 to 98

    Luca Giordano: Rooms 45, 85

FLEMISH BAROQUE PAINTING: Rooms 16 B, 20, 21, 61 B, 62 B, 63 B, 65,
67, 68, 79

    Rubens: Rooms 16 to 18, 18 A, 19 to 21, 65 B, 75
    Van Dyck and Jordaens: Rooms 16 A, 17 A
    Teniers: Room 66
    Bruegel de Velours: Room 67

DUTCH BAROQUE PAINTING: Rooms 22, 23
FRENCH PAINTING, XVII-XVIIIth CENTURIES: Rooms 31, 33 to 38
SPANISH PAINTING, XVIIIth CENTURY: Rooms 31, 81, 82

    Mengs: Room 80
    Goya: Rooms 32, 53, 54, 55, 55 A, 56, 56 A, 57, 57 A

ITALIAN PAINTING, XVIIIth CENTURY: Rooms 31, 39, 81, 82

    Tiepolo: Room 39

ENGLISH PAINTING, XVIII-XIXth CENTURIES: Room 84
FERNANDEZ DURAN LEGACY: Rooms 92 to 95
SCULPTURE: Rooms 1, 25 to 29, 39, 51, 70 to 75, 83
THE DAUPHIN'S TREASURE: Room 73

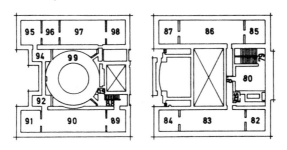

— SECOND FLOOR —

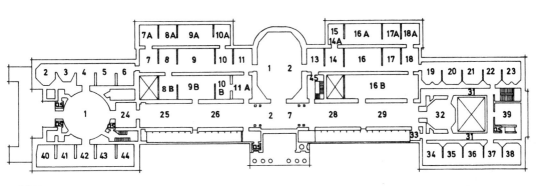

— MAIN FLOOR —

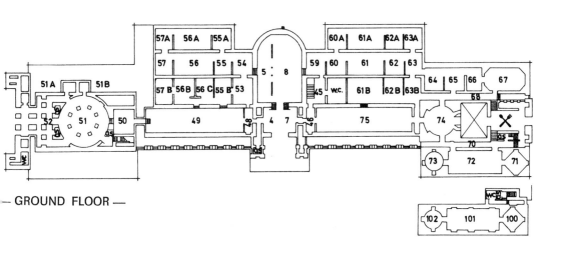

— GROUND FLOOR —

293

The length and variety of bibliography for the Prado Museum make it impossible to offer a list here, but we do not want to ignore its important Catalogs, especially the one on painting, the numbers from which we give after each work, so that the reader may broaden his knowledge of a certain piece not commented upon in the plates.

TRANSLATOR'S NOTE.—In Spanish numbering, a period is used in place of a comma for figures in the thousands; we retain this system for the numbers in our guide which correspond to Museum catalog numbers. It is also a Spanish custom to place other punctuation outside of quotation marks; after several unsuccessful bouts with the linotypist, we decided to follow the line of least resistance. Due to similar difficulties, the reader may also note rather unorthodox divisions of words at the ends of lines.